Pennsylvania Barn Quilt Coloring Book
John H. Lettau

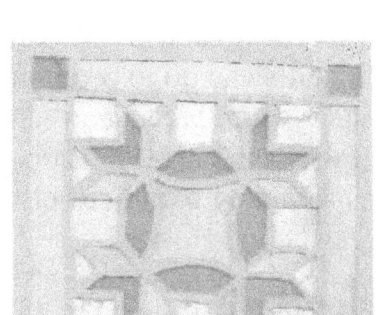 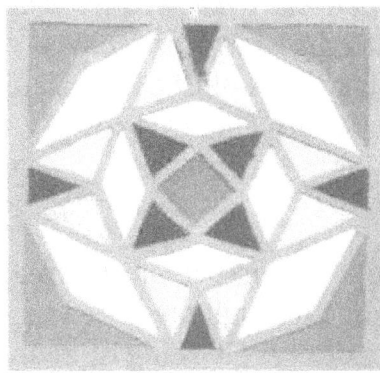 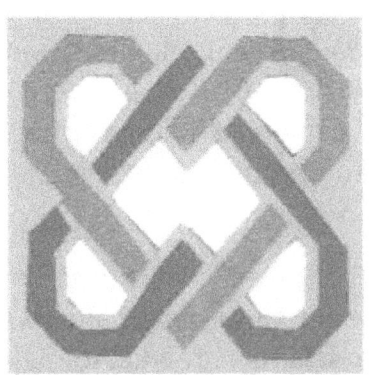

Featured Cover Barn Quilt Blocks
Maltese Cross   Turkey Tracks
Sunflower   Carpenter's Star

50 Barn Quilts in Frontier County Pennslyvania

2021 Copyright John Lettau

History of Barn Quilts

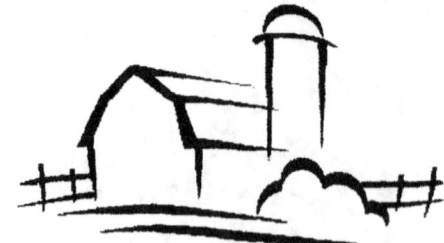

Today colorful barn quilts, also called quilt blocks, can be found along many highways, rural back roads and even in towns and cities through out America and Canada. The interest in this fast growing grass roots art movement started not many years ago in Ohio and continues to grow daily as communities, social clubs and clubs see what barn quilts can do to promote tourism and history/heritage. Brilliant barn quilt patterns are displayed on barns, corn cribs and other farm out-buildings through out farm country and even in towns and cities. This book is an opportunity for you to create many original color design patterns for many barn quilt blocks. book.

Barn Quilt Projects are usually supported and organized to educate, promote and celebrate the unique agricultural heritage of an area through the visual combination of barns and quilt patterns. Farms are vital to the economic well-being of many rural communities. Handmade barn quilt blocks provide warmth, beauty and an outlet for individual artistic expression. Plus, promoting tourism is a very important of all local barn quilt projects and trails,

How Barn Quilts are Constructed The Frontier County Barn Quilt Project

A barn quilt is usually made by painting a barn quilt design on MDO signboard suitable for weathering outdoors in all forms of weather. Prior to painting the barn quilt pattern two or three coats of primer are applied to front, back and edges of the signboard. Next, a selected barn quilt is drawn. Frog tape (painter tape) is applied to outline each section of the design. Two coats of each color paint is then applied to each section and allowed to dry over night. After all sections are painted the board is allowed to cure for two weeks before being mounted on barn or other structure,

Barn quilt blocks in Frontier County area of Pennsylvania are found in many different sizes...8 by 8, 4 by 4, 3 by 3 and 2 by 2 so they can be displayed on posts, sheds, businesses and even homes. Many are found in parks and yards. The Frontier County Barn Quilt Project promotes the barn quilt art through out the area as well as promoting the beauty and agricultural history of Frontier County and the state of Pennsylvania.

Each barn quilt design is usually painted by a team of volunteers and requires a willing farmer or property owner to donate hanging area on a barn, building or other structure, Making the quilt blocks allows volunteer groups from churches, schools, 4-H, other community service groups and even families the opportunity to create and paint their own quilt blocks. The chosen quilt block may represent a family created pattern or reminder of a beloved family quilt.

Interesting Facts On Barn Quilts

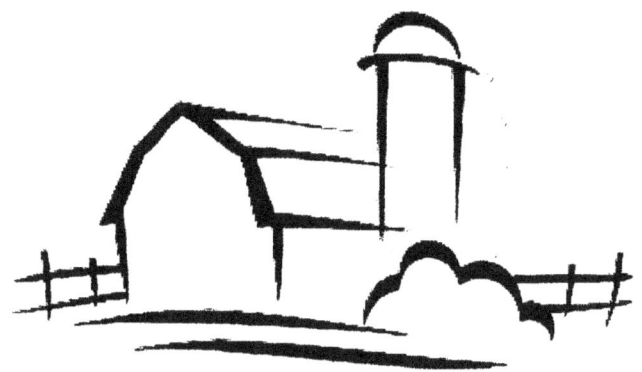

1. Common designs, such as Corn & Beans, are found in many states & rural areas.
2. The same quit pattern will be found with different color patterns.
3. It is not uncommon to find the same pattern with different names.
4. Some common patterns have small modification with a few extra lines.
5. Barn quilt patterns may honor individuals, families, and/or groups.
6. Many times color selections may have a special family meaning.
7. Quilts may be family designed and named.
8. Some city libraries and social clubs are organizing senior coloring programs.
9. Some select a common pattern and just change coloring pattern and/or name.
10. Some find popular patterns and change name and/or meaning.

Typical Barn Quilt Project Objectives

1. Reflects the agricultural heritage of the region.
2. Barns or buildings are highly visible from highway or road.
3. Bring pride to the area.
4. Notes well maintained barns and other farm buildings.
5. Promotes tourism for and in the area.

Objectives of Coloring Books

1. Provide a relaxing hobby for seniors and families.
2. Reduce tension in daily life.
3. Create a fun activity for all age groups.
4. Promote barn quilts around the country.

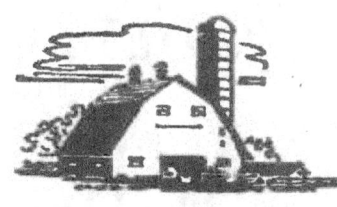

Frontier County Barn Quilt Listings

Name	Road	Township
Our Hearts	Knobsville Road	Todd Township
T Square	Sipes Mill Road	Licking Creek Township
Liberty	North 2nd Street	McConnellsburg Township
Shaffer Sunset	North 2nd Street	McConnellsburg Township
Turkey Tracks	North Valley Road	Wells Township
Hopes & Dreams	Great Cove Road	Ayr Township
Celtic Knot	Great Cove Road	Dublin Township
Becky's Own	Great Cove Road	Ayr Township
Friendship Basket	7th Street	McConnellsburg Township
Corn & Beans	South Valley Road	Brush Creek Township
Endless Chain	Pleasant Valley Road	Brush Creek Township
Hither & Yon	Lions Park Drive	Todd Township
My Favorite	Fulton Drive	Ayr Township
Penn's Best	Great Cove Road	Todd Township
Flowers of Friendship	Buchanan Trail	Ayr Township
Gem Star	Gem Bridge Road	Belfast Township
Horseshoe Star	Great Cove Road	Belfast Township
Sunflower	Union Church Road	Ayr Township
Art & Soul	Lincoln Way East	Todd Township
Carpenter's Star	Church Road	Brush Creek Township
Churn Dash	Layton Road	Brush Creek Township
Arrowhead	Great Cove Road	Todd Township
Steps to Knowledge	East Maple Street	McConnellsburg Township
Bear Paw	Dent Road	Thompson Township
Buckwheat	South Valley Road	Brush Creek Township
America's Bird	Knobsville Road	Todd Township
Six Windows of Sunshine	North 3rd Street	McConnellsburg Township
Pig Tail	Great Cove Road	Todd Township
North, South, East & West	North 3rd Street	McConnellsburg Township
Irish Green	East Patterson Street	Todd Township
Zelda's Ins & Outs	Black Bear Road	Belfast Township
J & B Star	Cito Road	Ayr Township
Cathy's Star Patchwork	Timber Ridge Road	Thompson Township
Hands All Around	Great Cove Road	Belfast Township
Pigeon Cove Cross	Alpine Road	Bethel Township
Nova	Great Cove Road	Belfast Township
Kansas	Black Mountain Road	Taylor Township
Crown of Thorns	Cito Road	Ayr Township

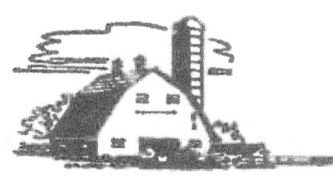

Frontier County Barn Quilt Listings

Blazing Star	Circle Drive	Taylor Township
County Fair	Lincoln Way East	Todd Township
Scout's Sunflower	Big Cove Tannery Road	Ayr Township
Union Star	Spring Road	Bethel Township
Horn of Plenty	Horton Drive	Ayr Township
Maryland, Old Line State	Battle Ridge Road	Dublin Township
Farmer Fields	Great Cove Road	Aye Township
Mill Wheel	Grist Mill Road	Dublin Township
Dickey's Mountain Star	Big Cove Tannery Road	Thompson Township
Maltese Cross	East Maple Street	McConnellsburg Township
Jacques Illinois Star	Circle Drive	Licking Creek Township
Northcraft's	Buck Valley Road	Union Township

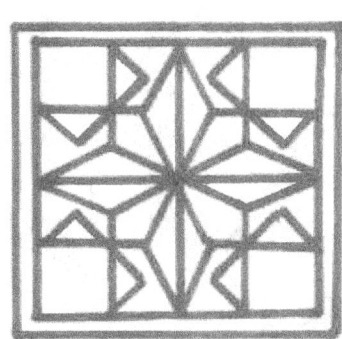 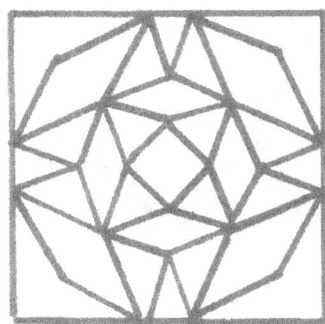 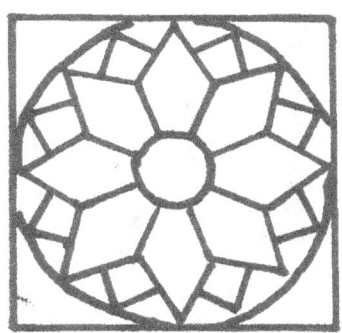

Barn Quilt Our Hearts
Frontier County Barn Quilt Trail

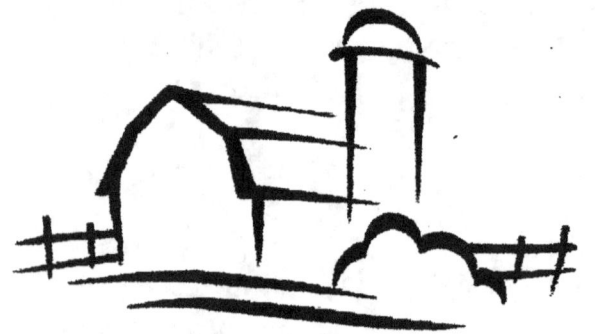

**Barn Quilt Location
Knobsville Road
Todd Township**

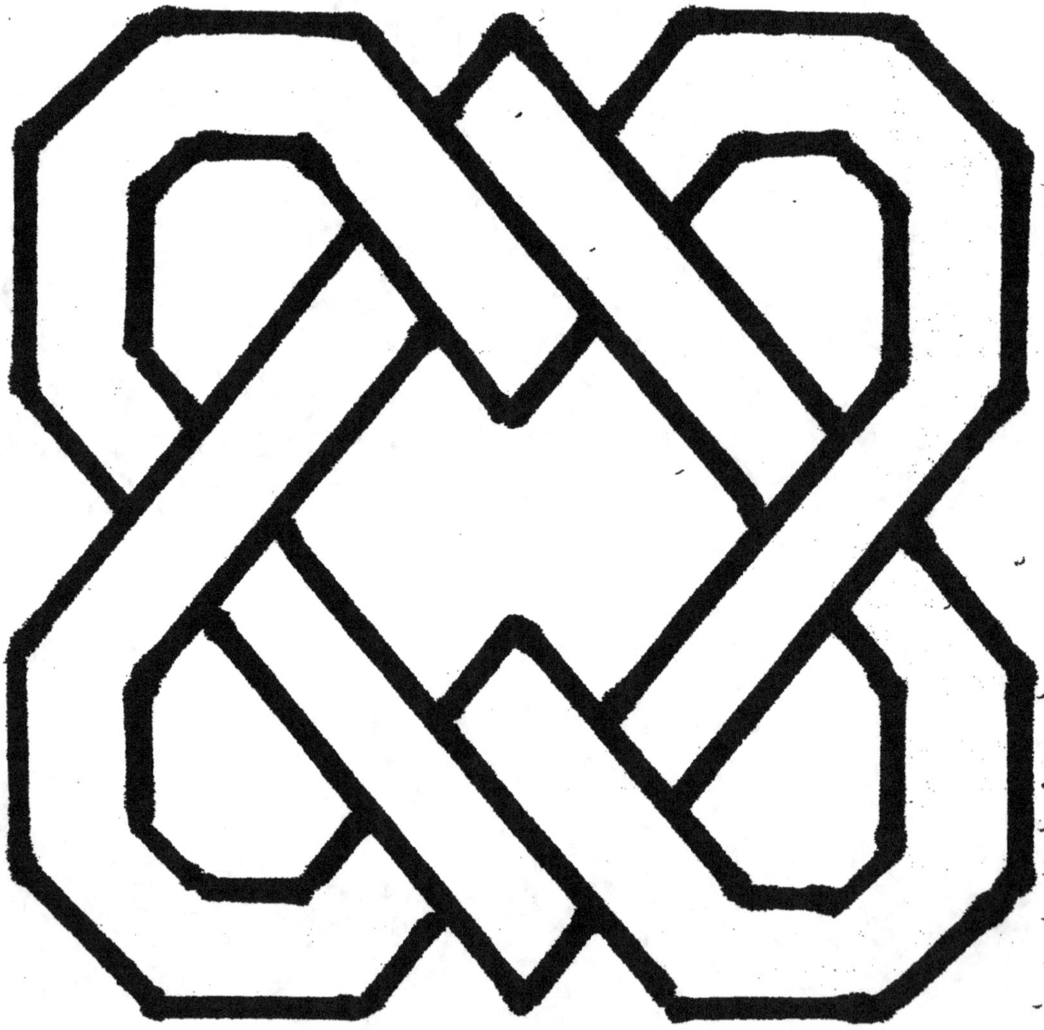

Frontier County Barn Quilt Our Hearts

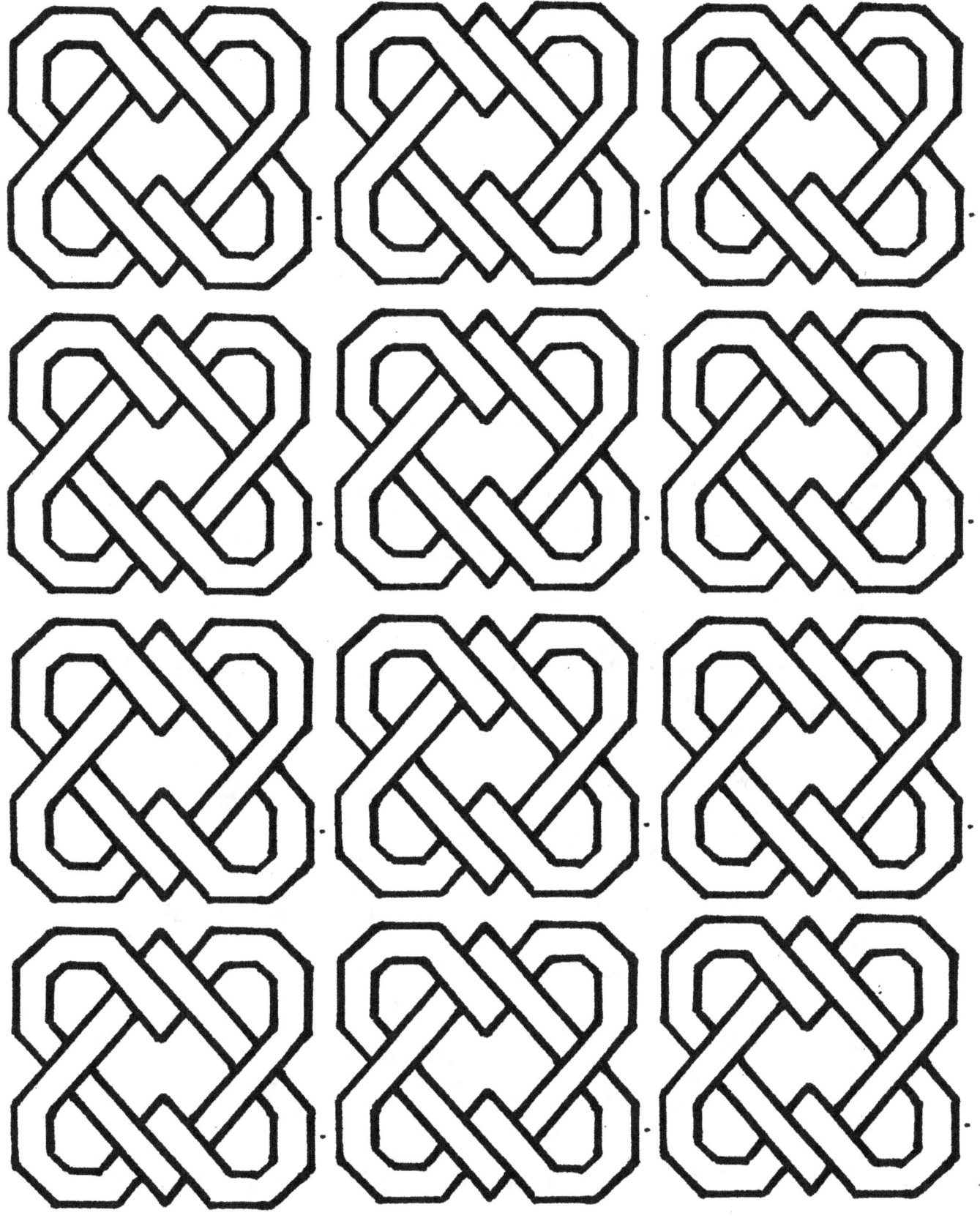

Barn Quilt T Square
Frontier County Barn Quilt Trail

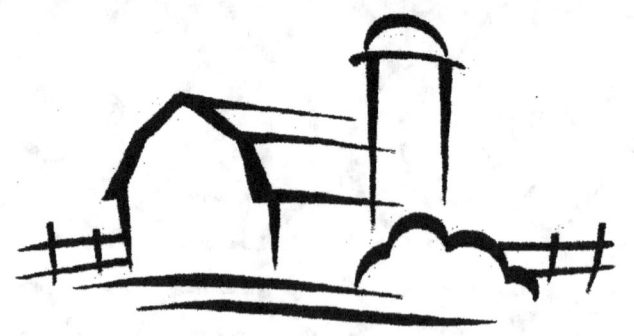

Barn Quilt Location
Sipes Mill Road
Licking Creek Township

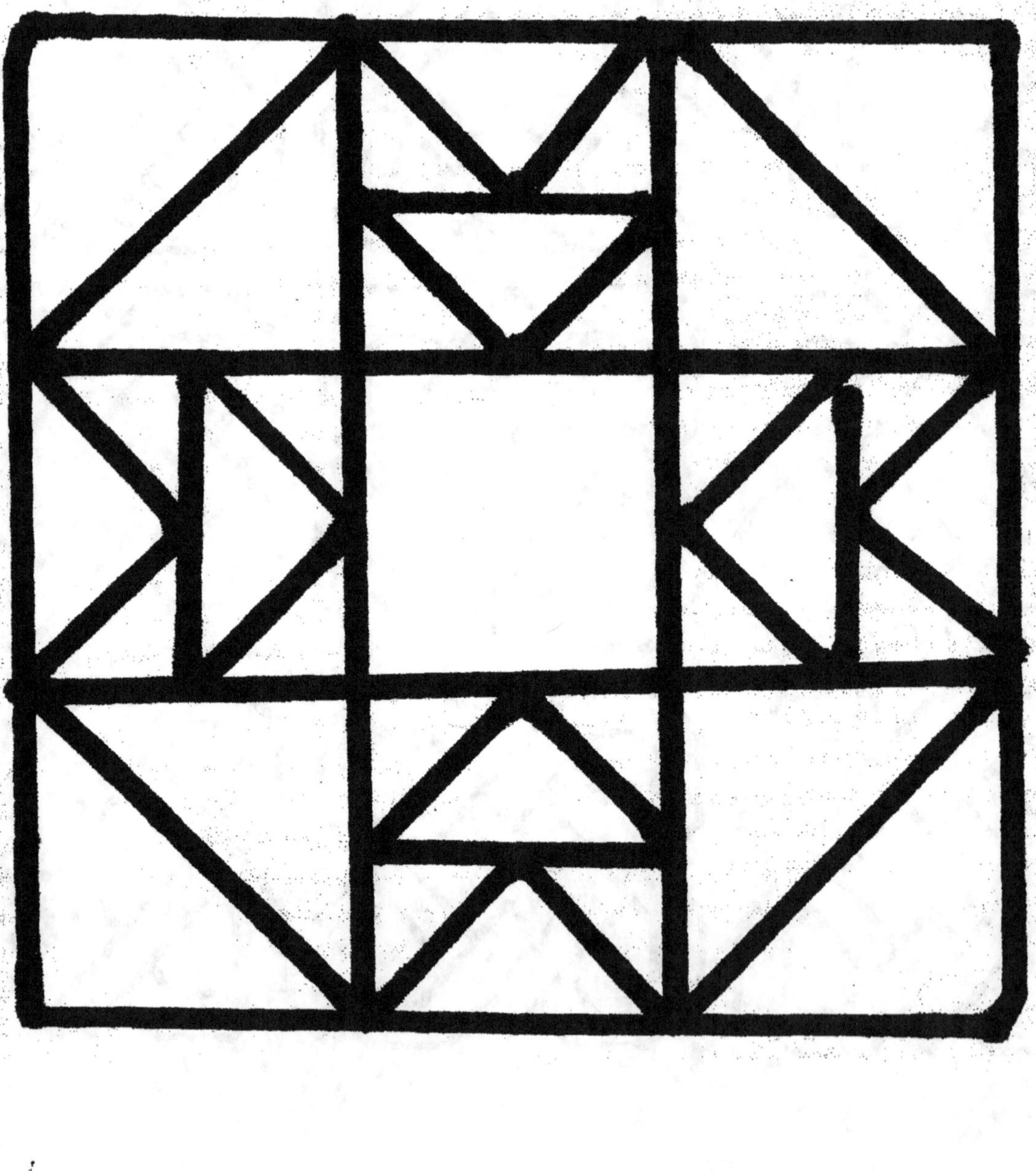

Frontier County Barn Quilt T Square

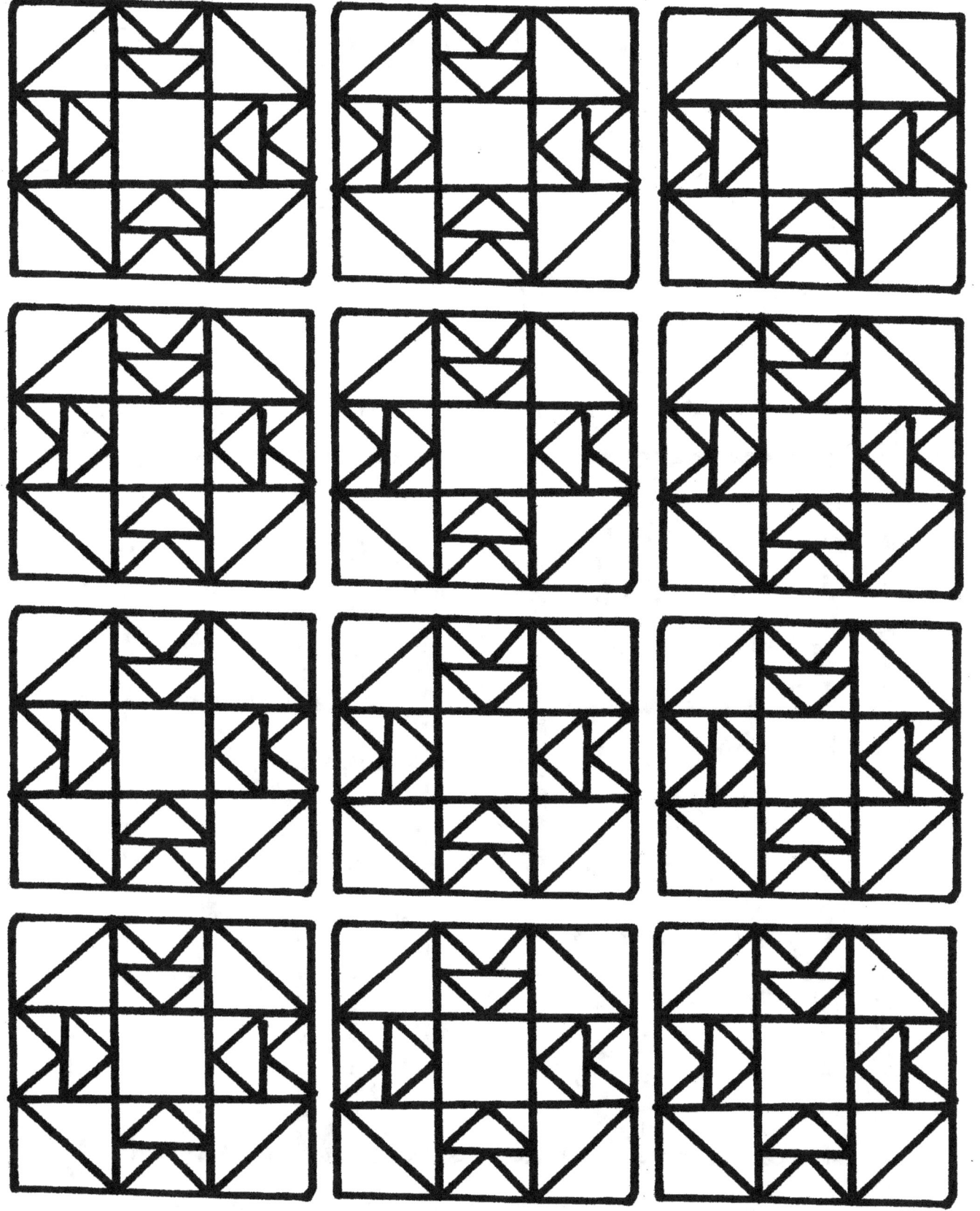

Barn Quilt Liberty
Frontier County Barn Quilt Trail

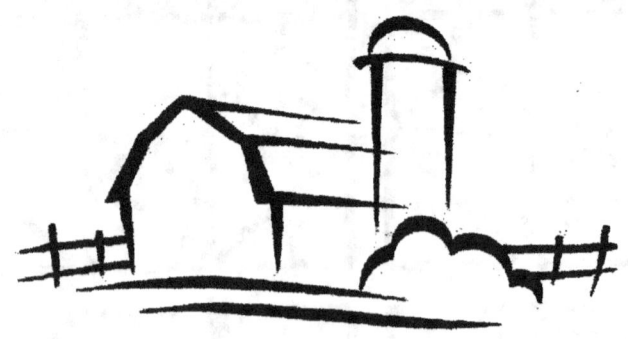

Barn Quilt Location
North 2ⁿᵈ Street
McConnellsburg Township

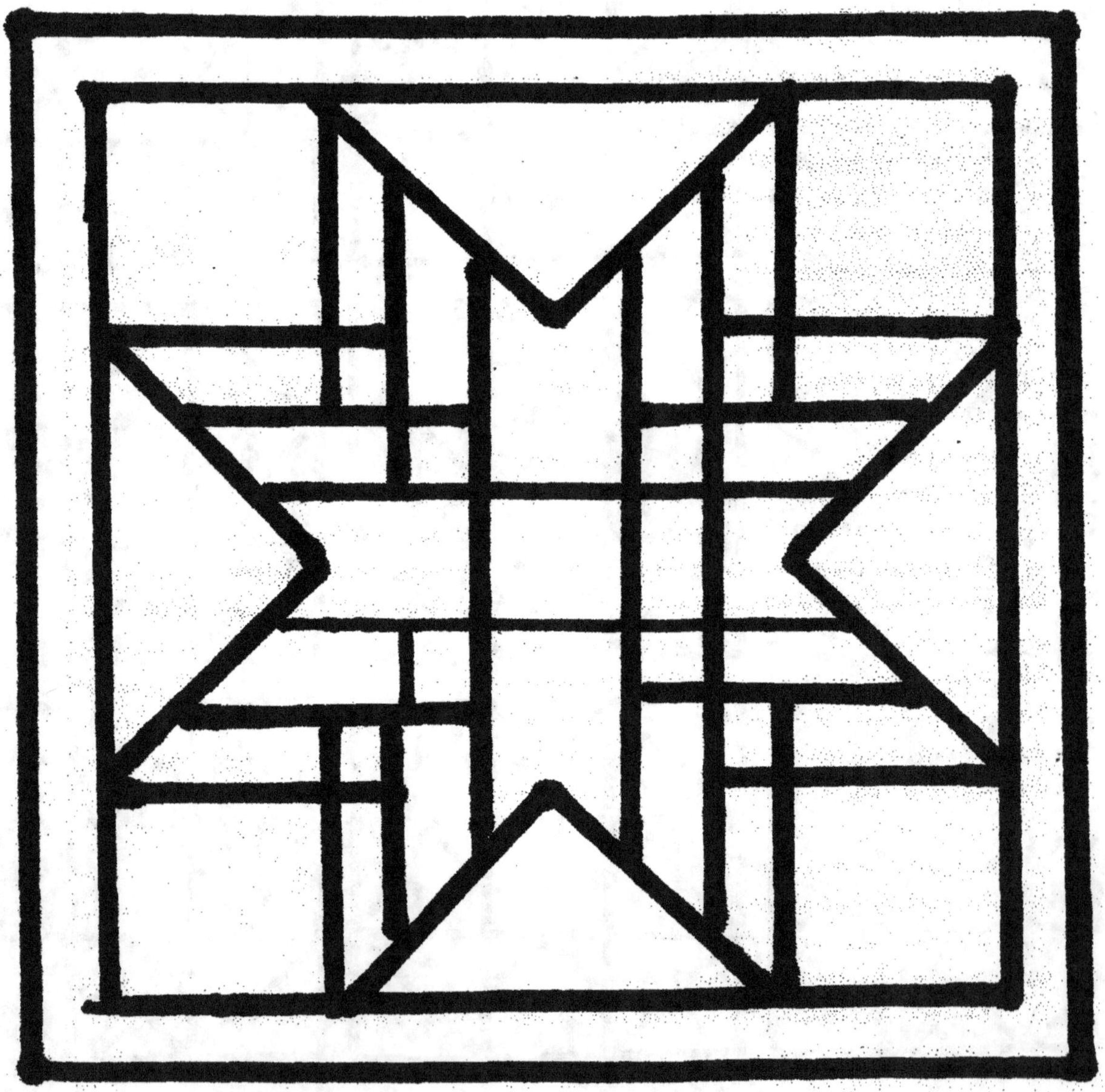

Frontier County Barn Quilt Liberty

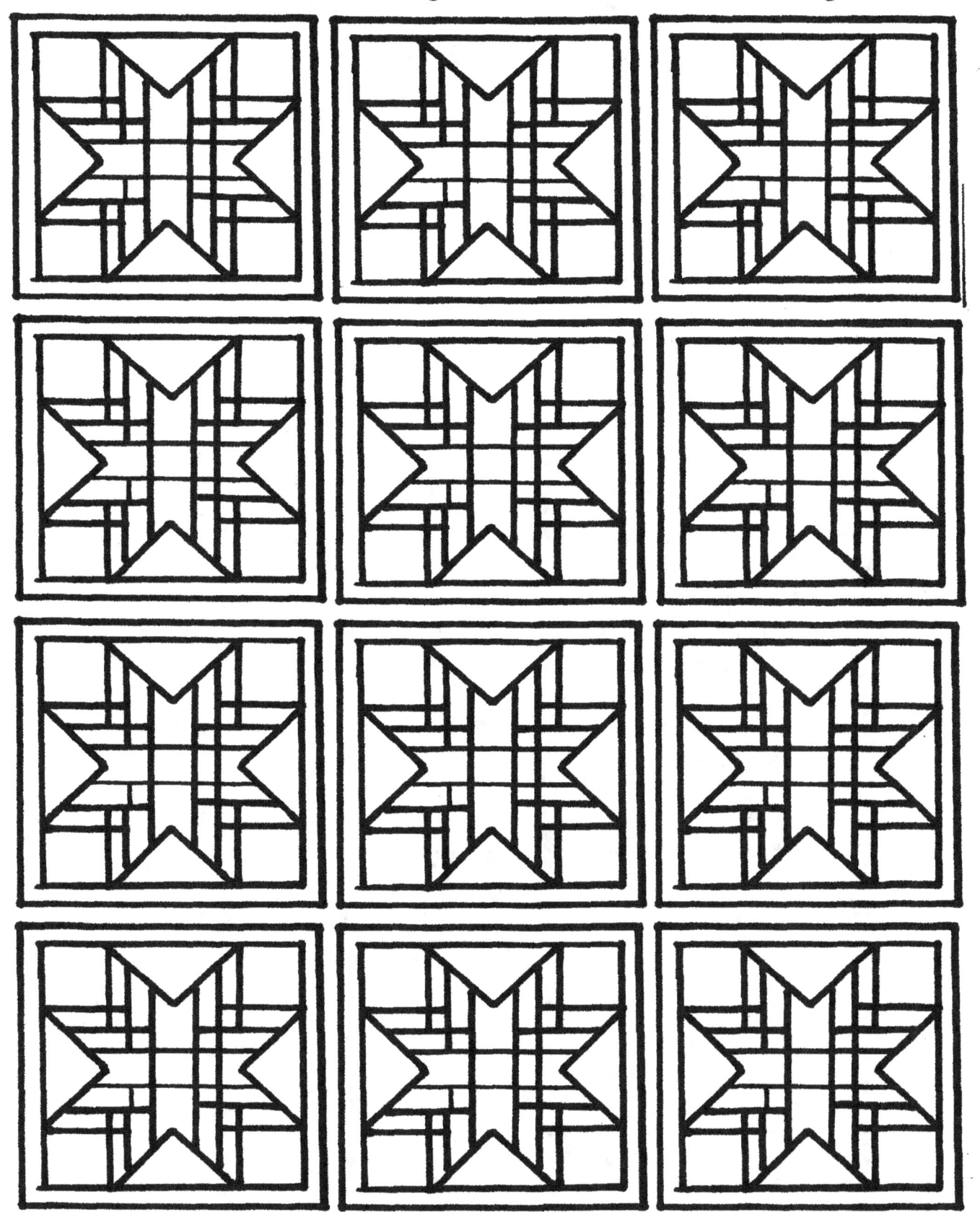

Barn Quilt Shaffer Sunset
Frontier County Barn Quilt Trail

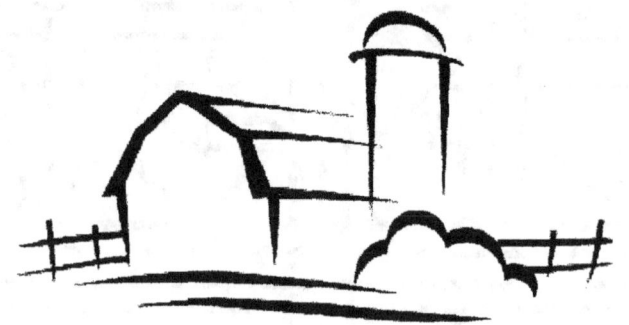

Barn Quilt Location
North 2nd Street
McConnellsburg Township

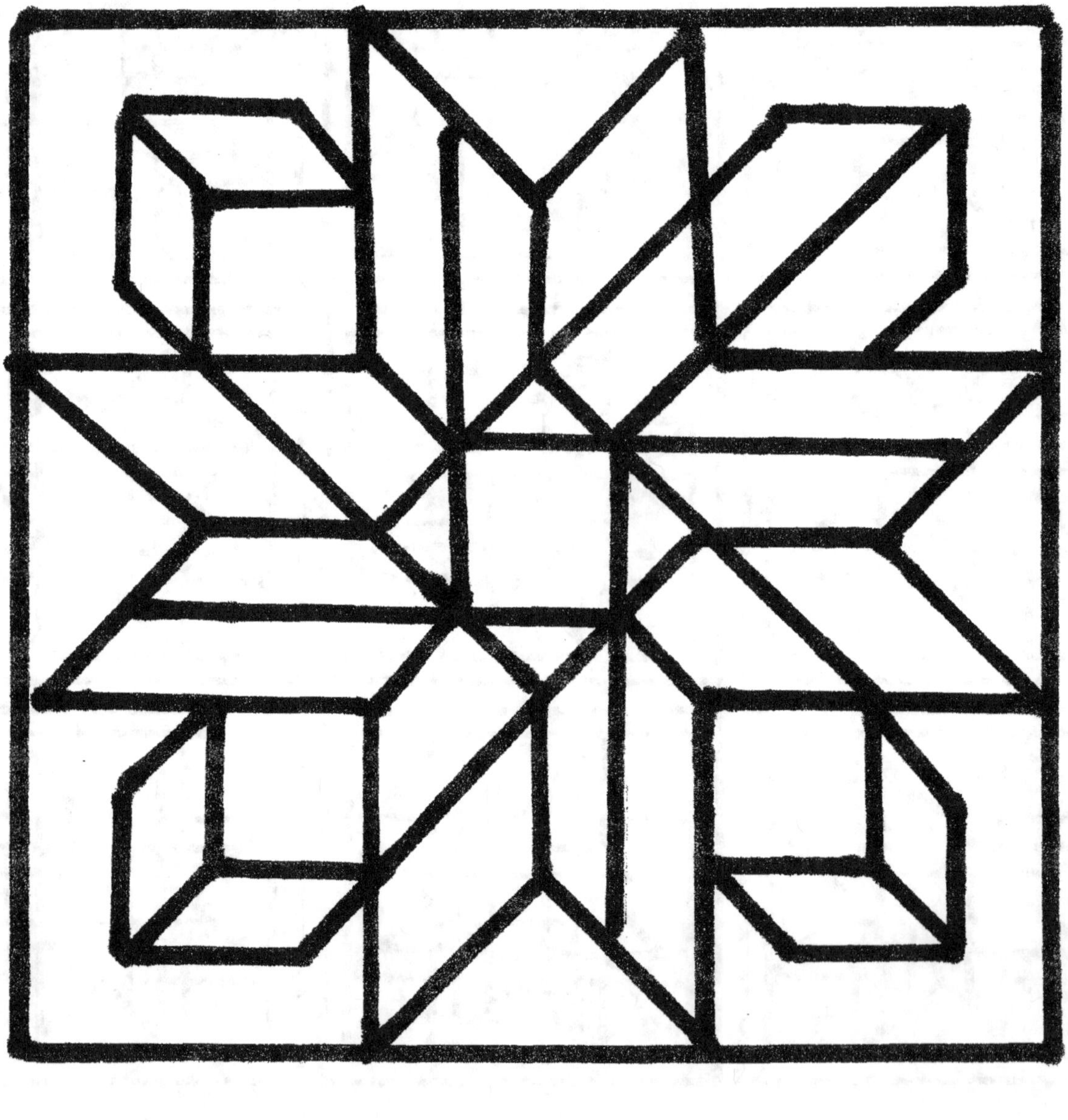

Frontier County Barn Quilt Shaffer Sunset

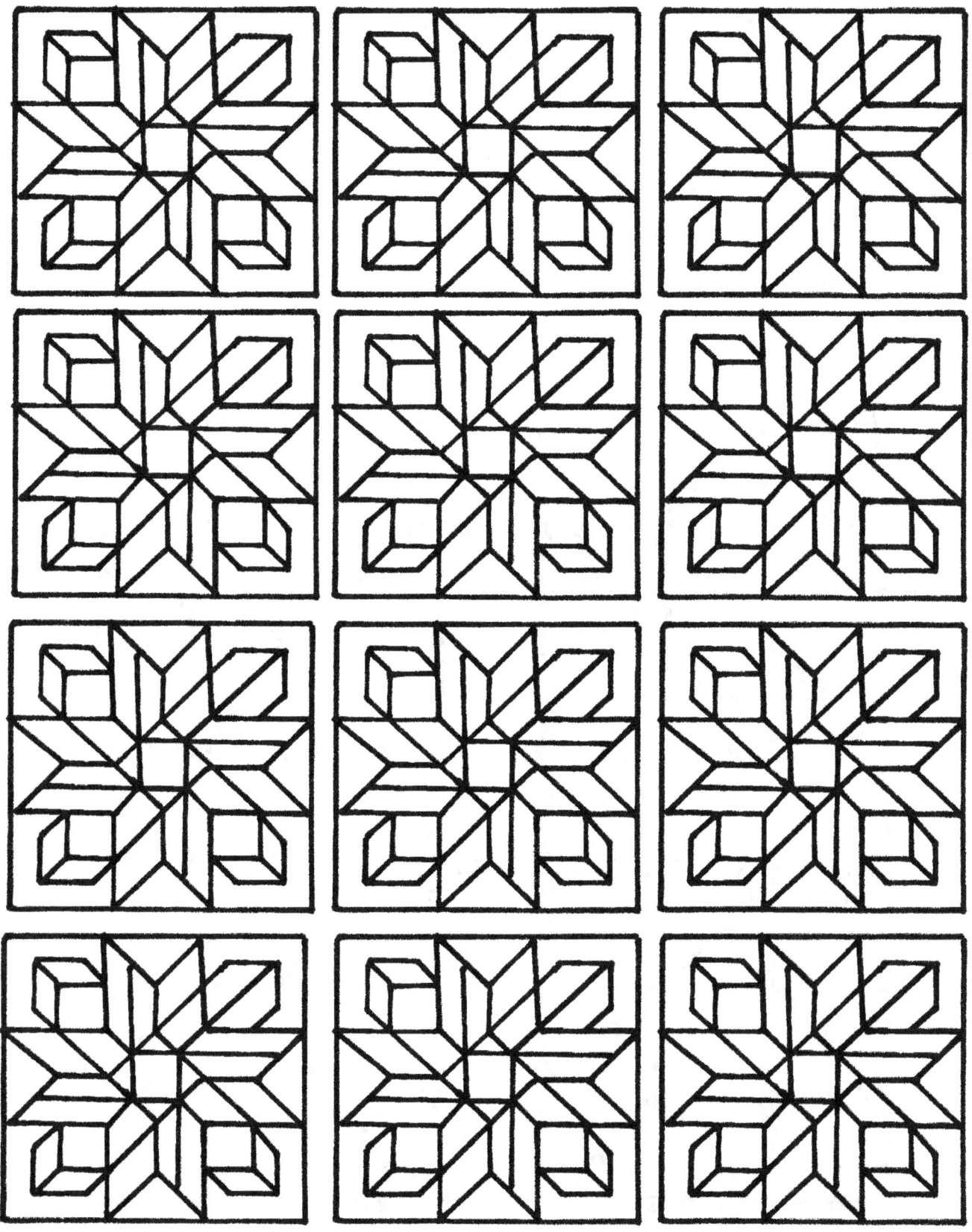

Barn Quilt Turkey Tracks
Frontier County Barn Quilt Trail

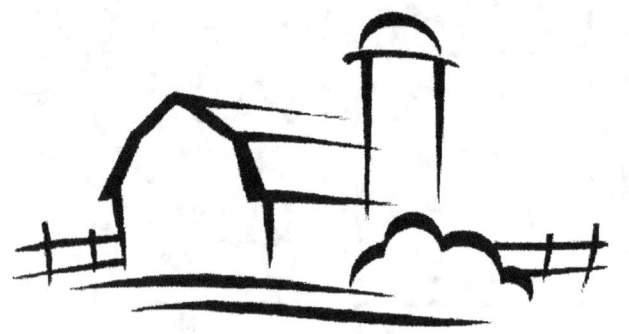

Barn Quilt Location
North Valley Road
Wells Township

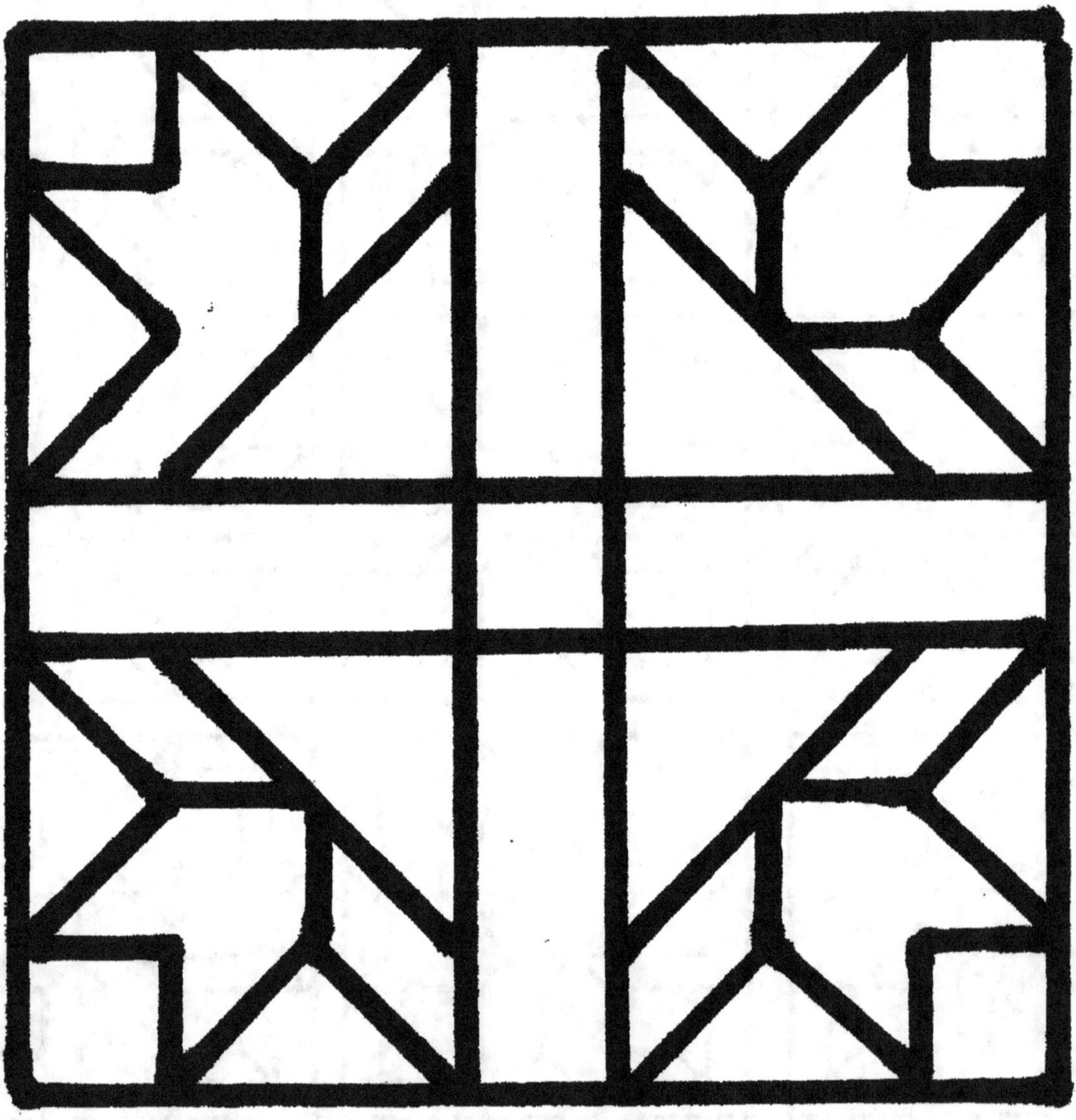

Frontier County Barn Quilt Turkey Tracks

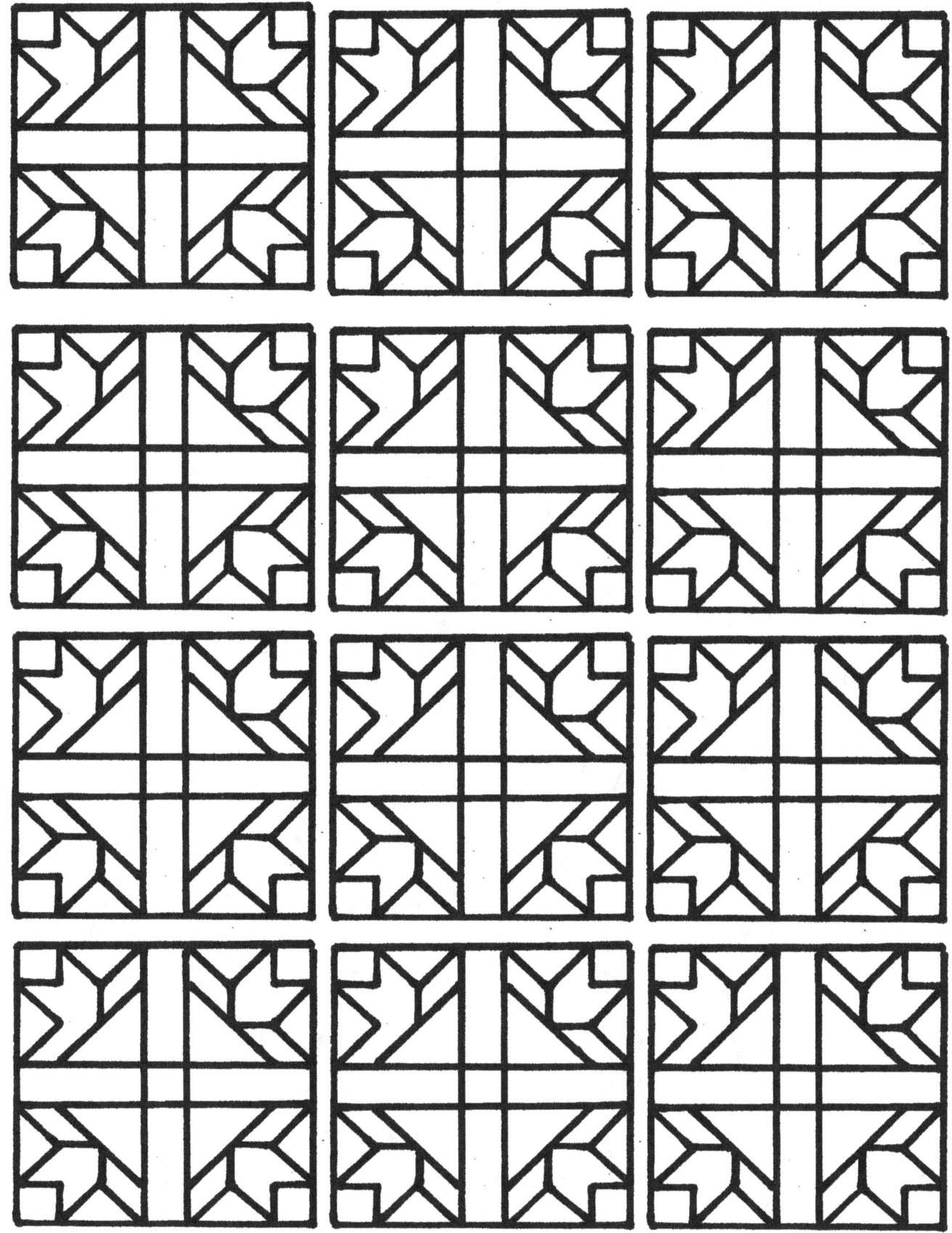

Barn Quilt Hopes & Dreams
Frontier County Barn Quilt Trail

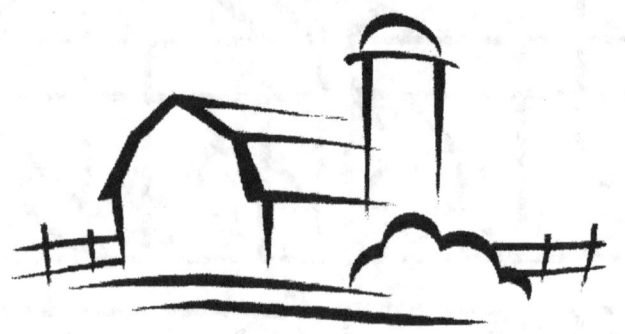

Barn Quilt Location
Great Cove Road
Ayr Township

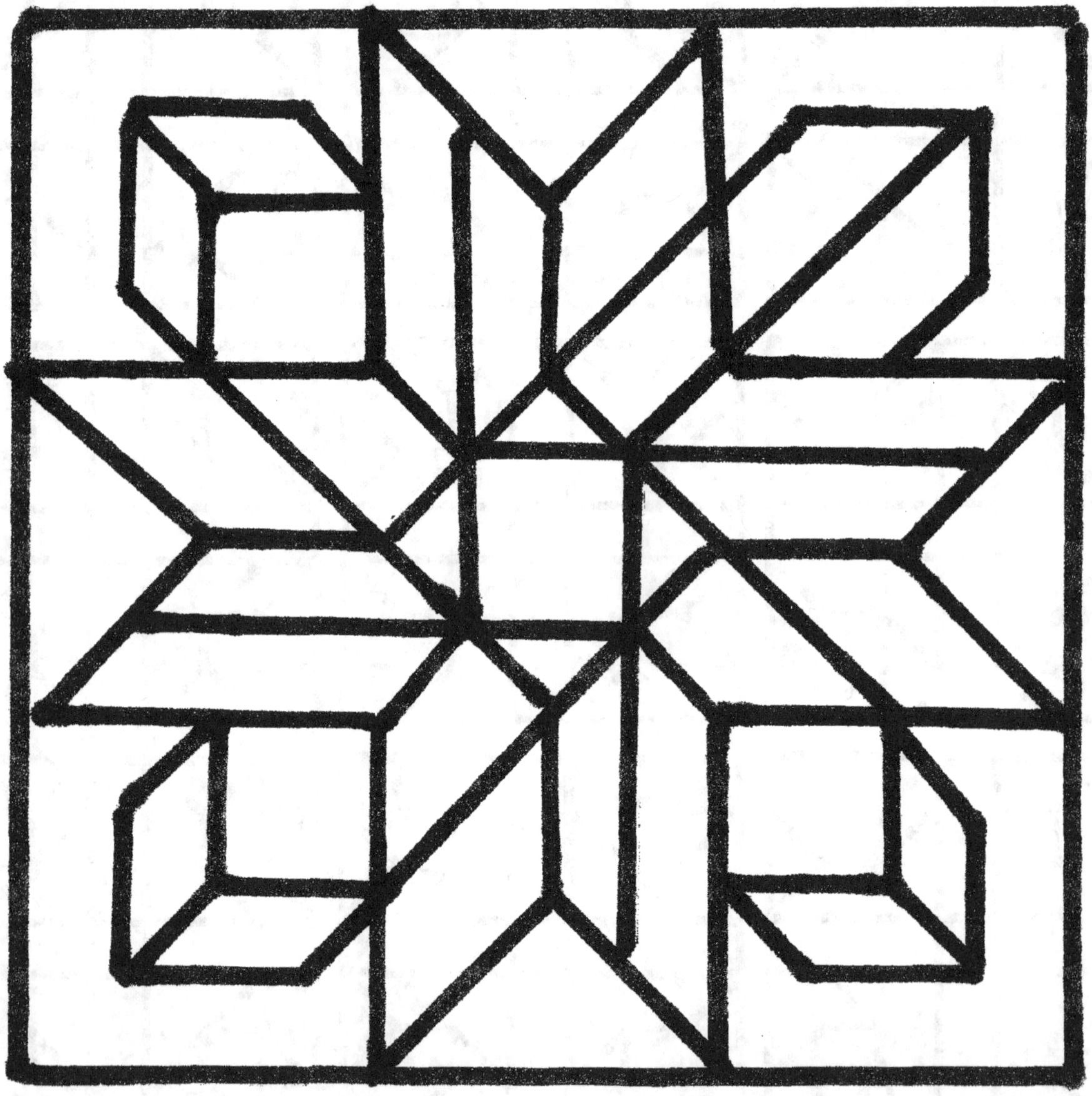

Frontier County Barn Quilt Hopes & Dreams

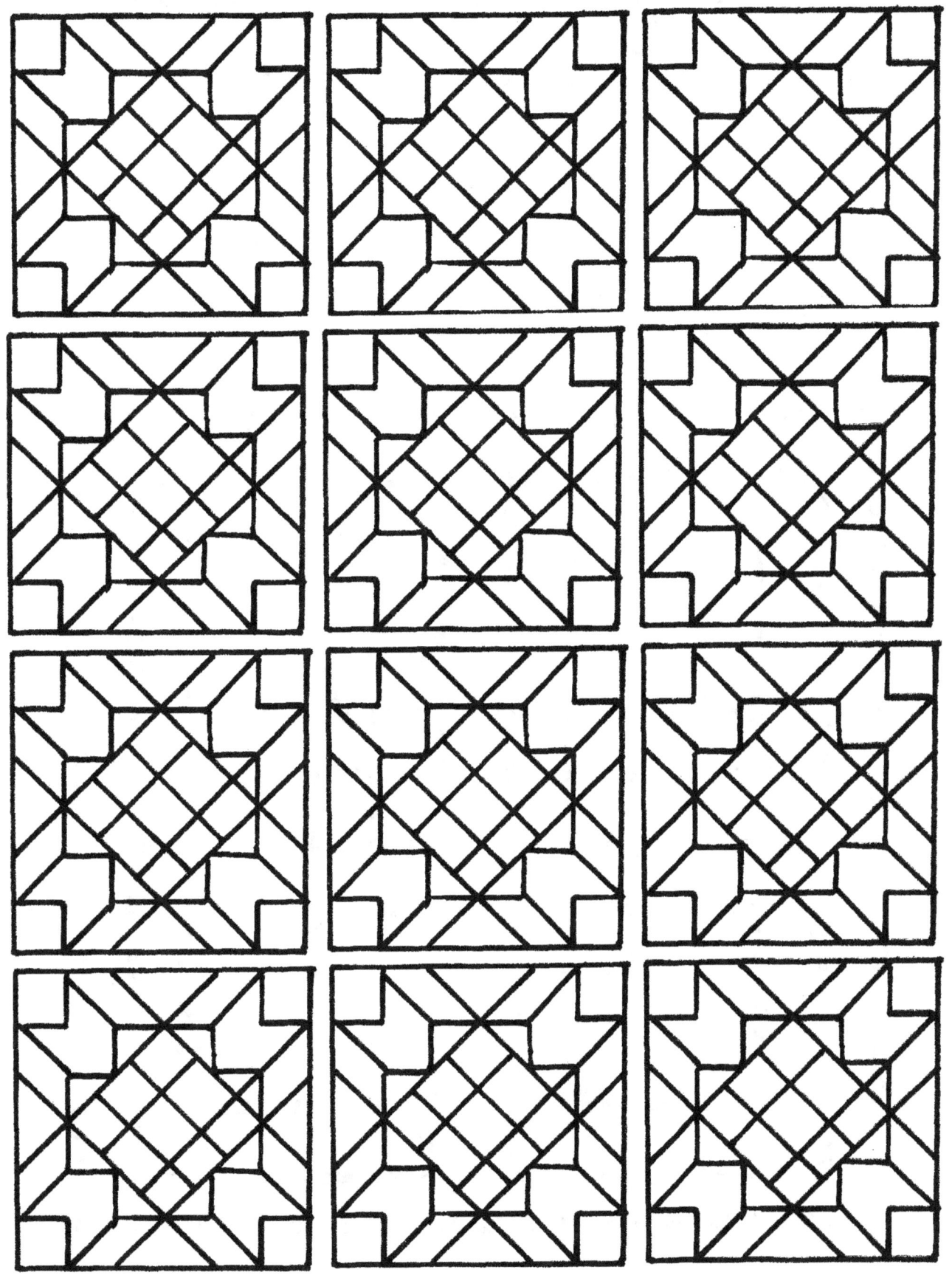

Barn Quilt Celtic Knot
Frontier County Barn Quilt Trail

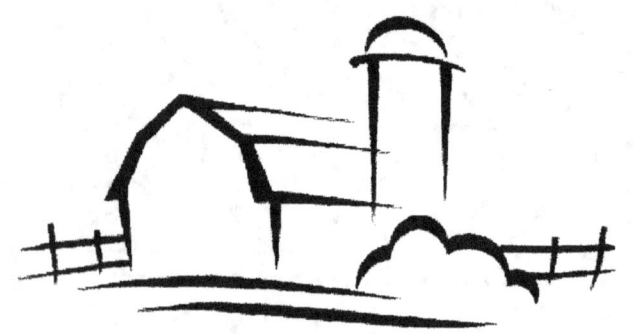

Barn Quilt Location
Great Cove Road
Dublin Township

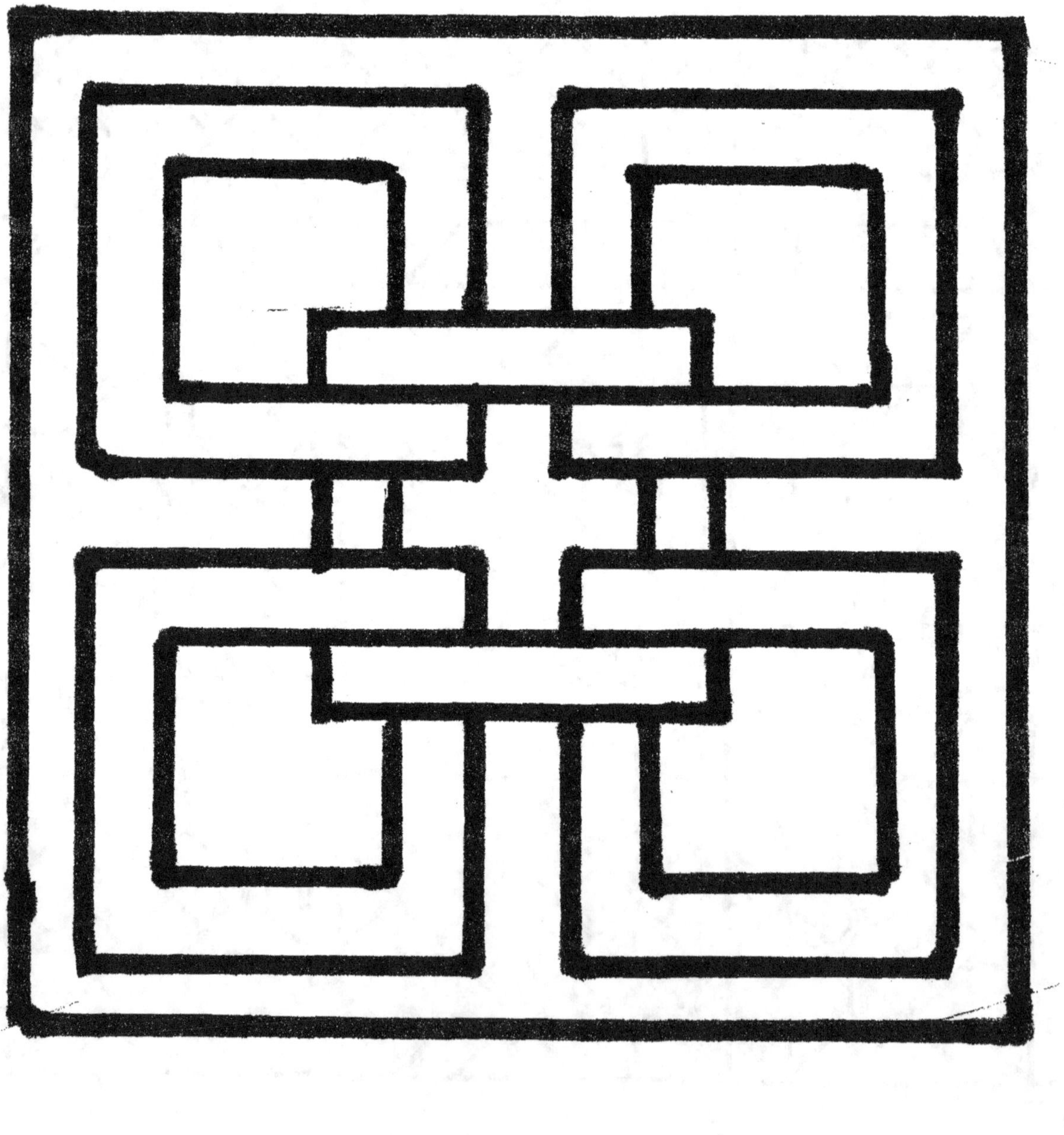

Frontier County Barn Quilt Celtic Knot

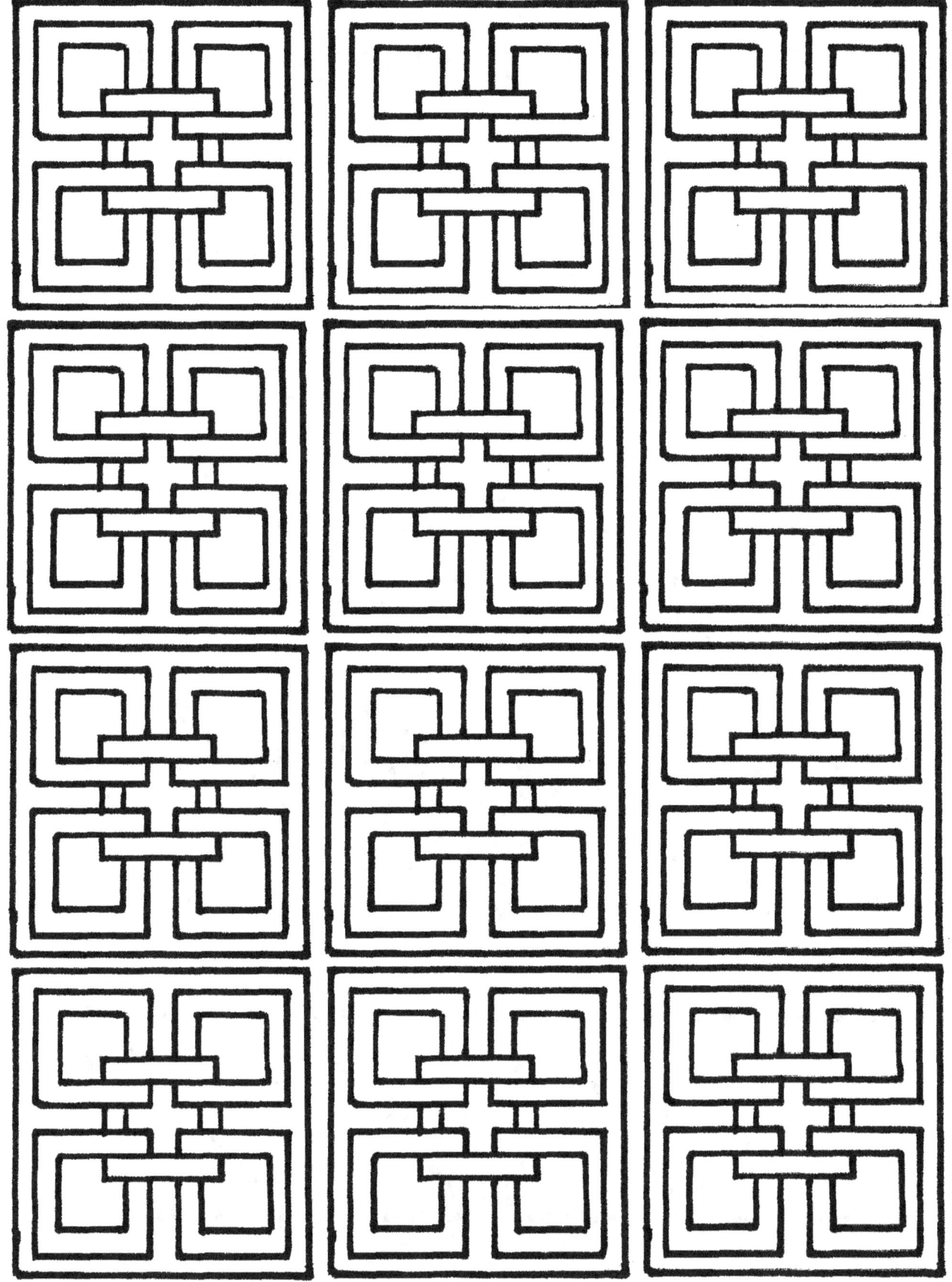

Barn Quilt Becky's Own
Frontier County Barn Quilt Trail

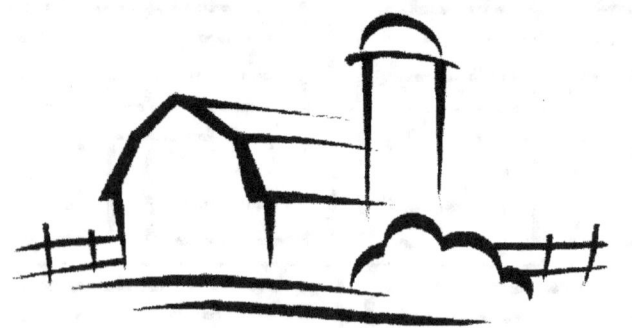

Barn Quilt Location
Great Cove Road
Ayr Township

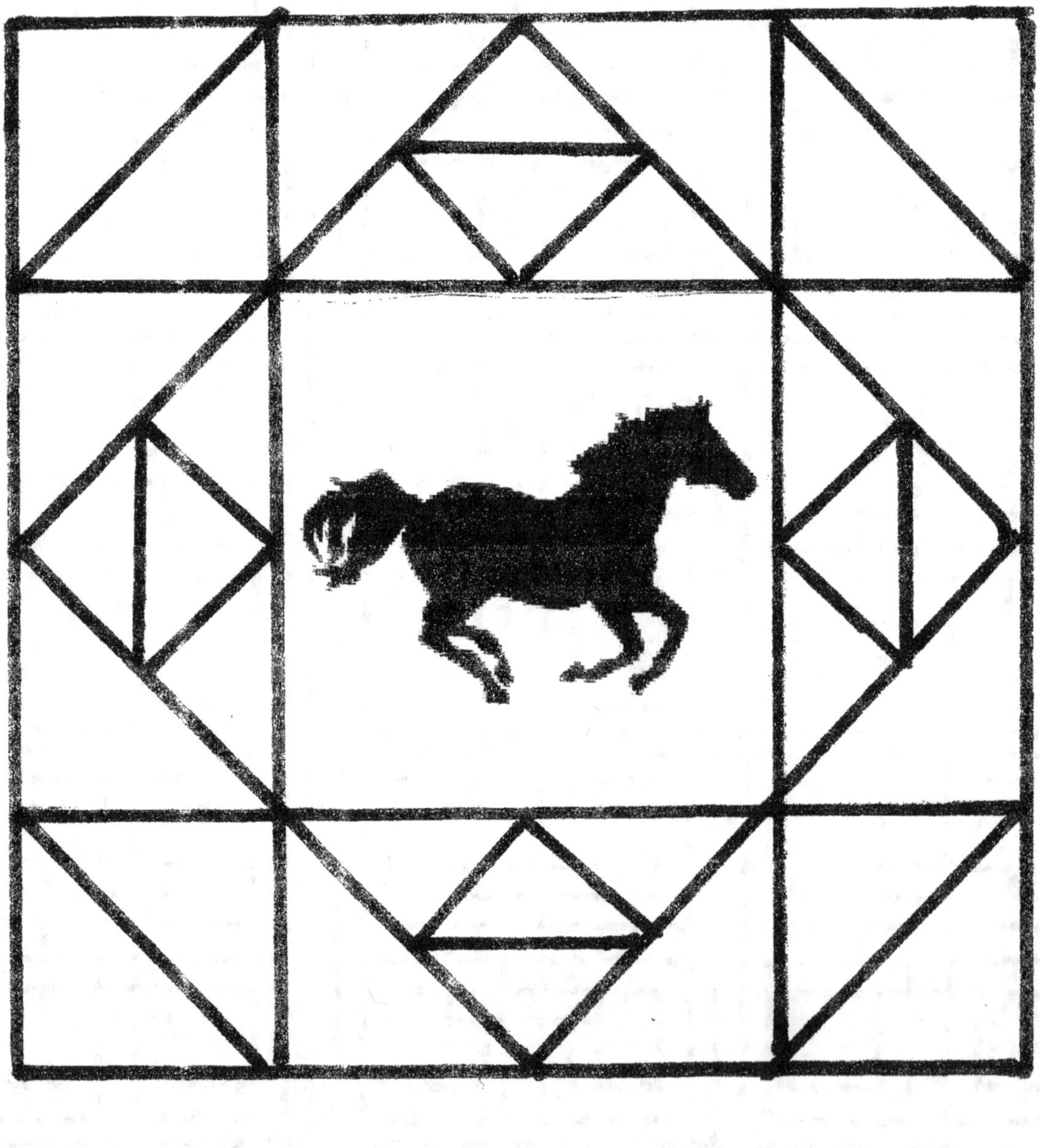

Frontier County Barn Quilt Becky's Own

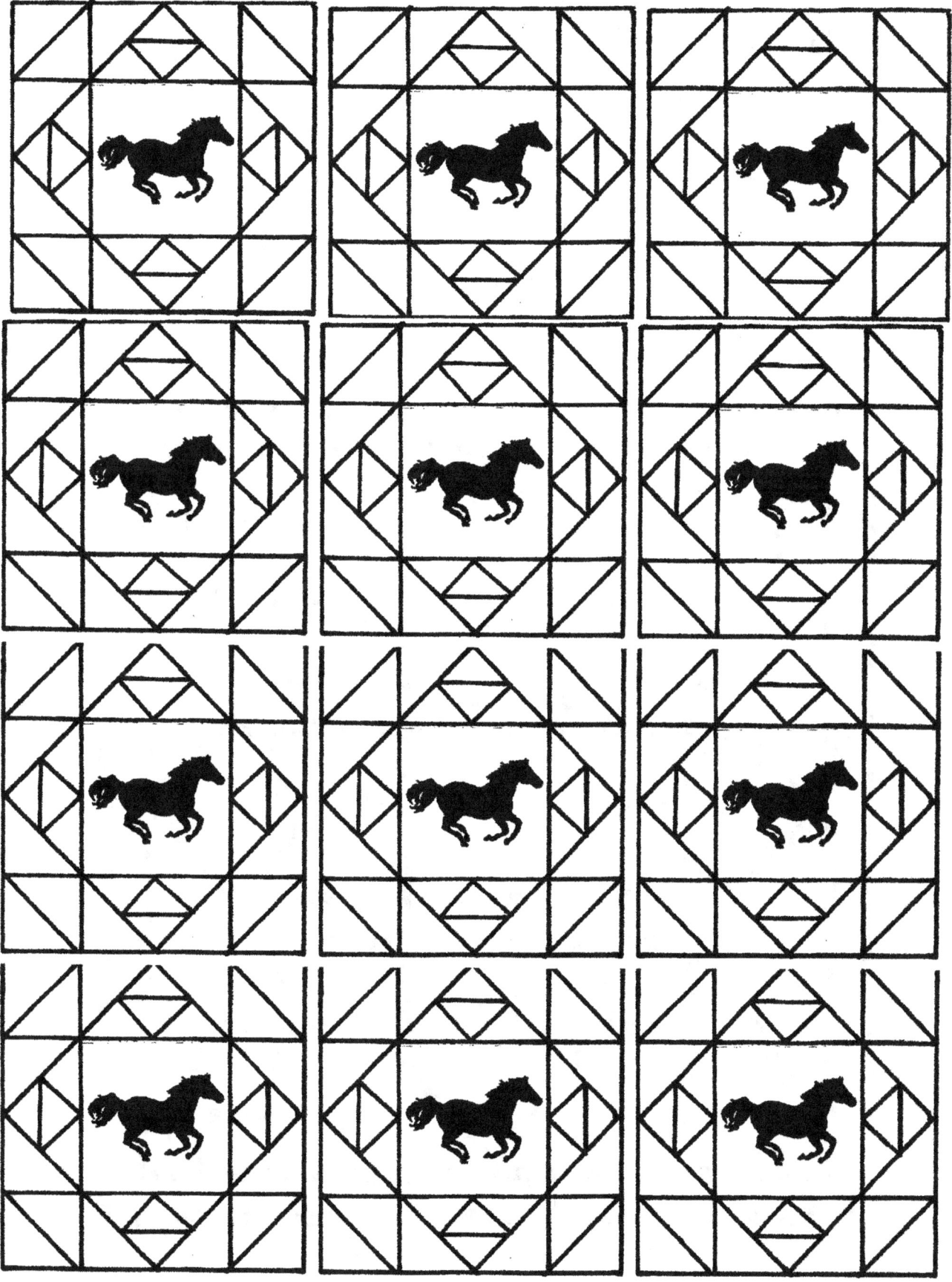

Barn Quilt Still Here...Still Strong
Frontier County Barn Quilt Trail

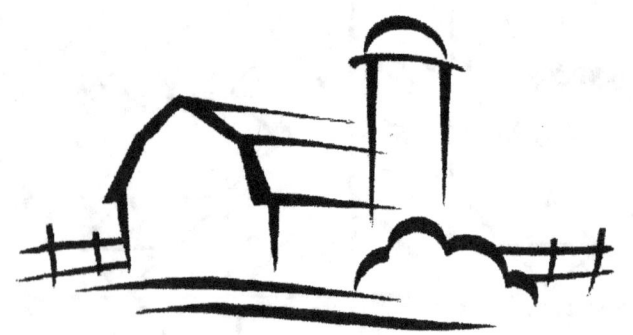

Barn Quilt Location
Cito Road
Ayr Township

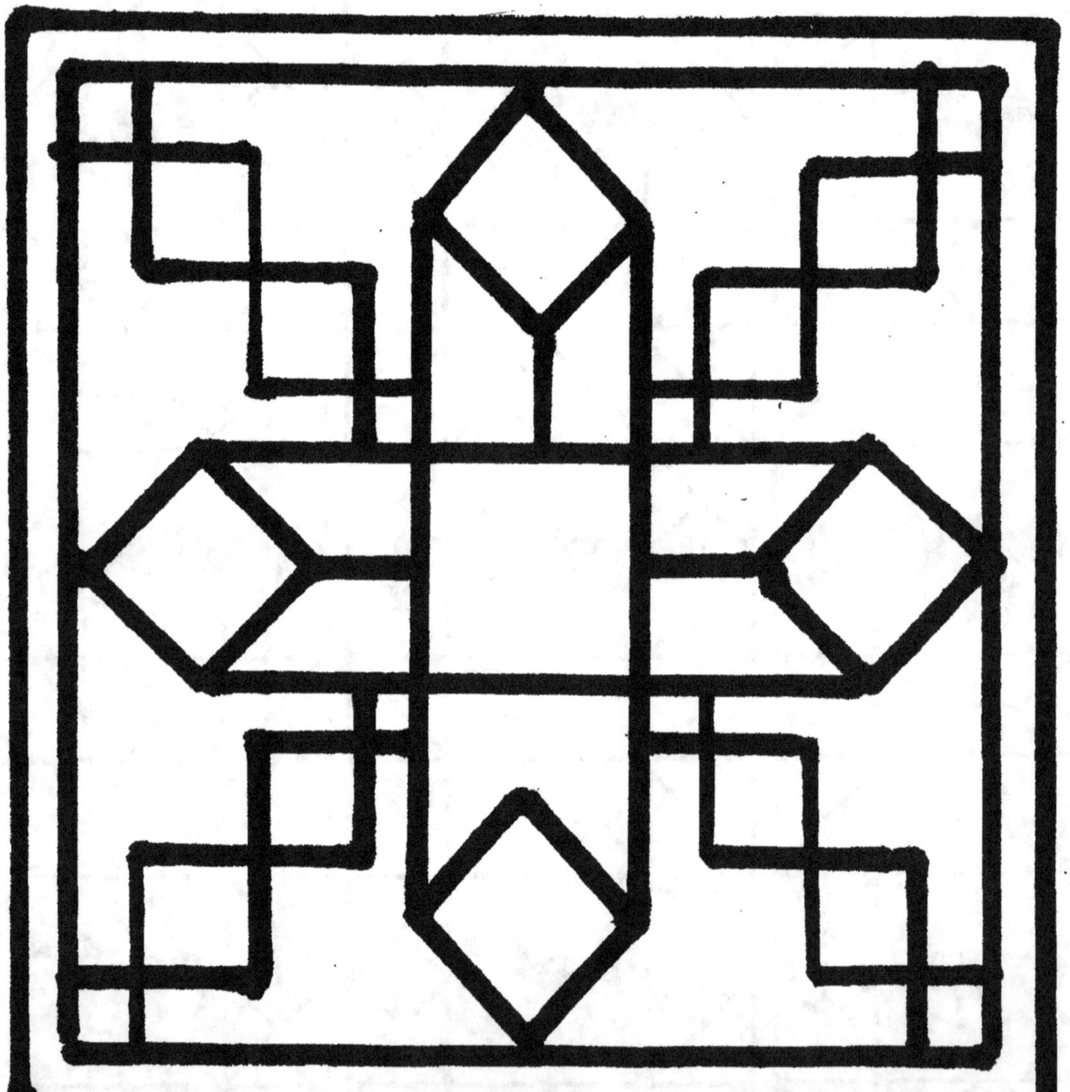

Frontier County Barn Quilt Still Here...Still Strong

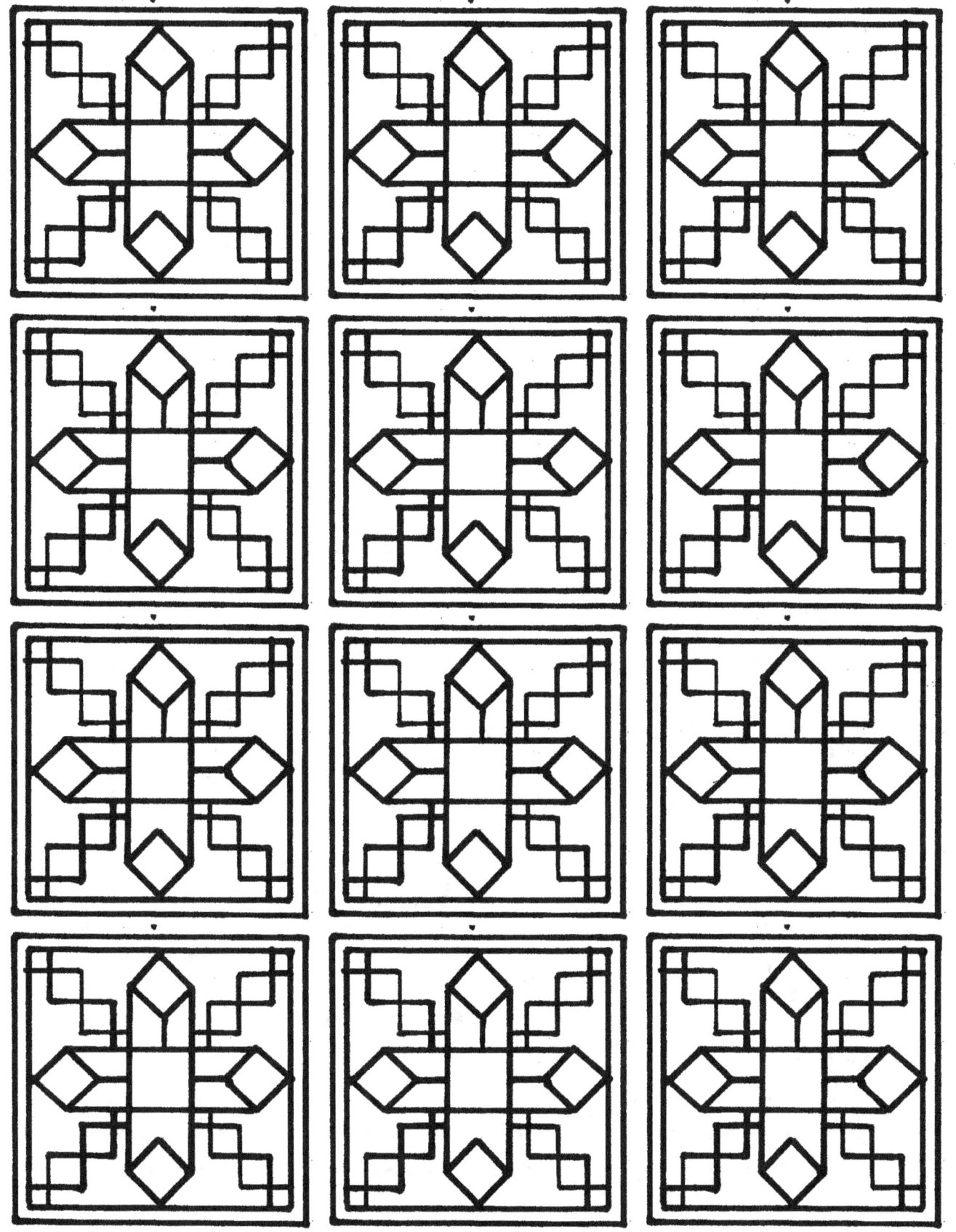

Barn Quilt Corn Beans
Frontier County Barn Quilt Trail

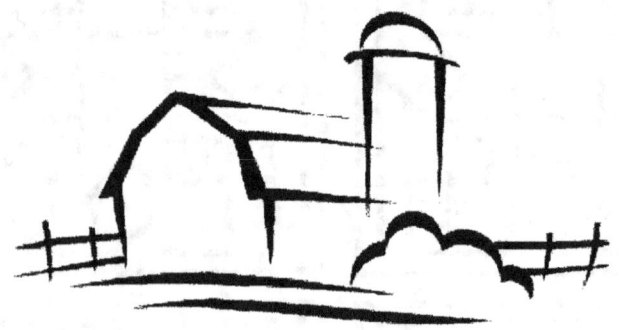

Barn Quilt Location
South Valley Road
Brush Creek Township

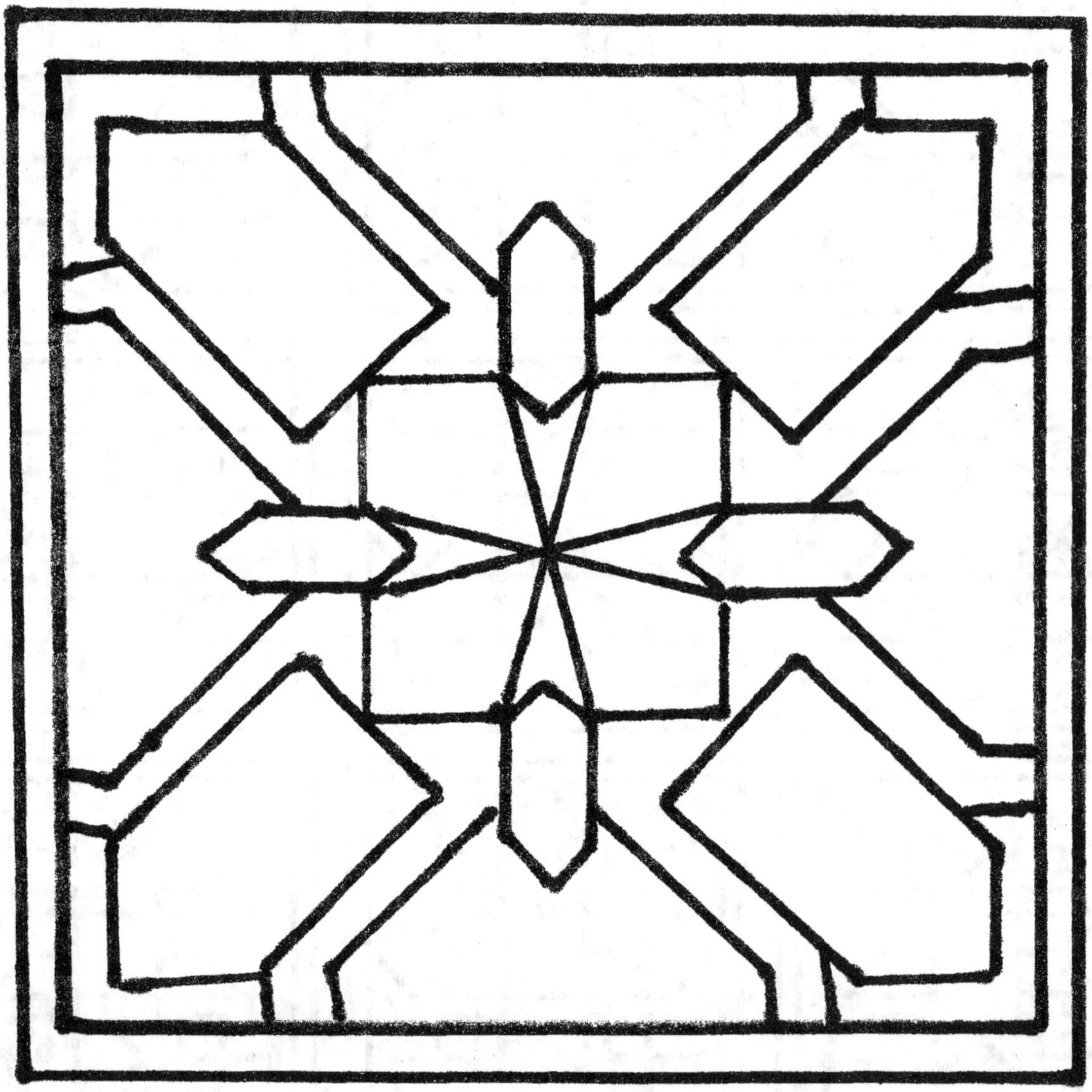

Frontier County Barn Quilt Corn & Beans

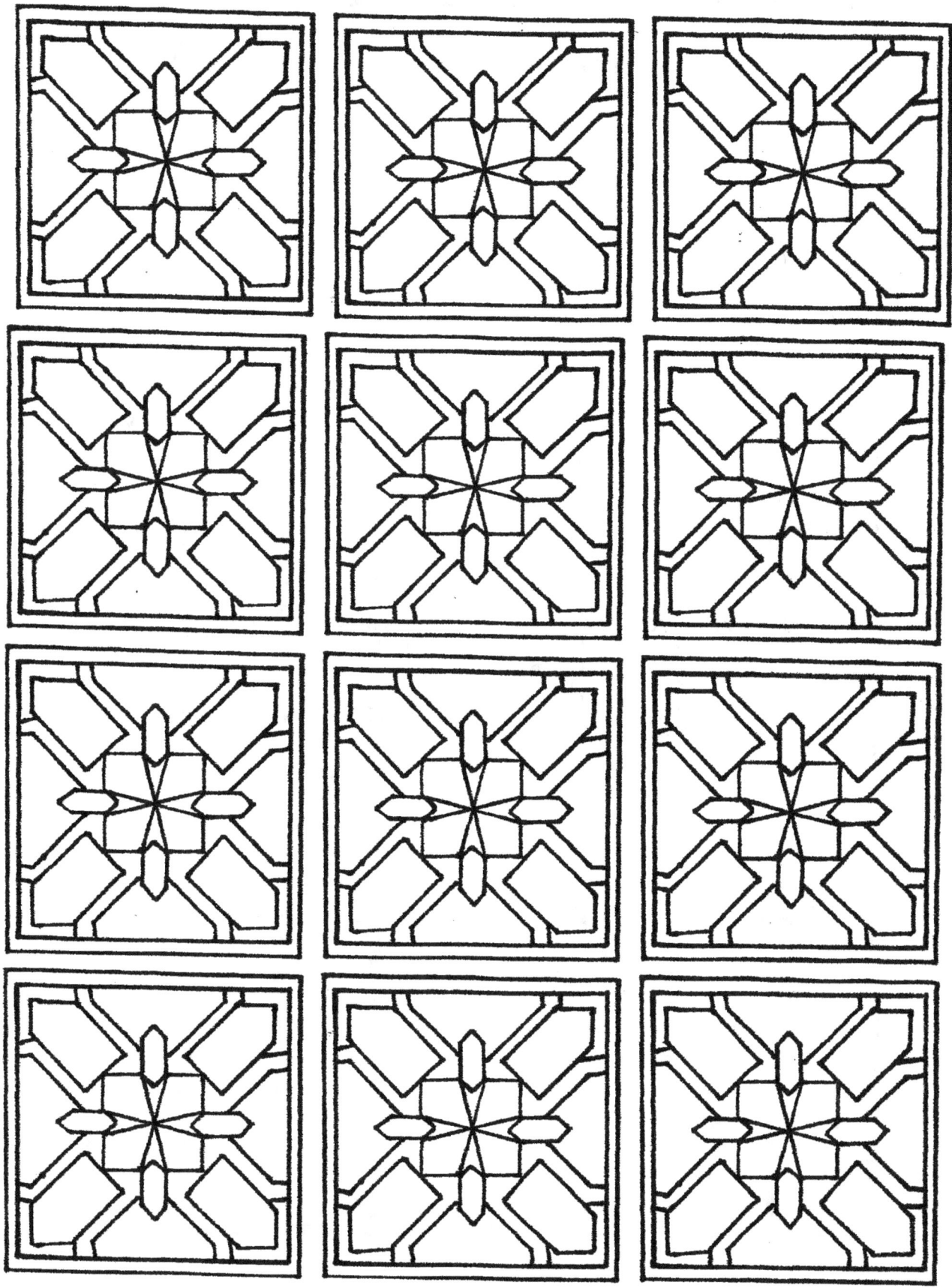

Barn Quilt Endless Chain
Frontier County Barn Quilt Trail

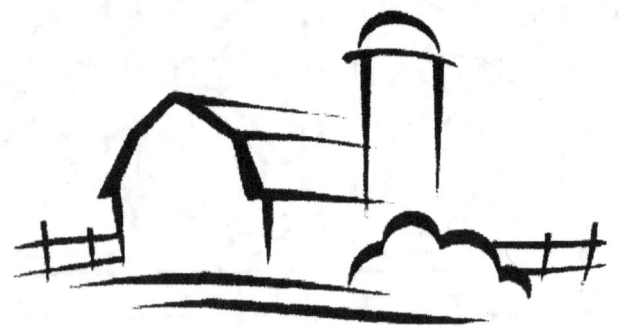

Barn Quilt Location
Pleasant Valley Road
Brush Creek Township

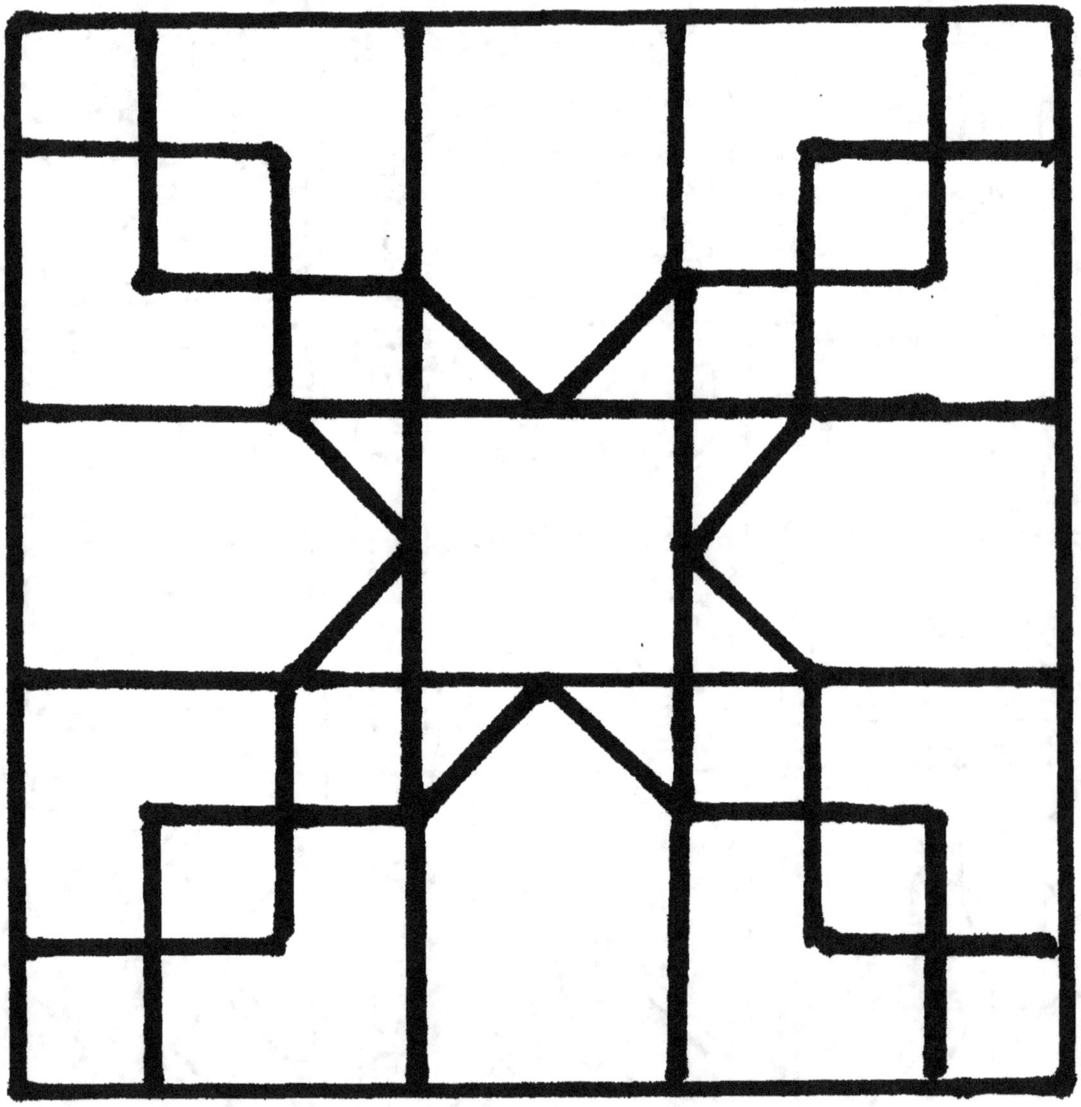

Frontier County Barn Quilt Endless Chain

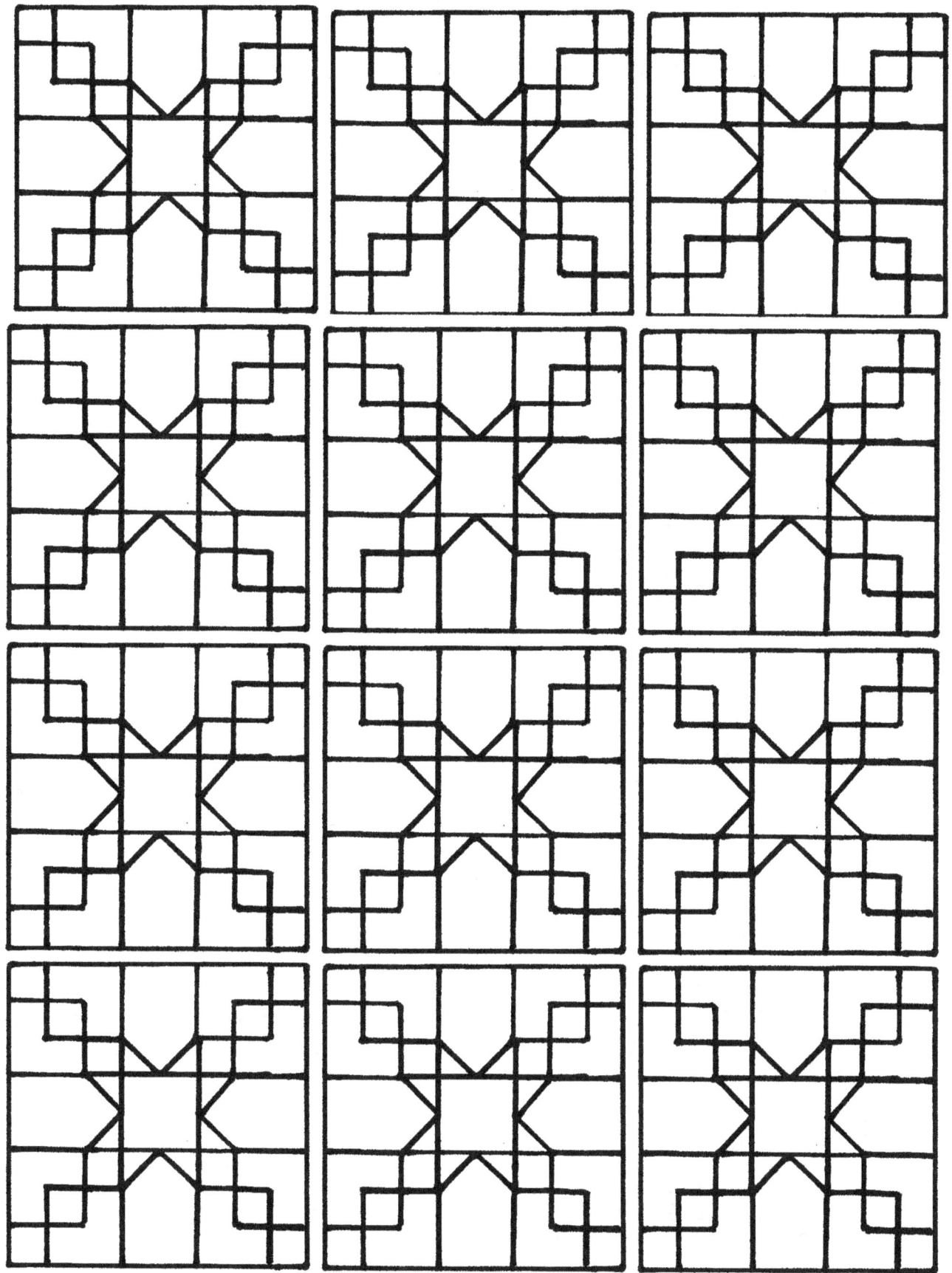

Barn Quilt Hither & Yon
Frontier County Barn Quilt Trail

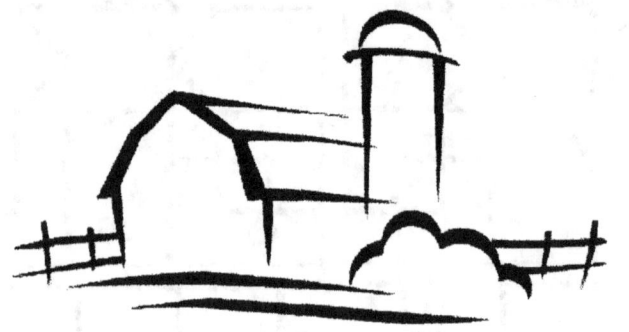

**Barn Quilt Location
Lions Park Drive
Todd Township**

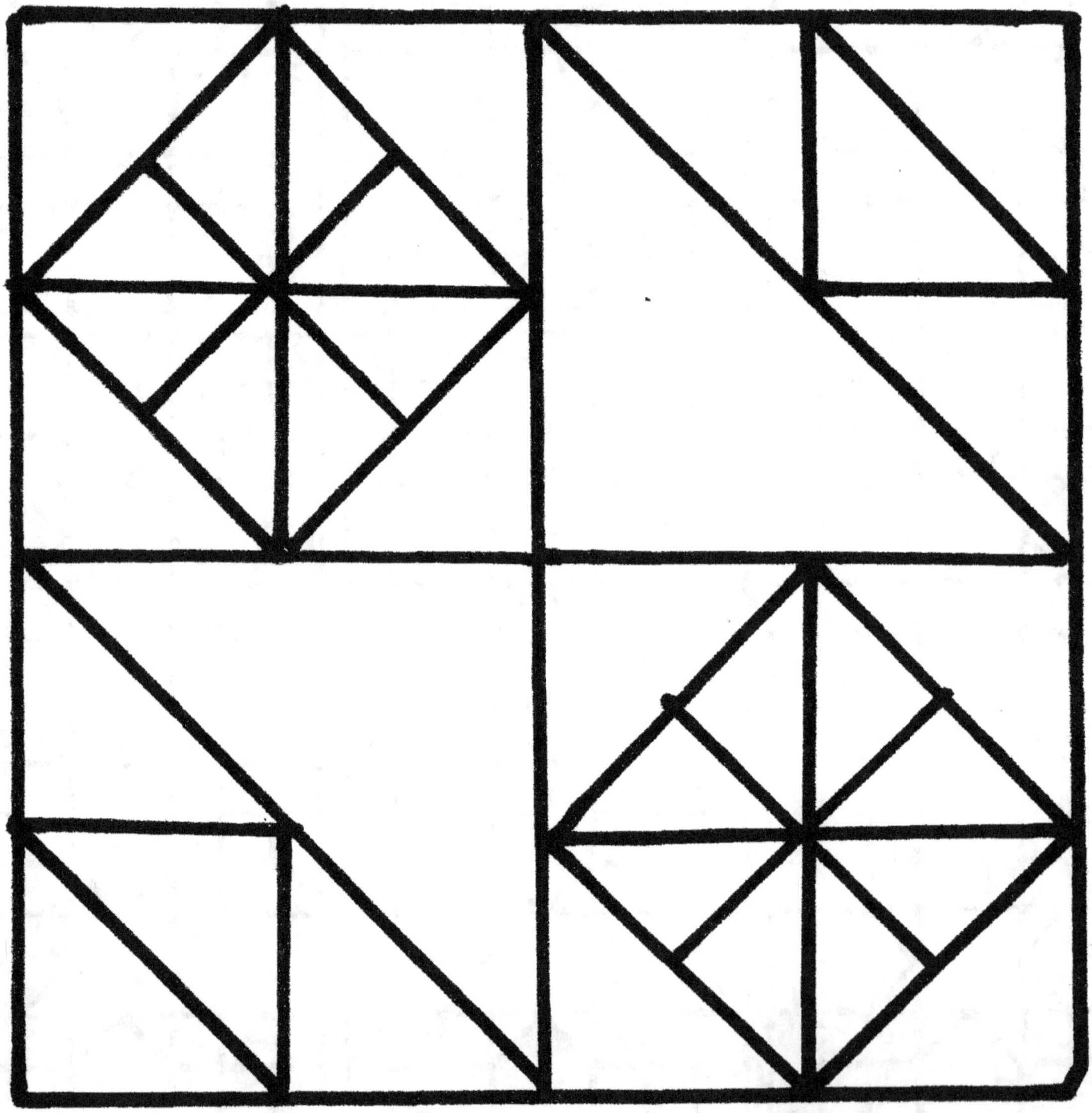

Frontier County Barn Quilt Hither & Yon

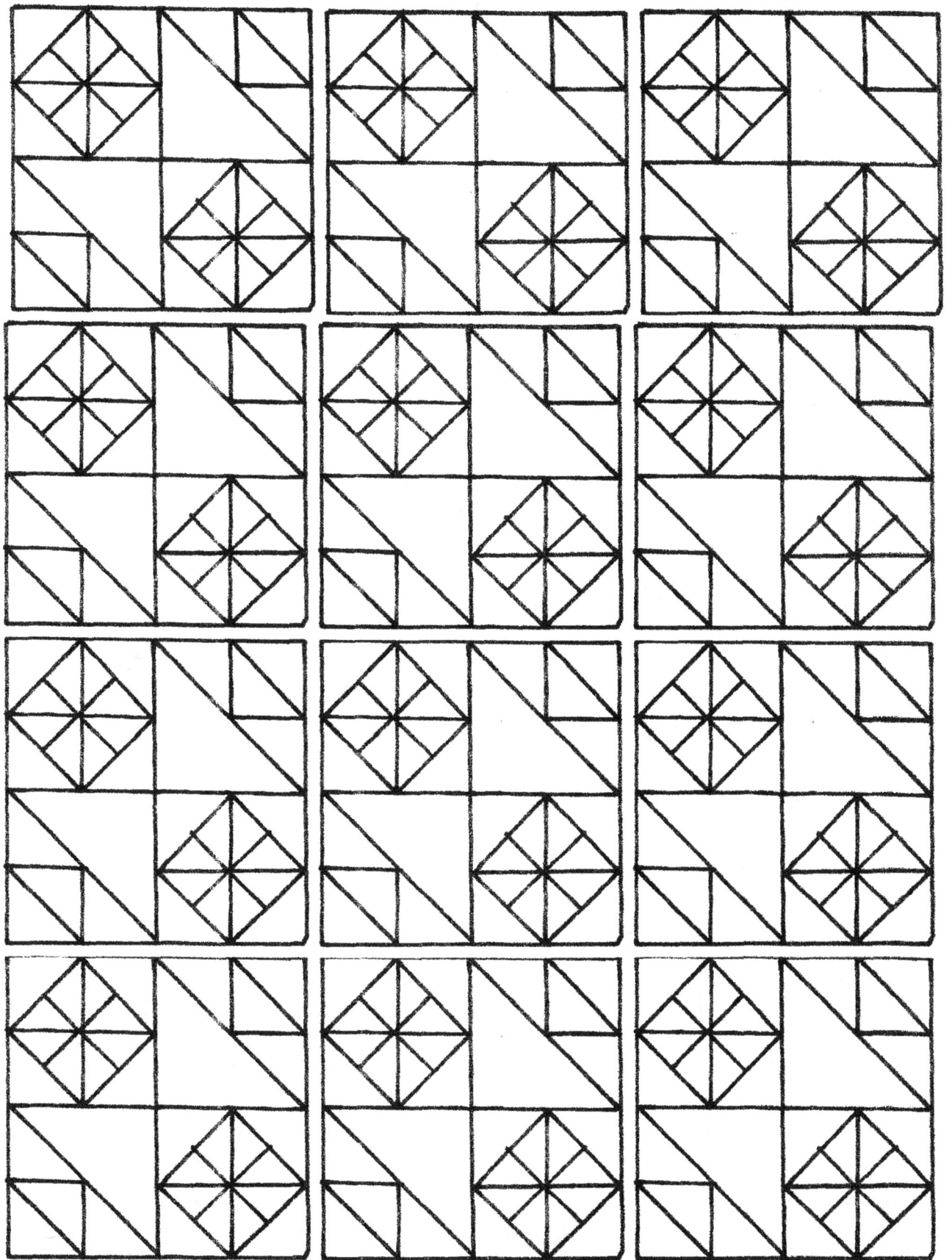

Barn Quilt My Favorite
Frontier County Barn Quilt Trail

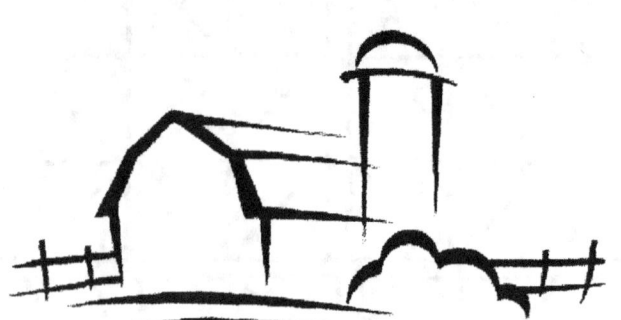

Barn Quilt Location
Fulton Drive
Ayr Township

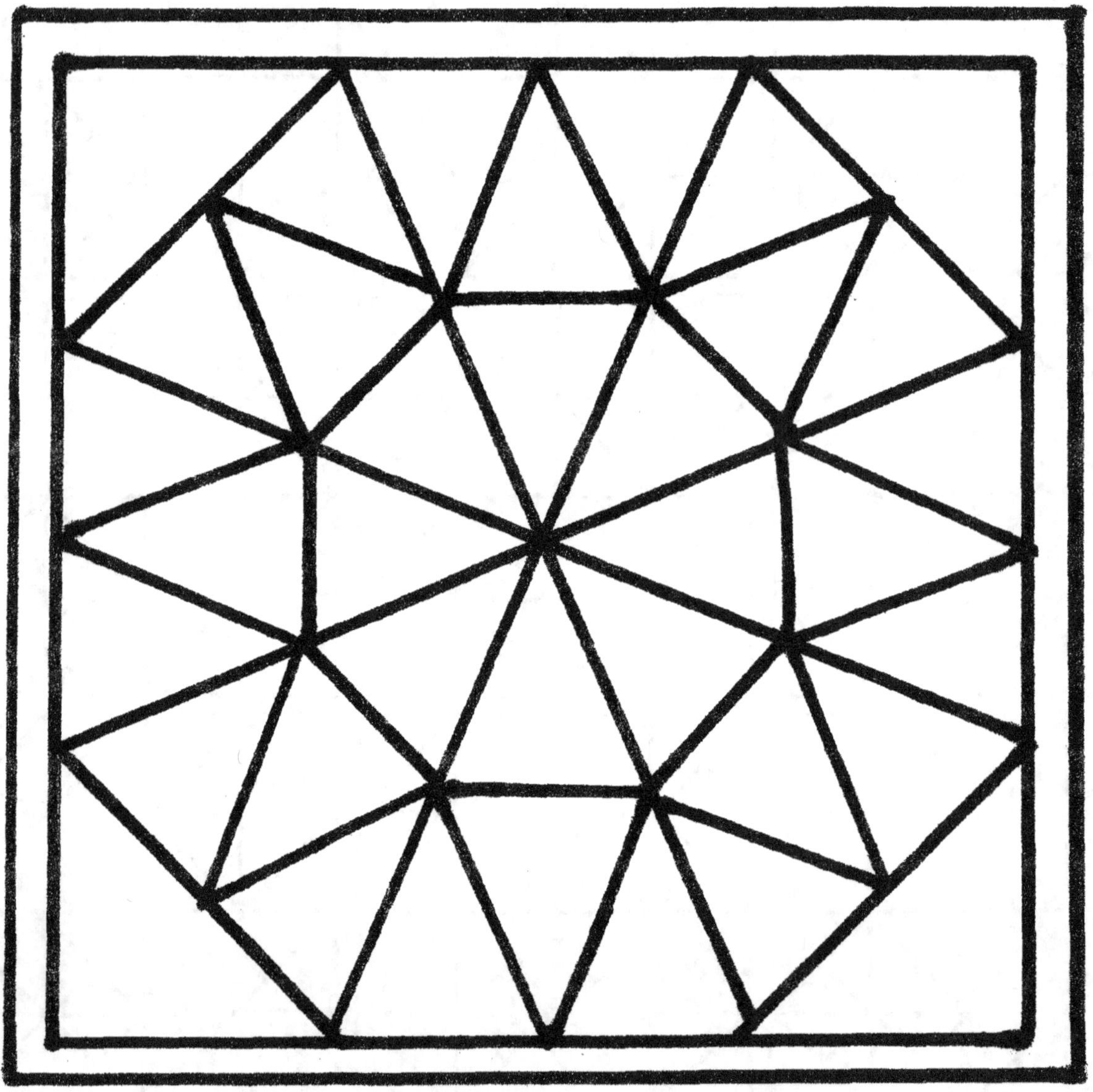

Frontier County Barn Quilt My Favorite

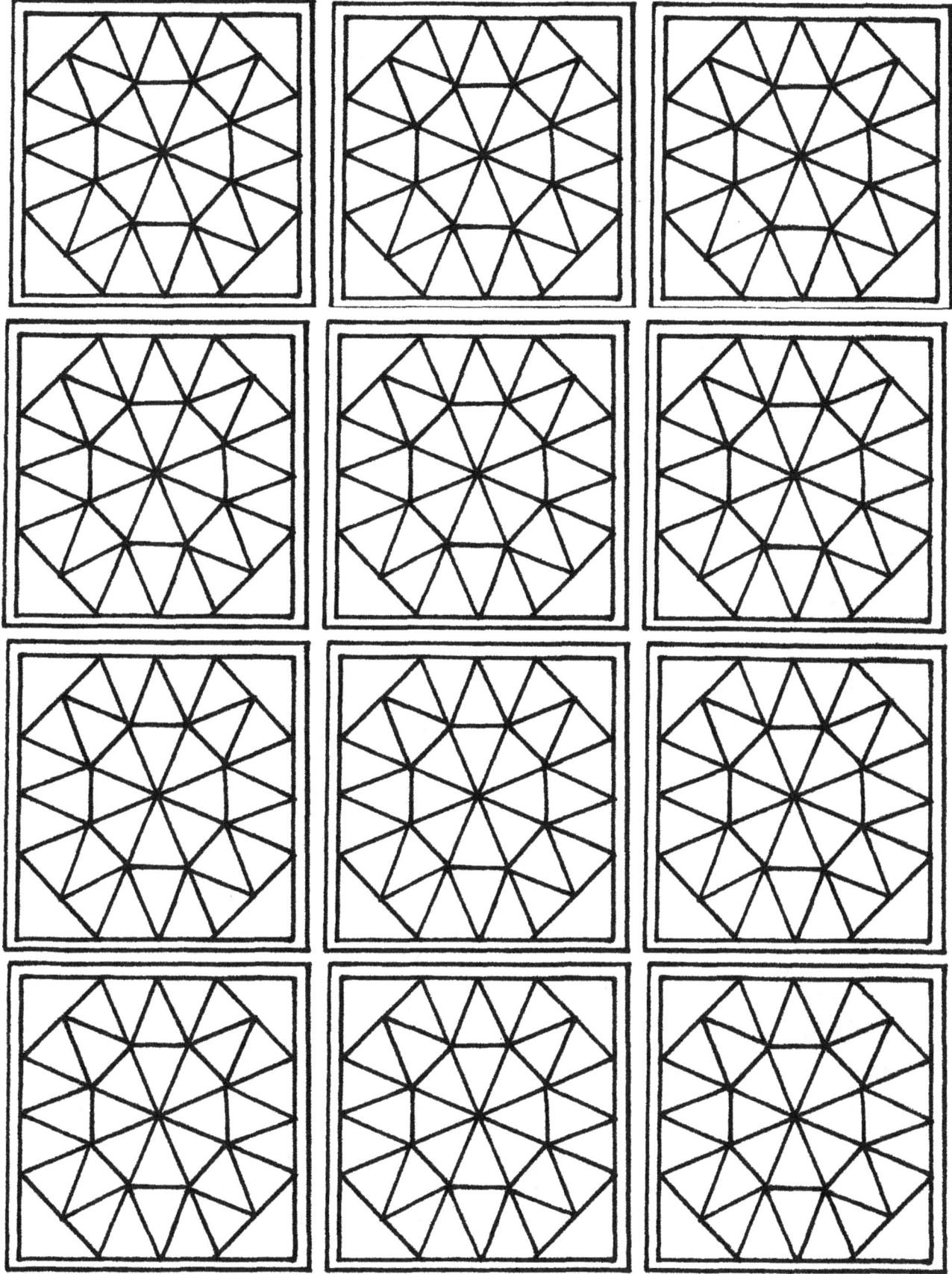

Barn Quilt Penn's Best
Frontier County Barn Quilt Trail

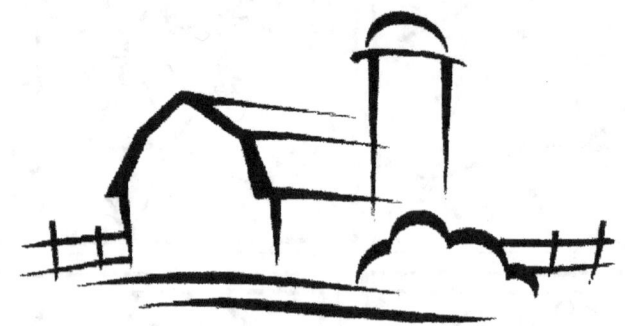

Barn Quilt Location
Great Cove Road
Todd Township

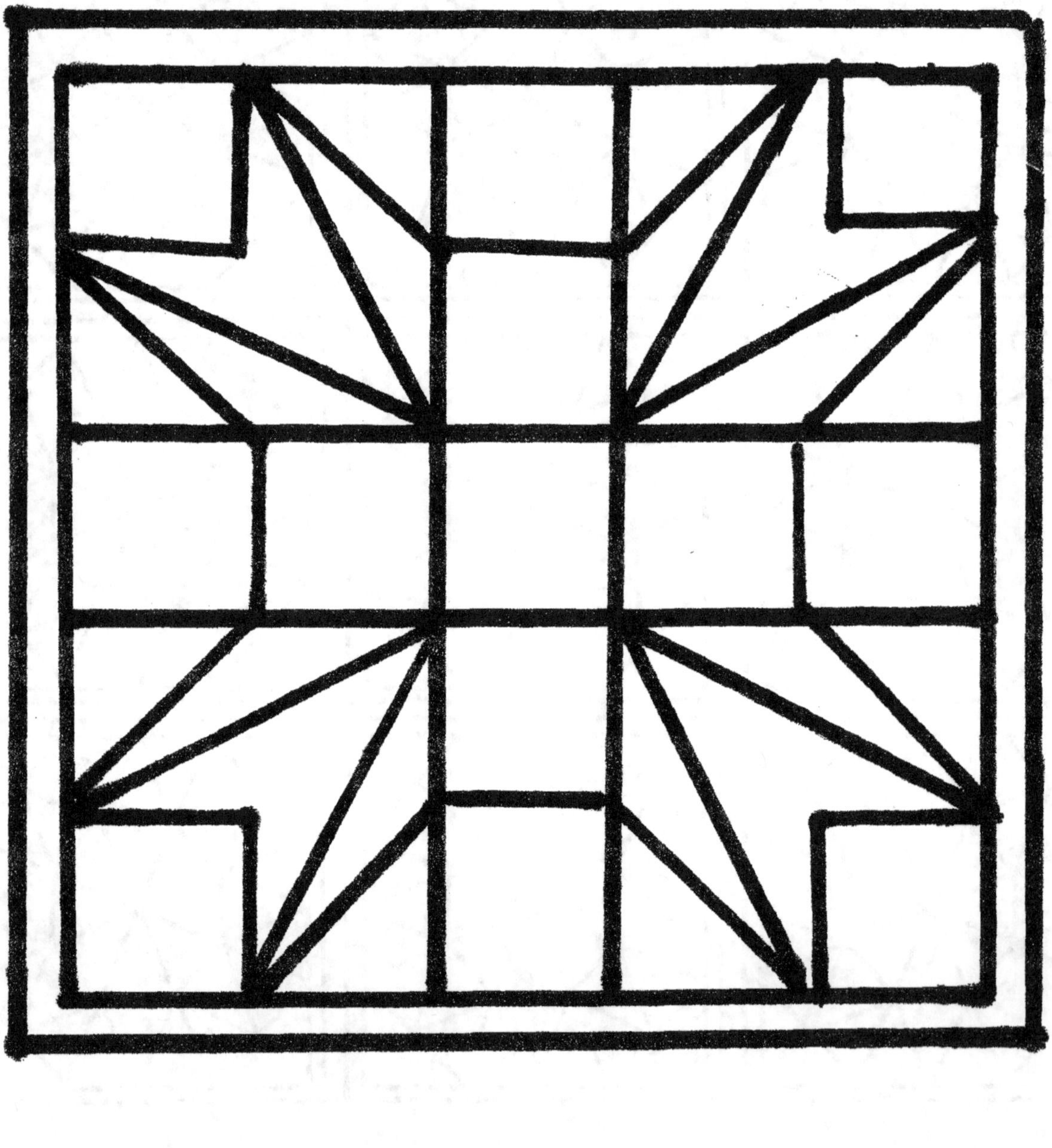

Frontier County Barn Quilt Penn's Best

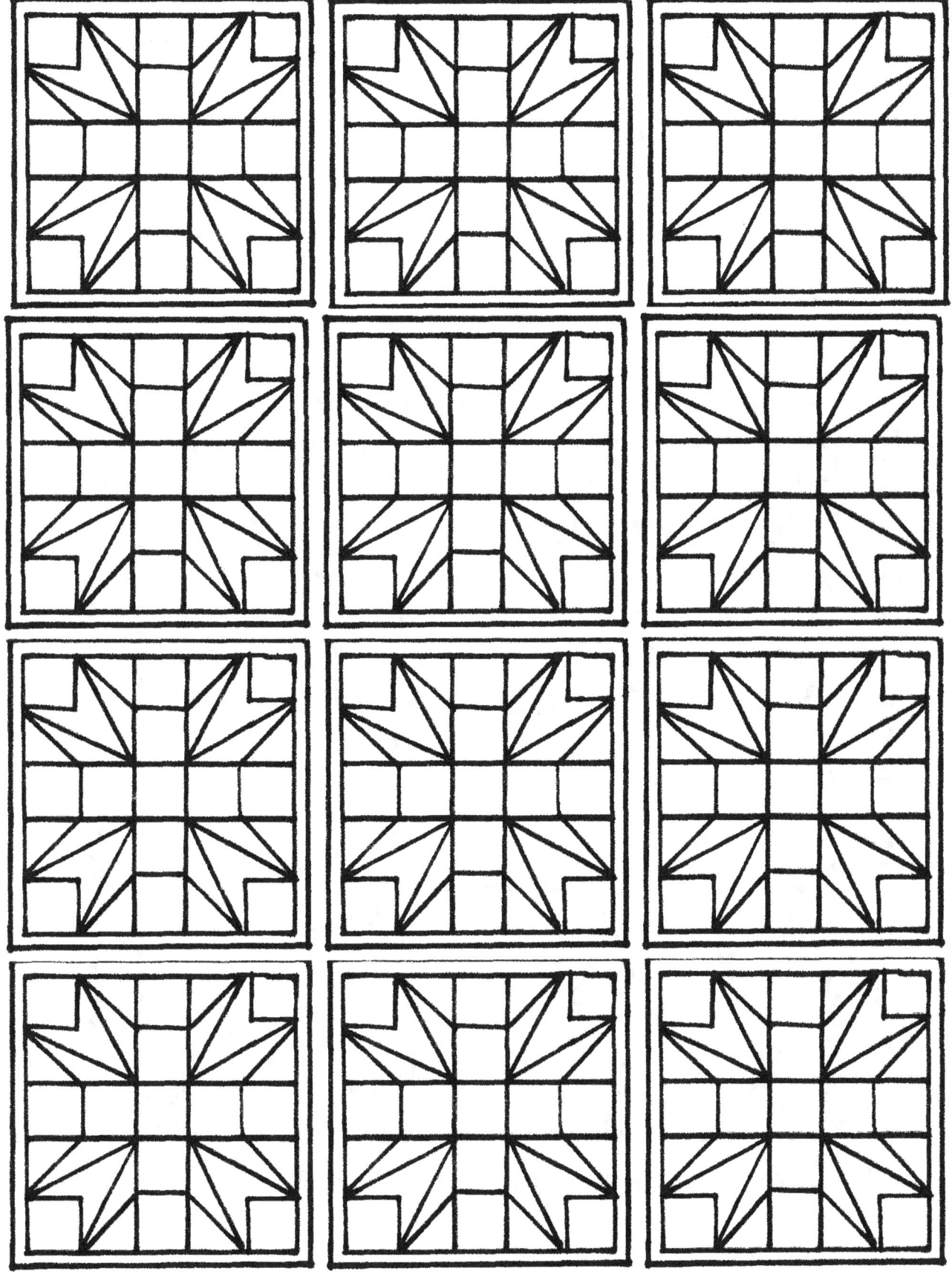

Barn Quilt Flowers of Friendship
Frontier County Barn Quilt Trail

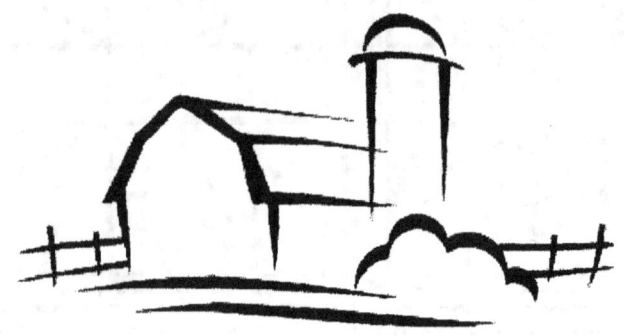

**Barn Quilt Location
Buchanan Trail
Ayr Township**

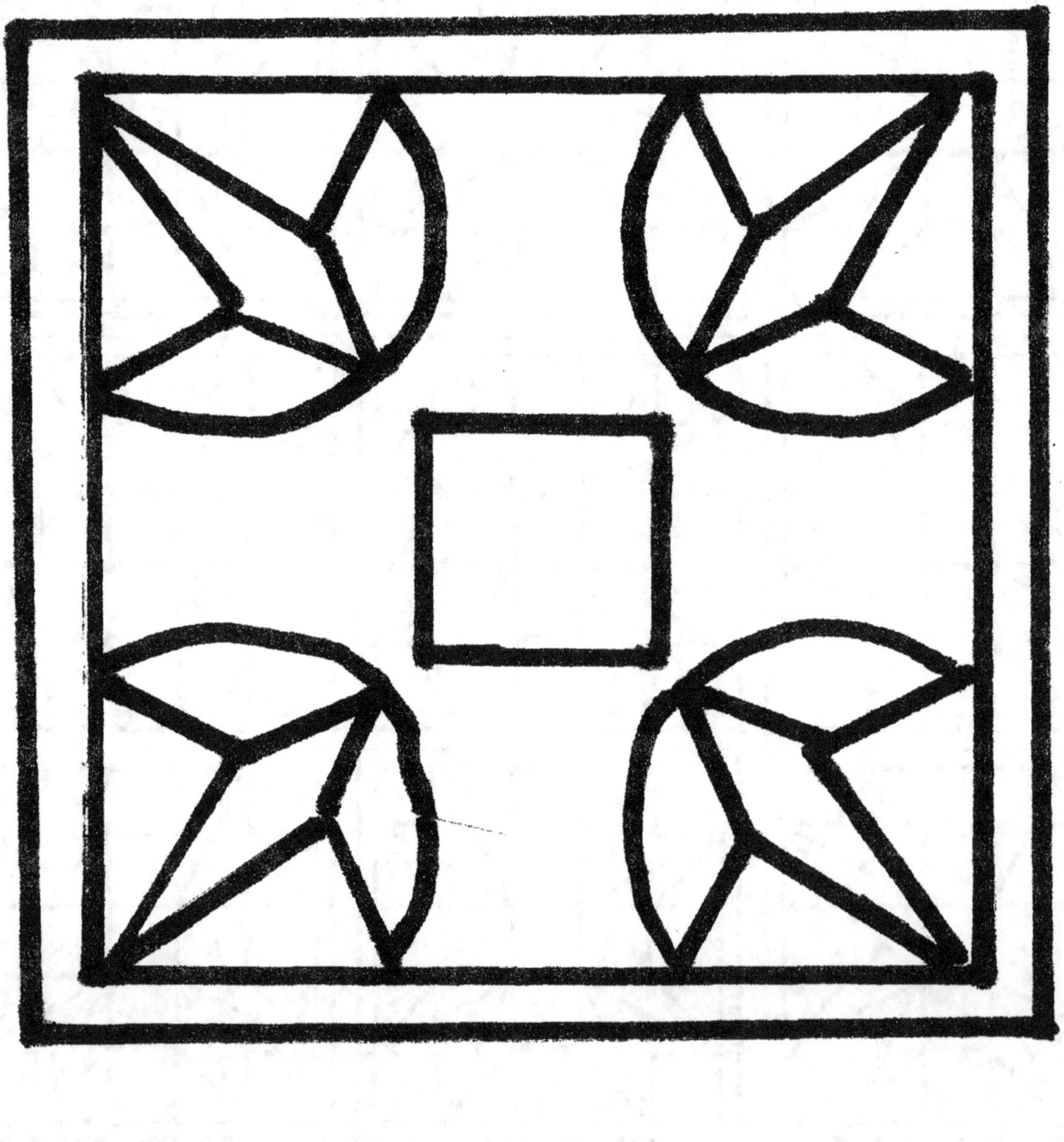

Frontier County Barn Quilt Flowers of Friendship

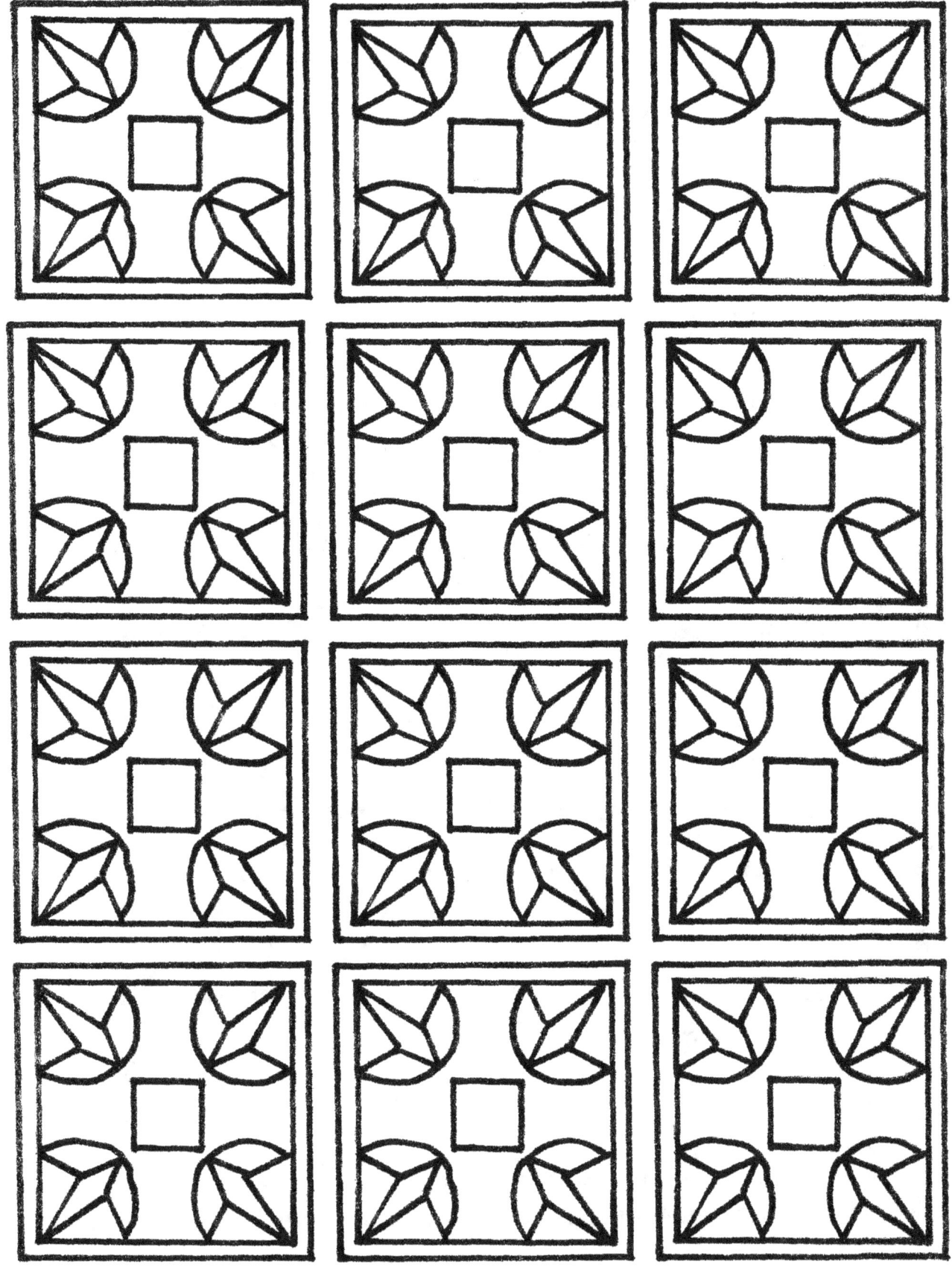

Barn Quilt Gem Star
Frontier County Barn Quilt Trail

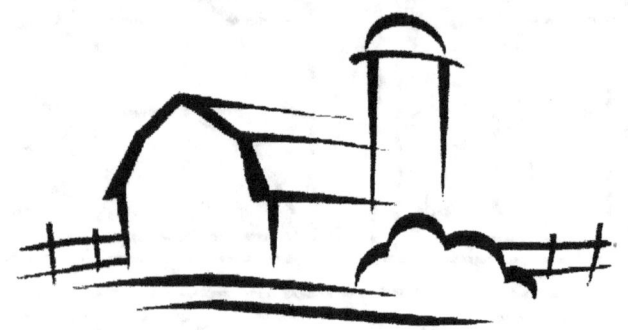

Barn Quilt Location
Gem Bridge Road
Belfast Township

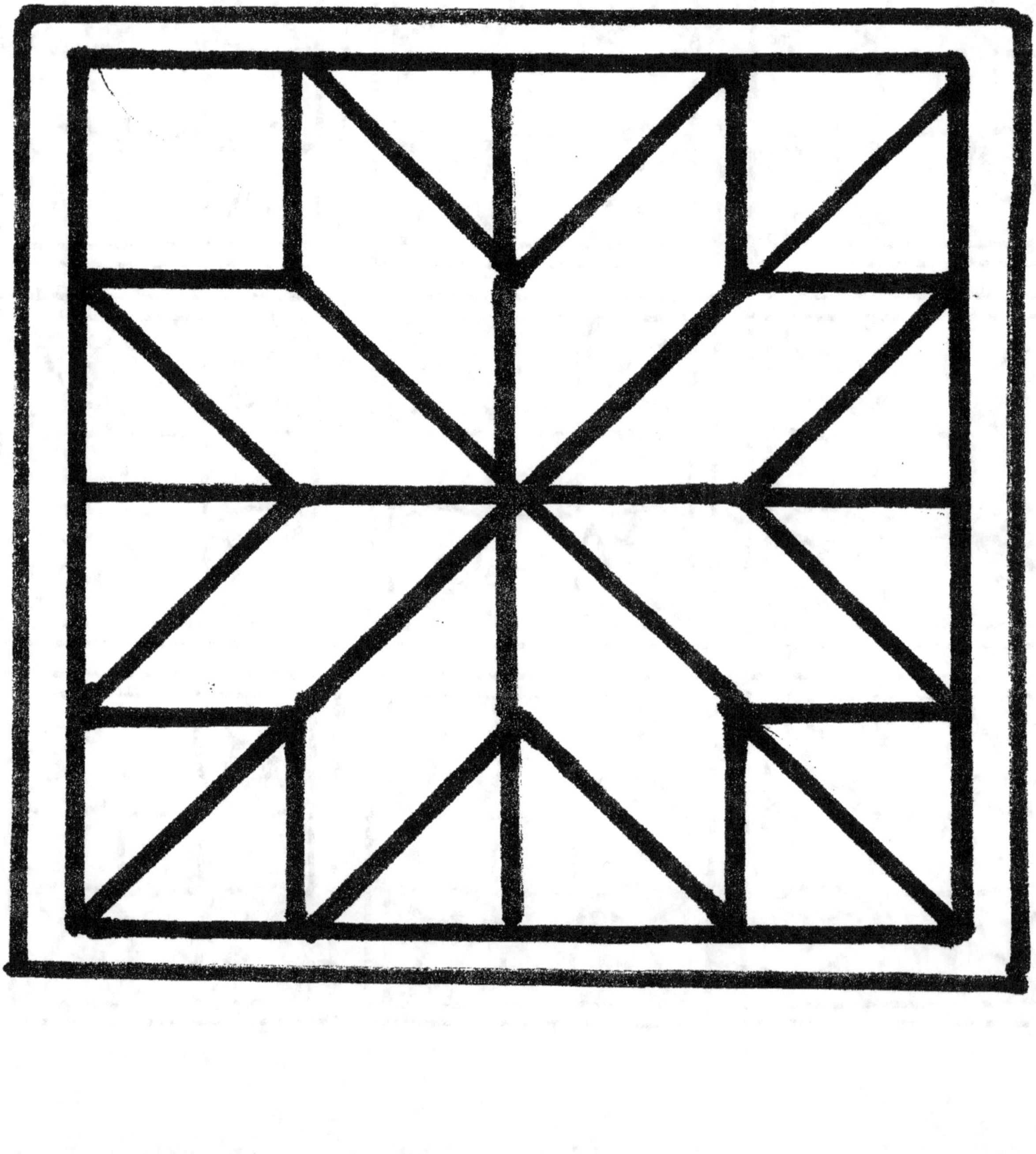

Frontier County Barn Quilt Gem Star

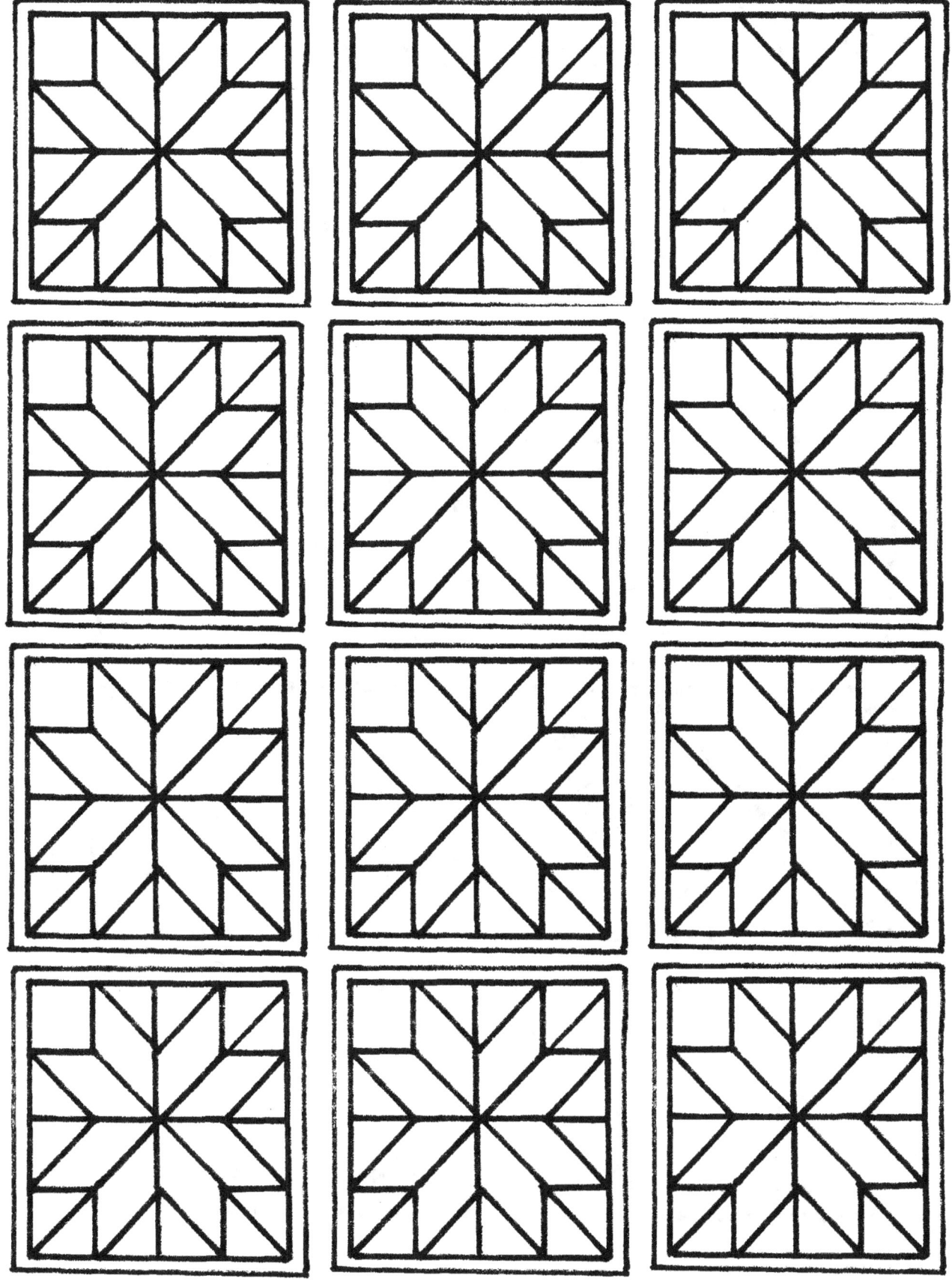

Barn Quilt Horseshoe Star
Frontier County Barn Quilt Trail

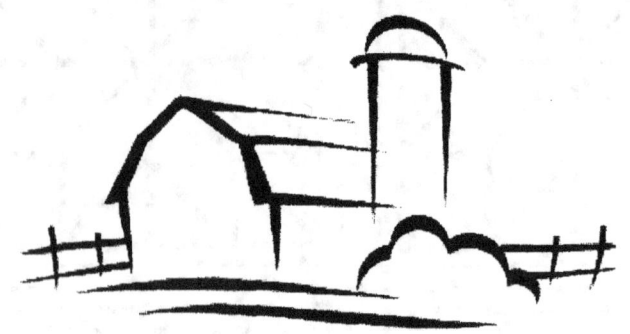

Barn Quilt Location
Great Cove Road
Belfast Township

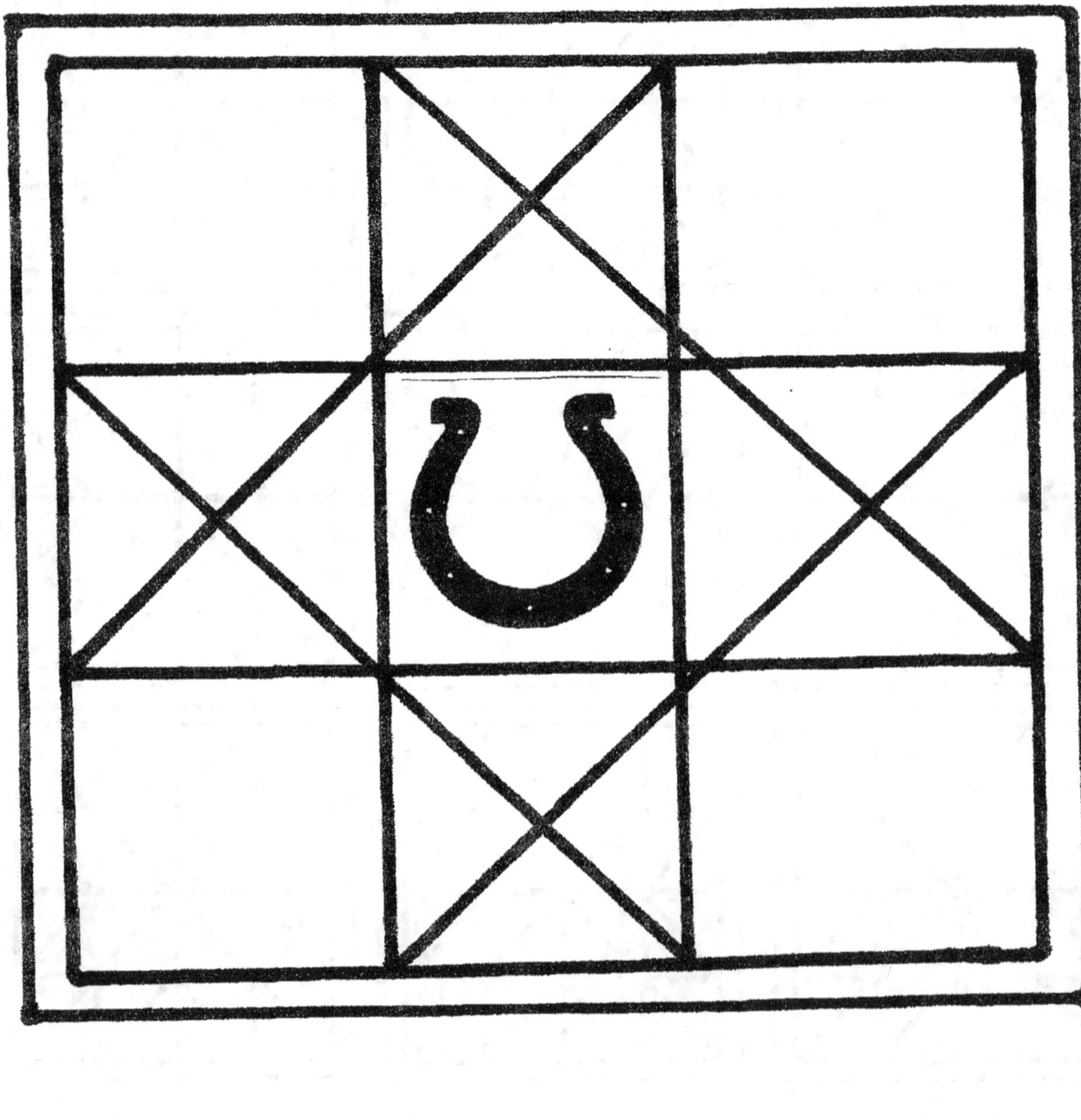

Frontier County Barn Quilt Horseshoe Star

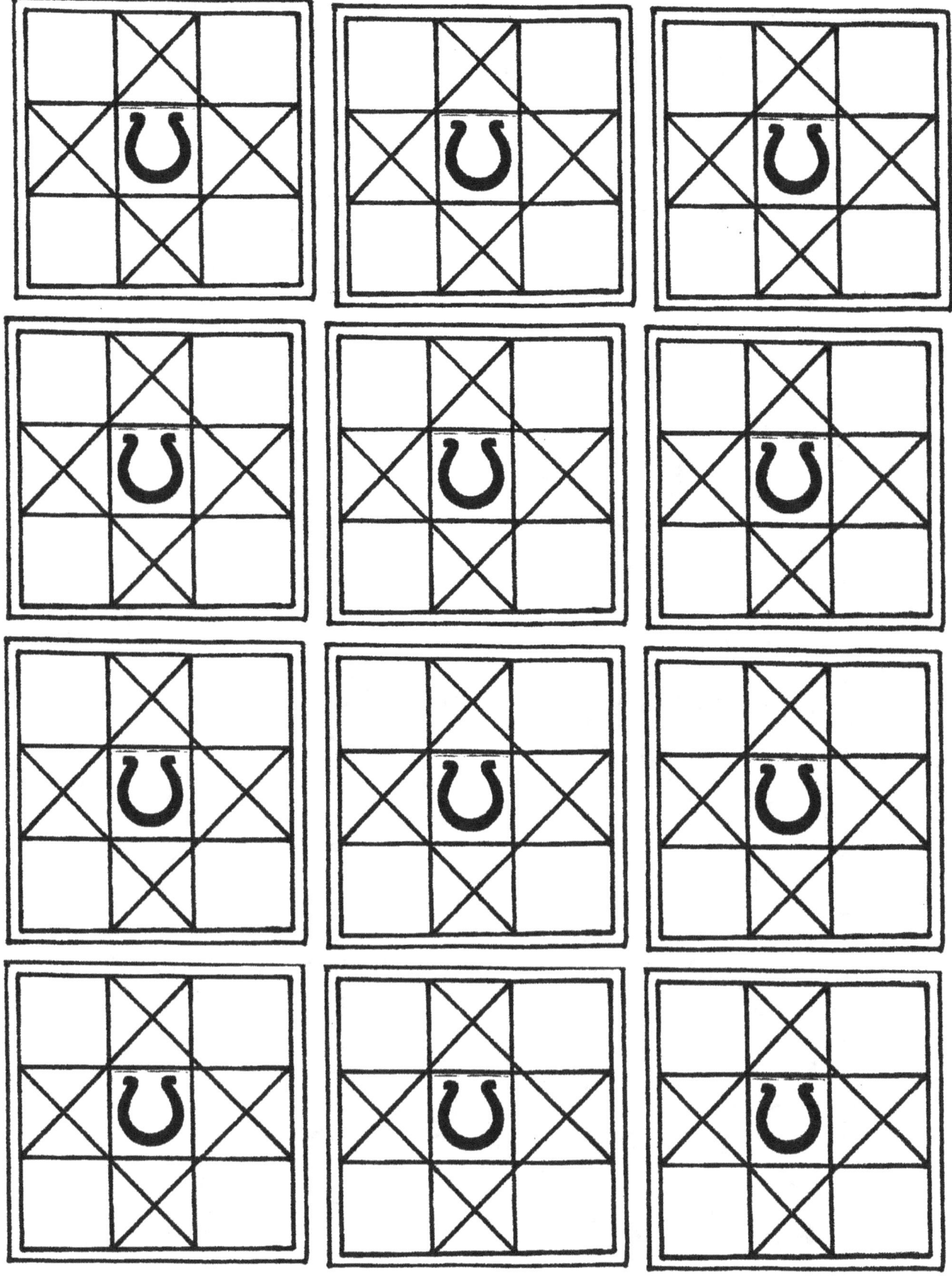

Barn Quilt Sunflower
Frontier County Barn Quilt Trail

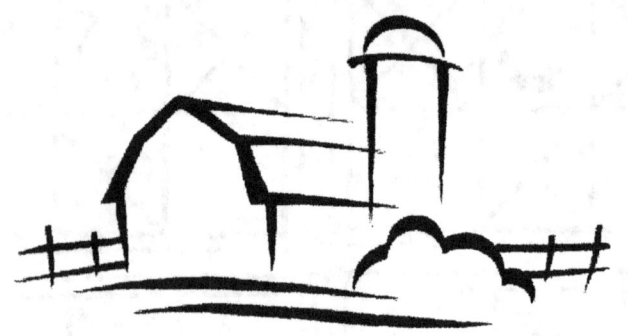

**Barn Quilt Location
Union Church Road
Ayr Township**

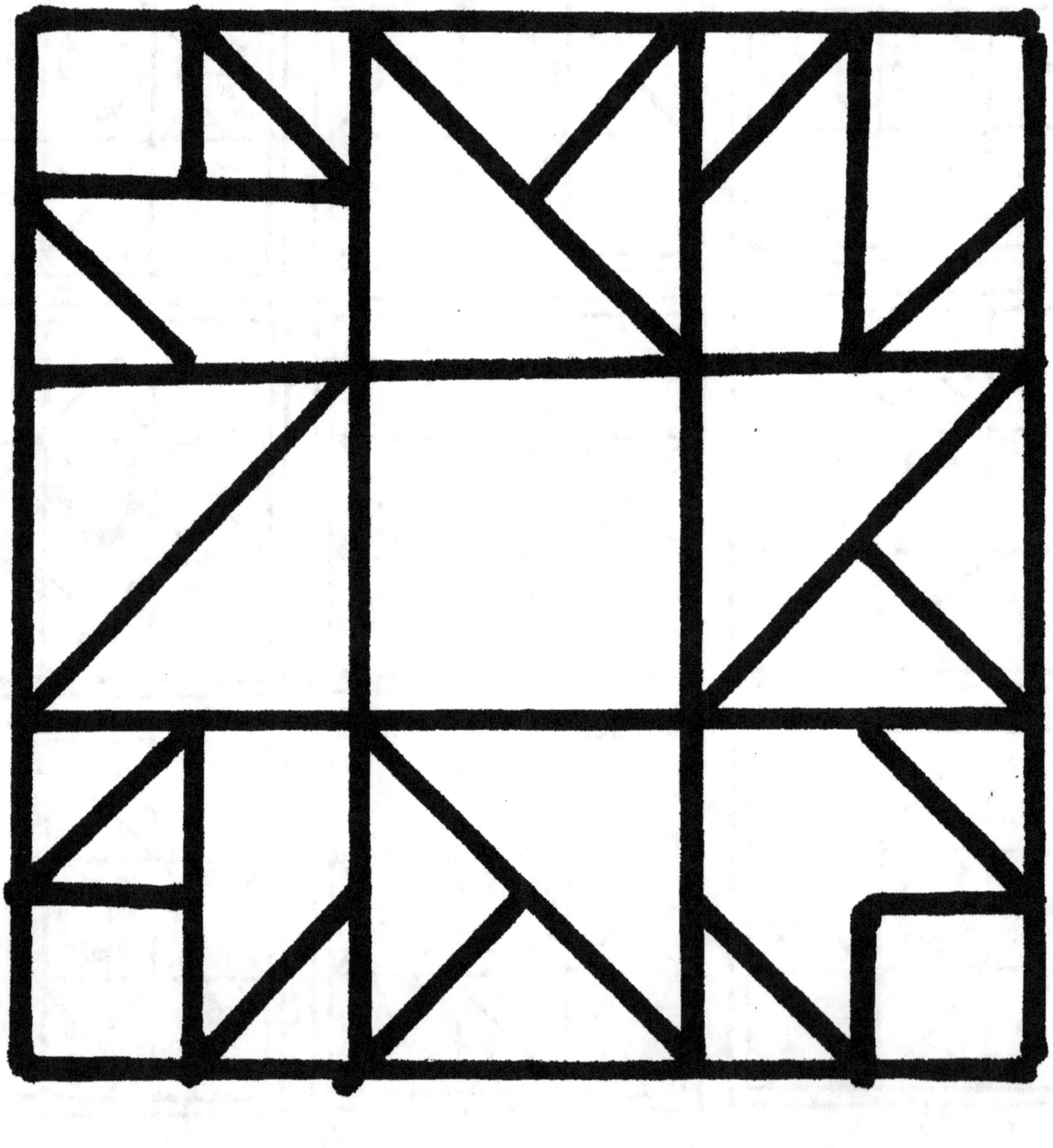

Frontier County Barn Quilt Sunflower

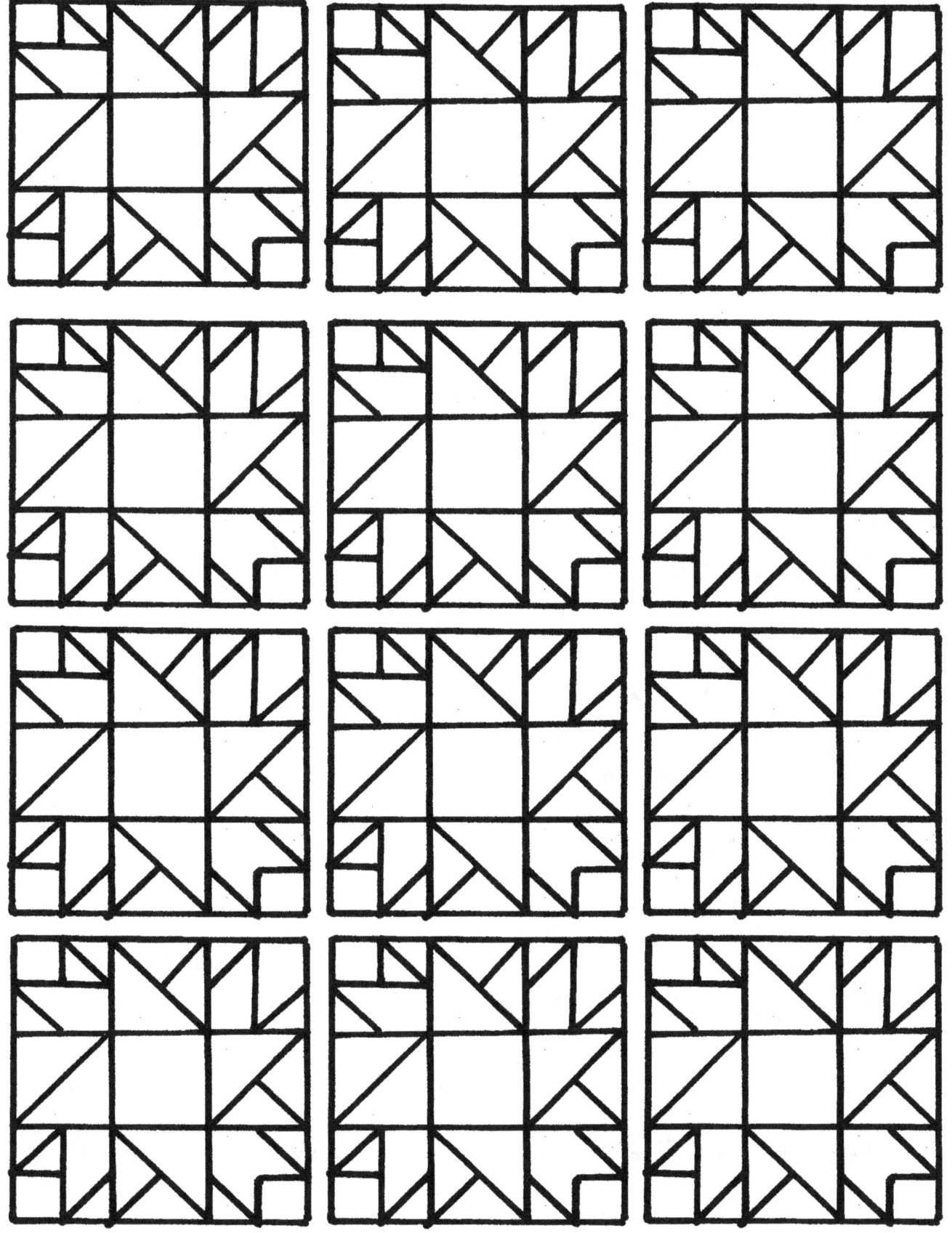

Barn Quilt Art & Soul
Frontier County Barn Quilt Trail

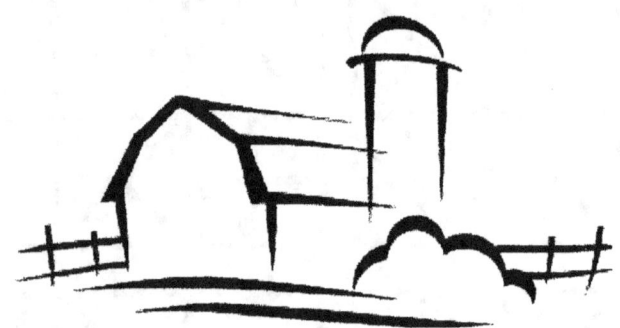

Barn Quilt Location
Lincoln Way East
Todd Township

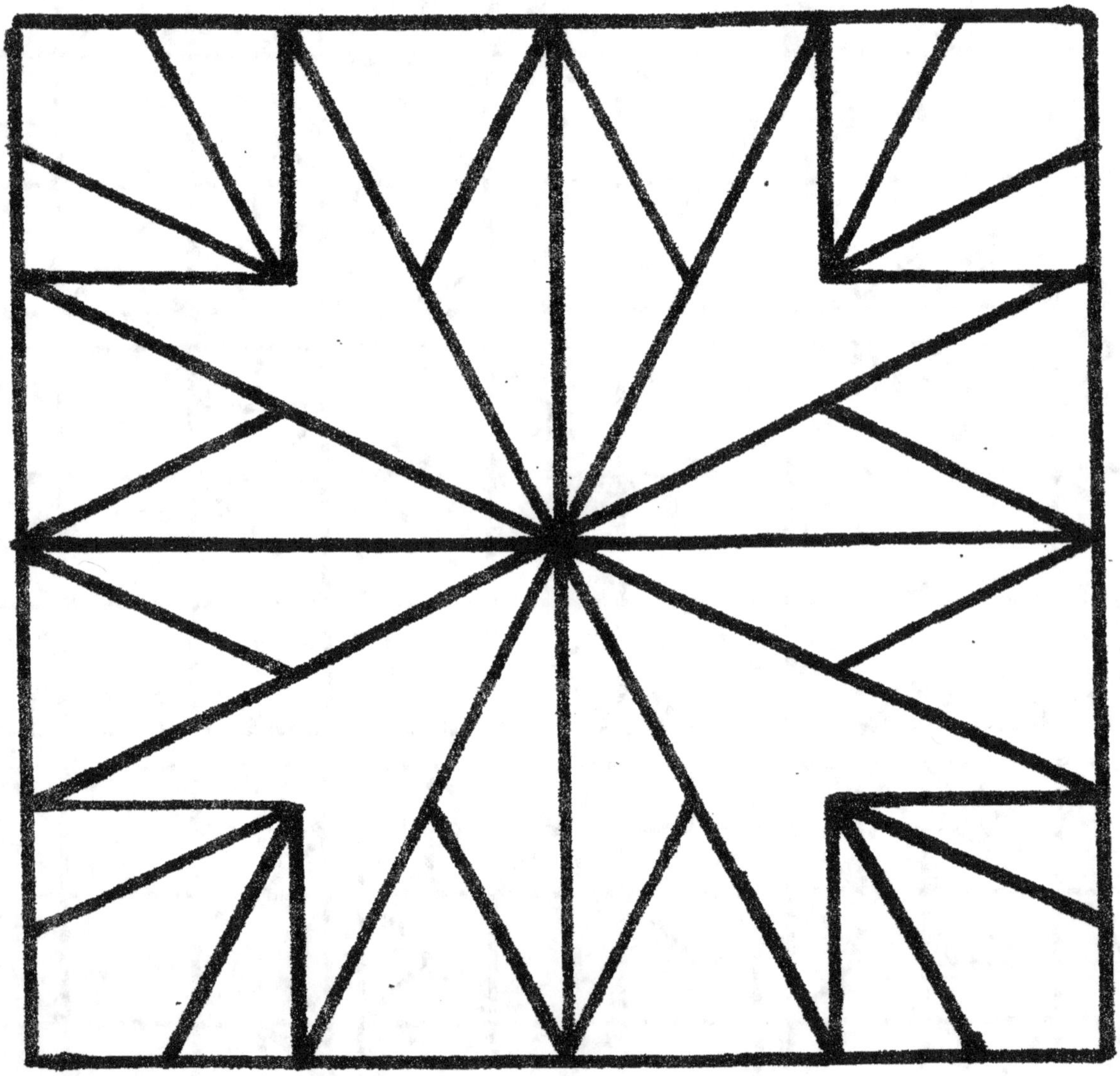

Frontier County Barn Quilt Art & Soul

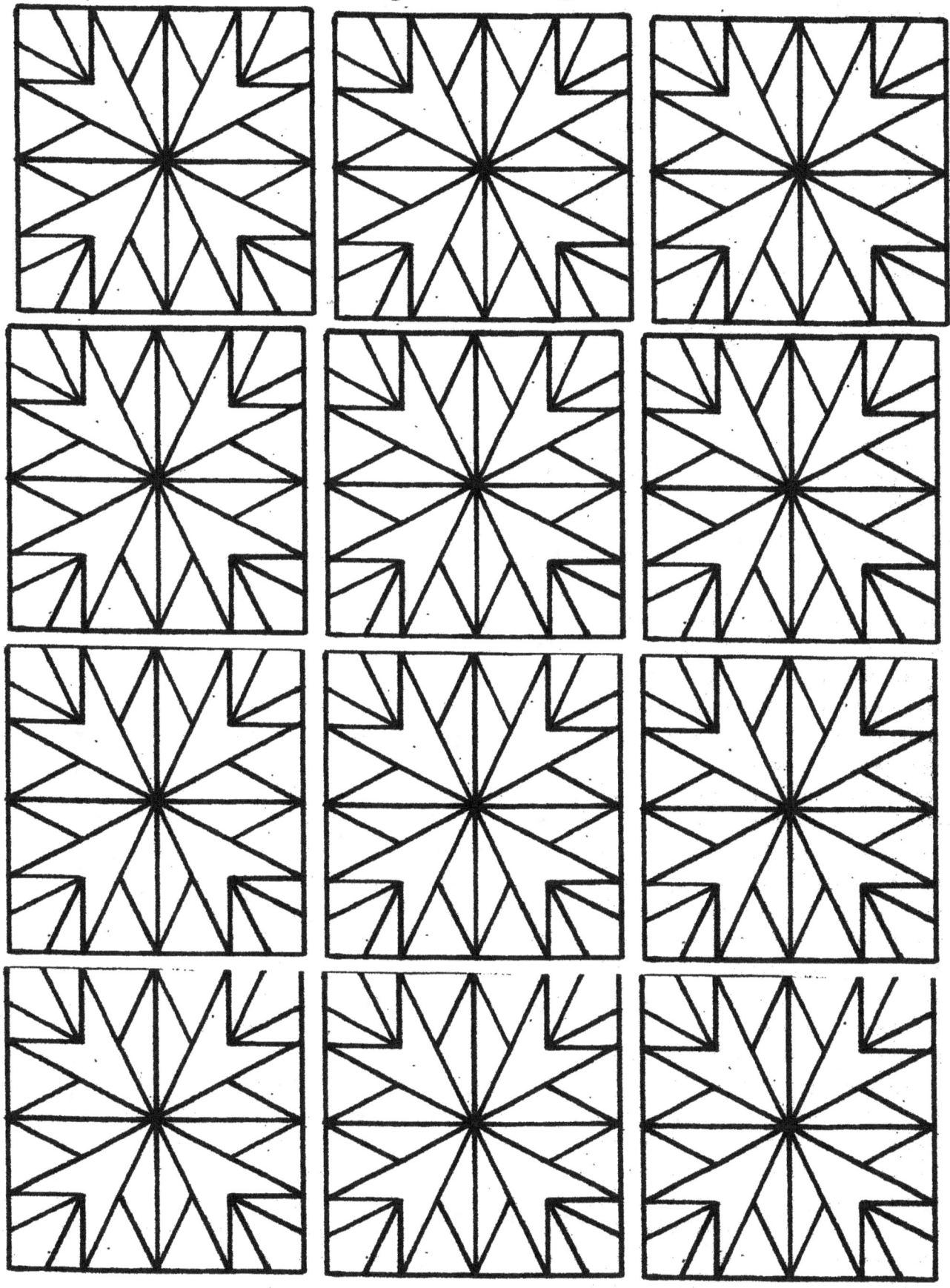

Barn Quilt Carpenter's Star
Frontier County Barn Quilt Trail

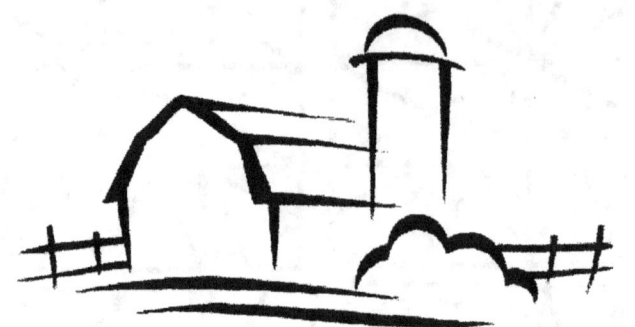

Barn Quilt Location
Church Street
Brush Creek Township

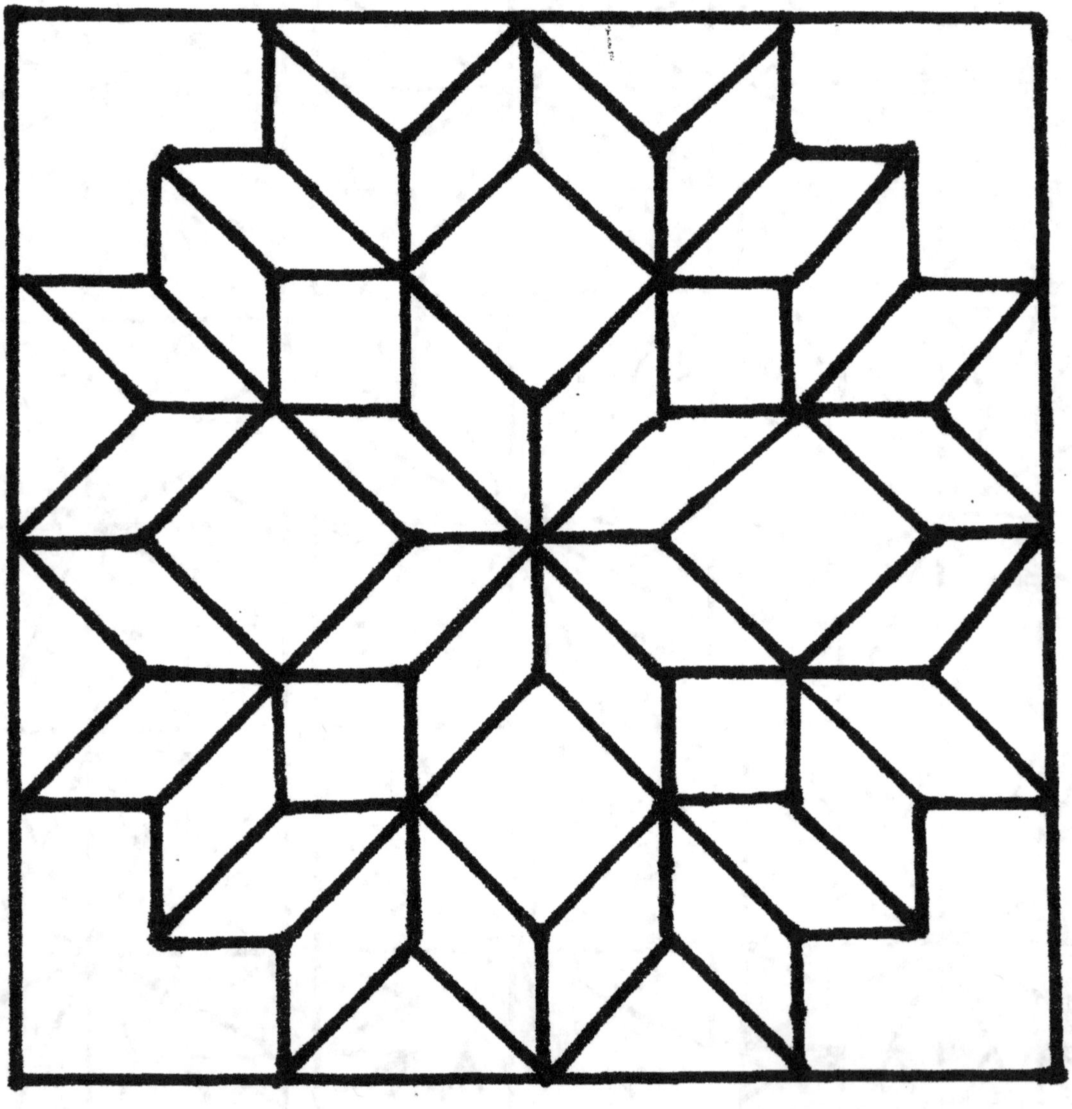

Frontier County Barn Quilt Carpenter's Star

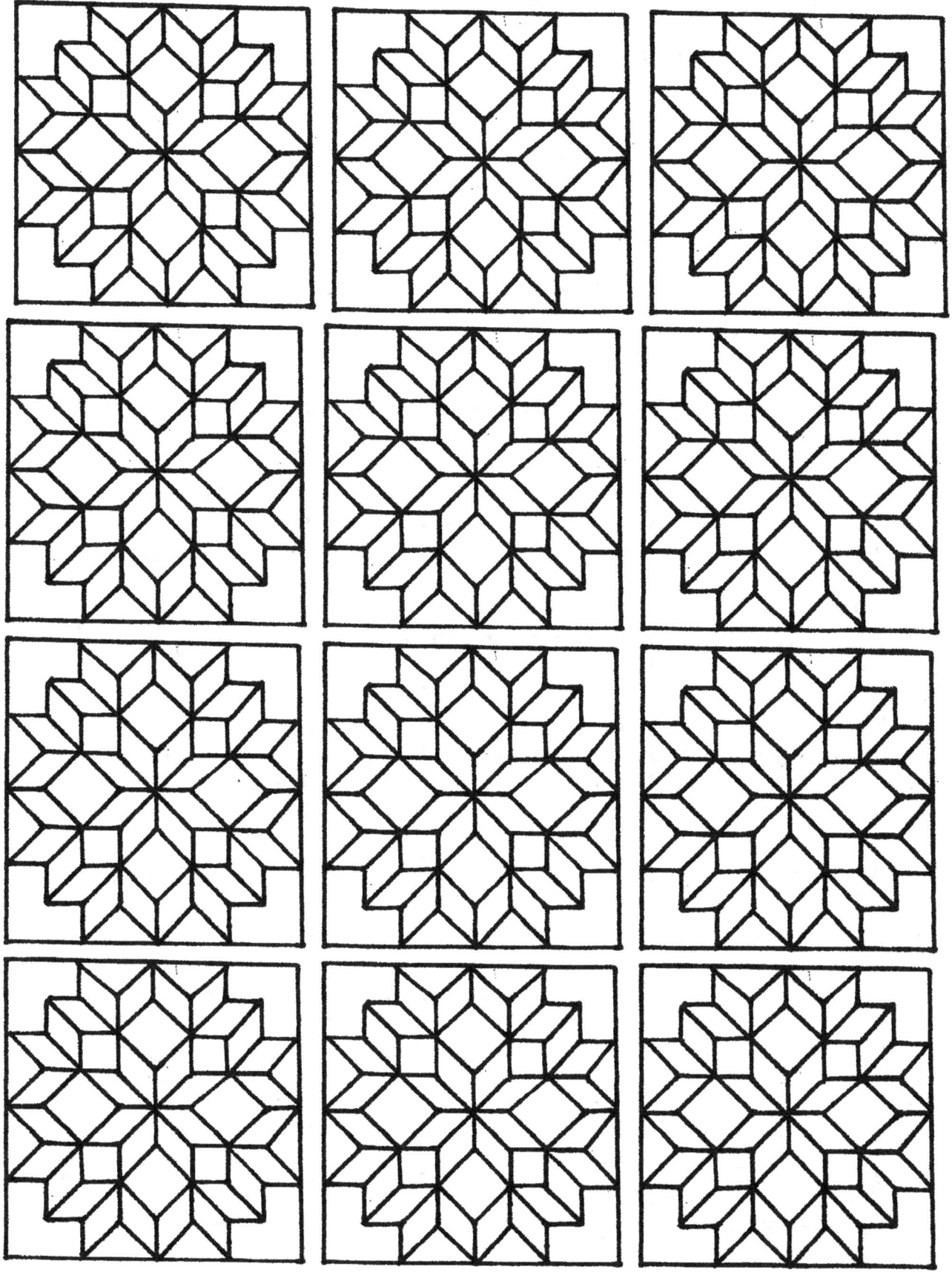

Barn Quilt Churn Dash
Frontier County Barn Quilt Trail

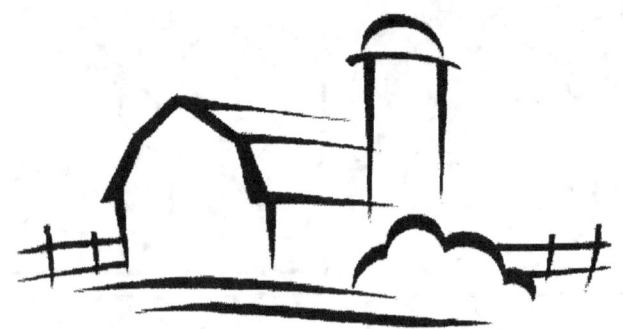

**Barn Quilt Location
Layton Road
Brush Creek Township**

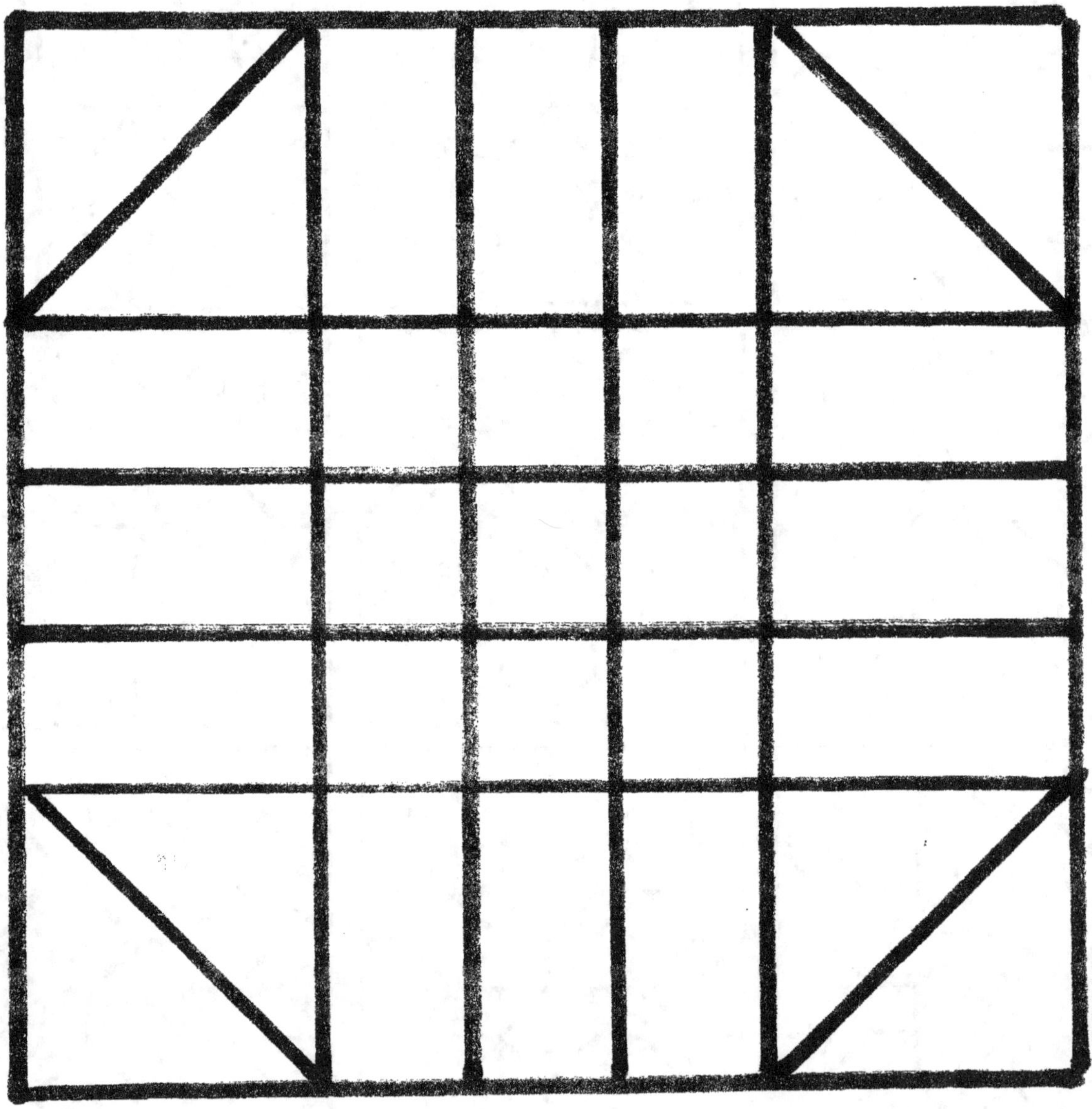

Frontier County Barn Quilt Churn Dash

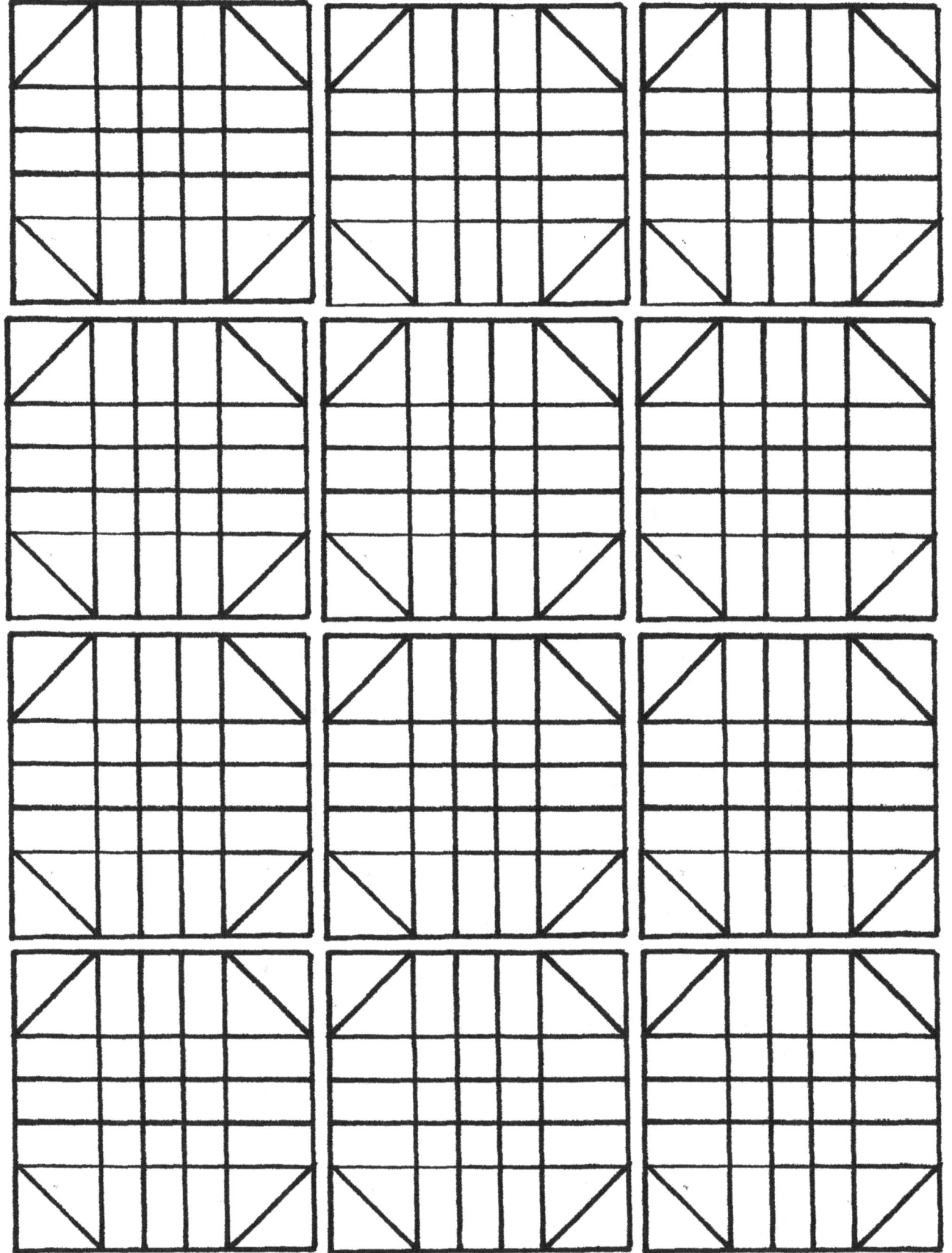

Barn Quilt Arrowhead
Frontier County Barn Quilt Trail

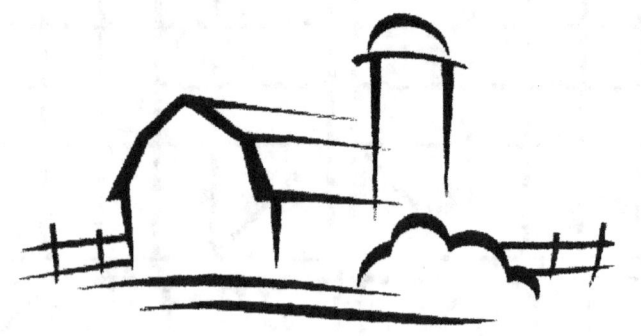

Barn Quilt Location
Great Cove Road
Todd Township

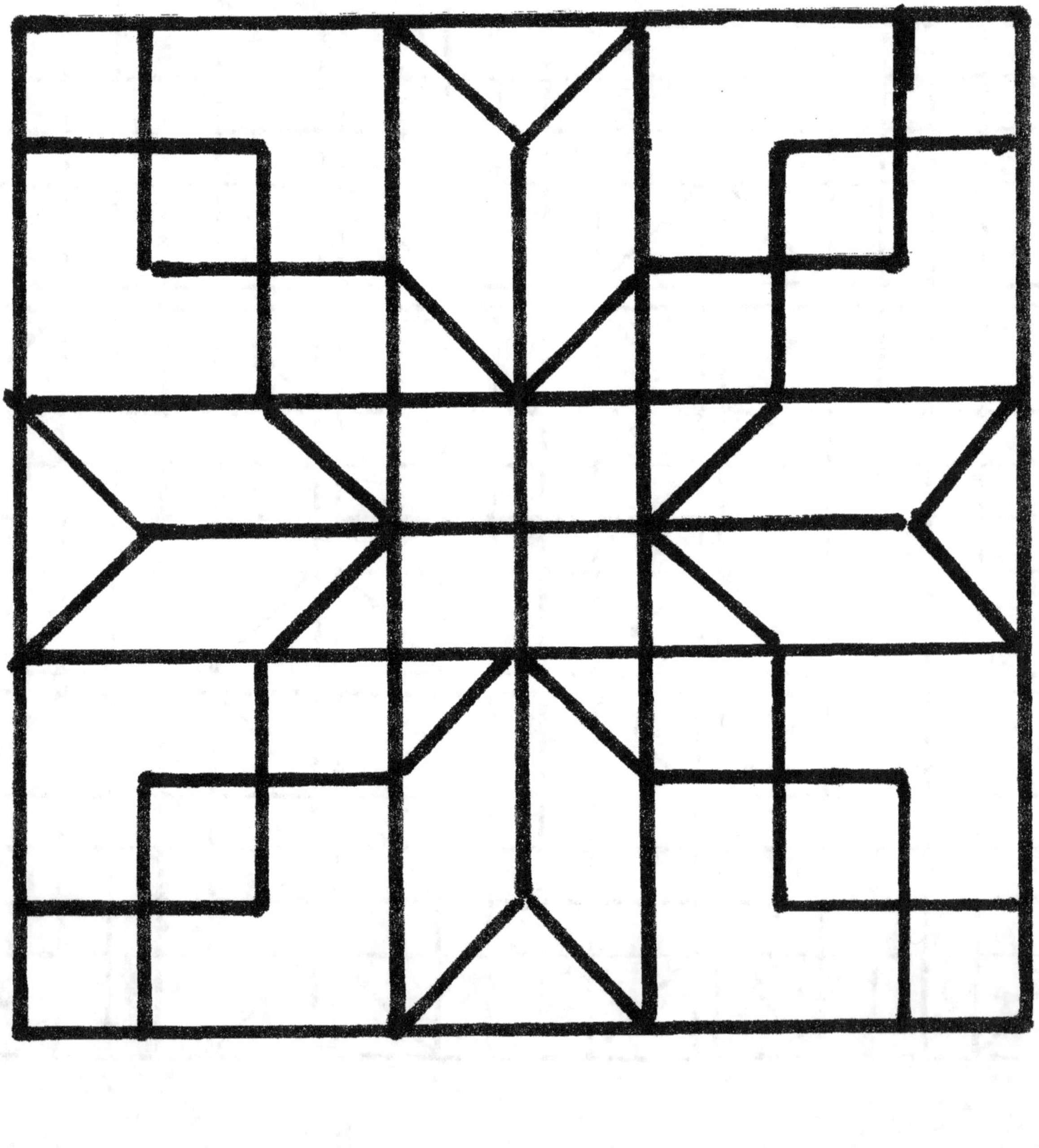

Frontier County Barn Quilt Arrowhead

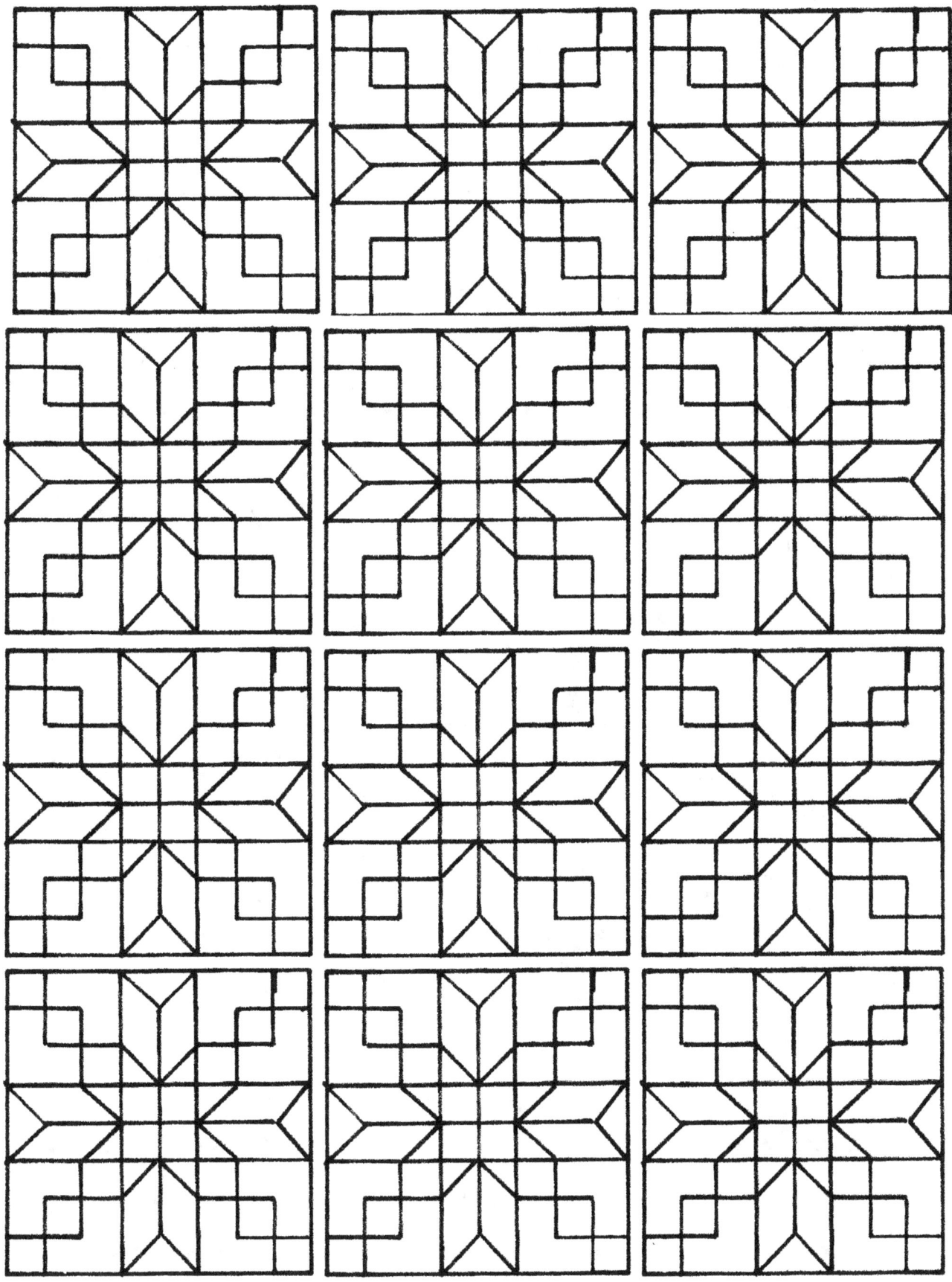

Barn Quilt Steps to Knowledge
Frontier County Barn Quilt Trail

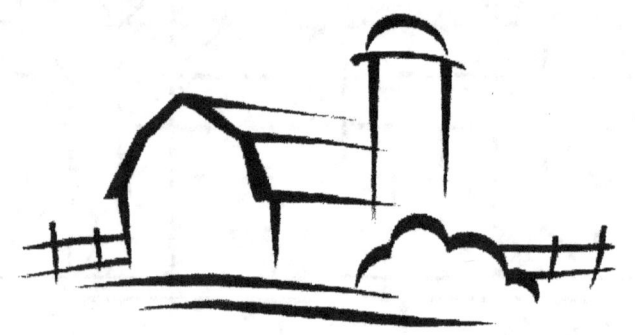

Barn Quilt Location
East Maple Street
McConnellsburg Township

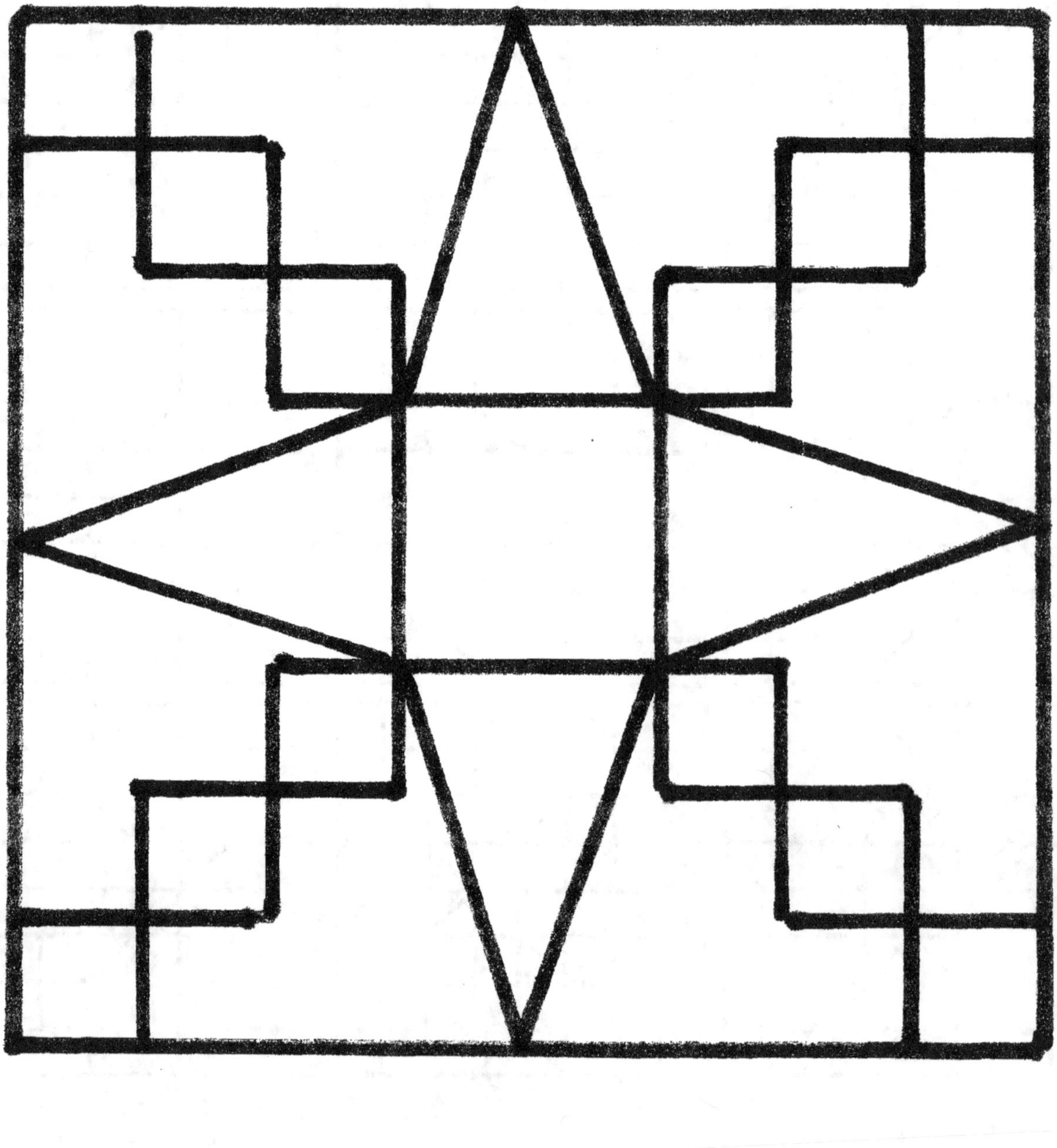

Frontier County Barn Quilt Steps to Knowledge

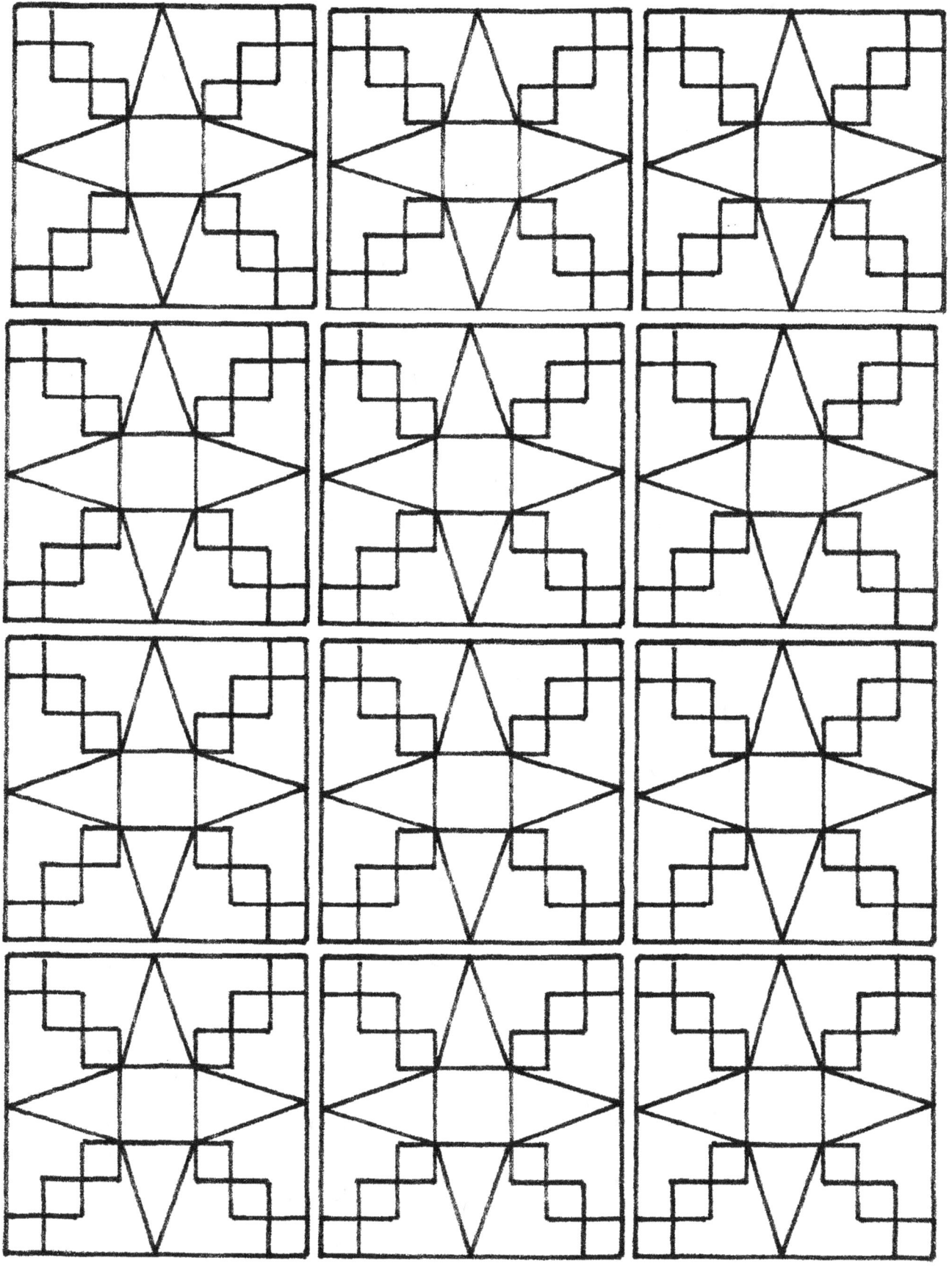

Barn Quilt Bear Paw
Frontier County Barn Quilt Trail

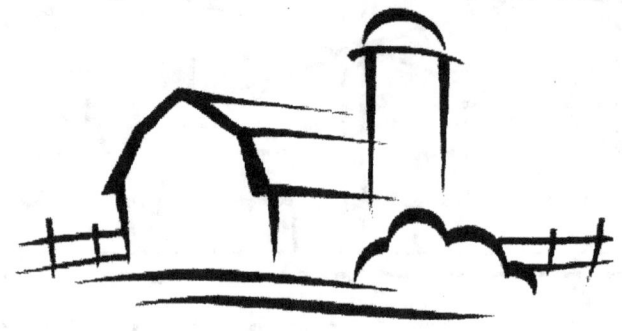

Barn Quilt Location
Dent Road
Thompson Township

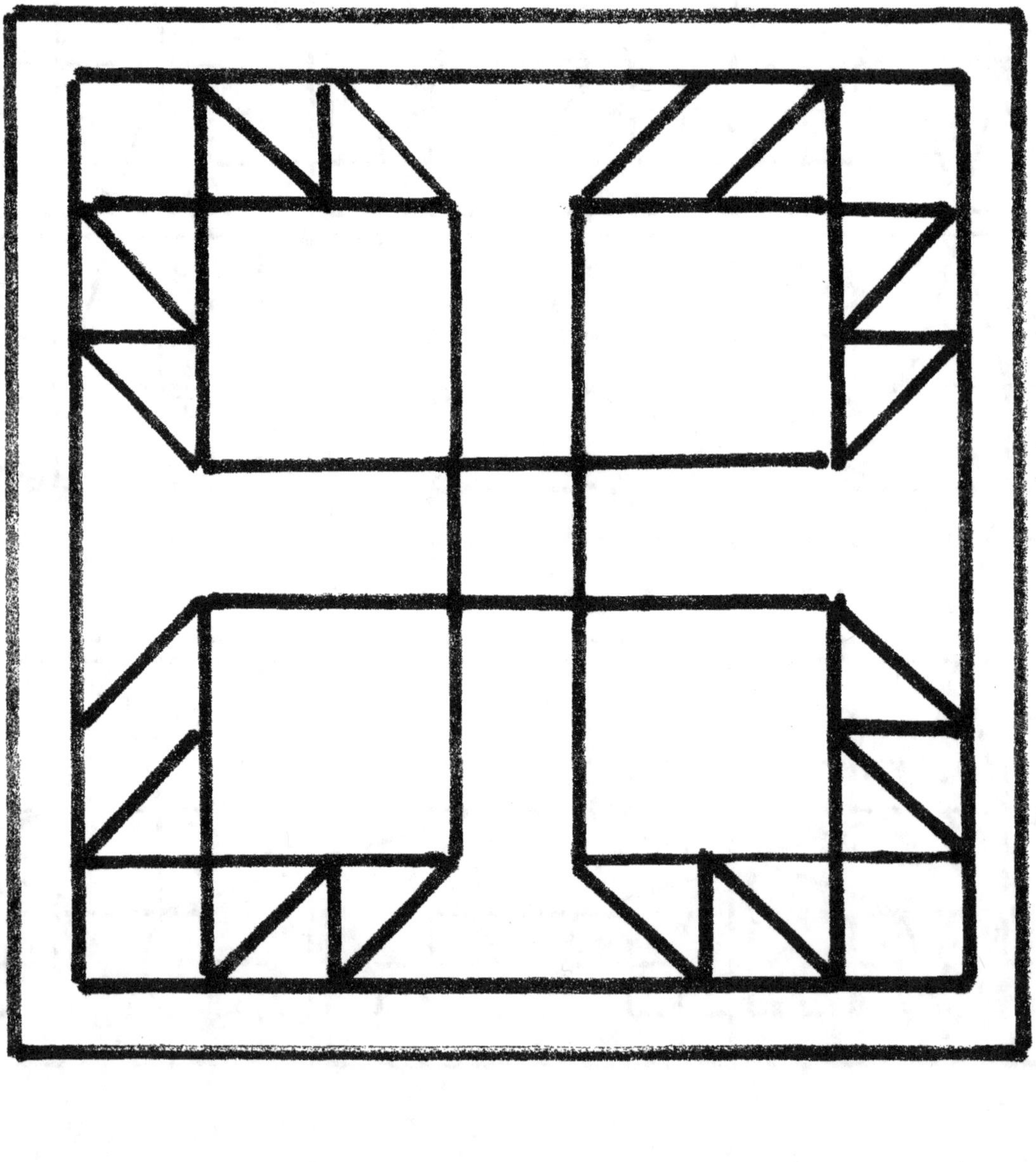

Frontier County Barn Quilt Bear Paw

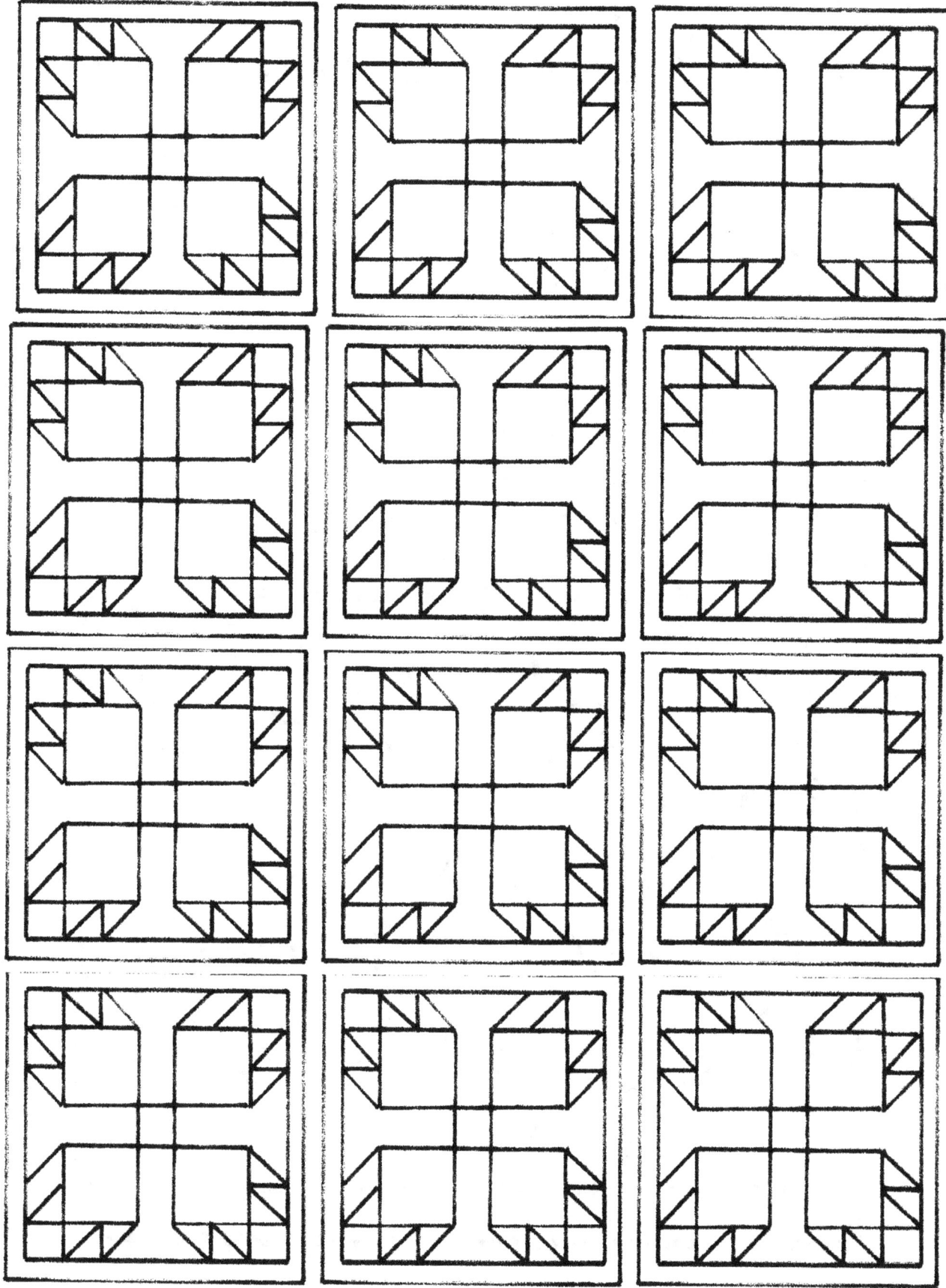

Barn Quilt Buckwheat
Frontier County Barn Quilt Trail

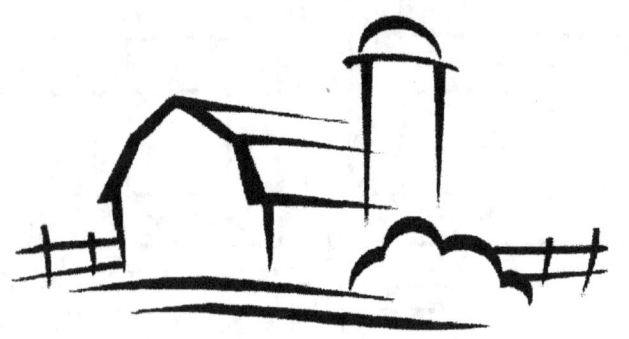

Barn Quilt Location
South Valley Road
Brush Creek Township

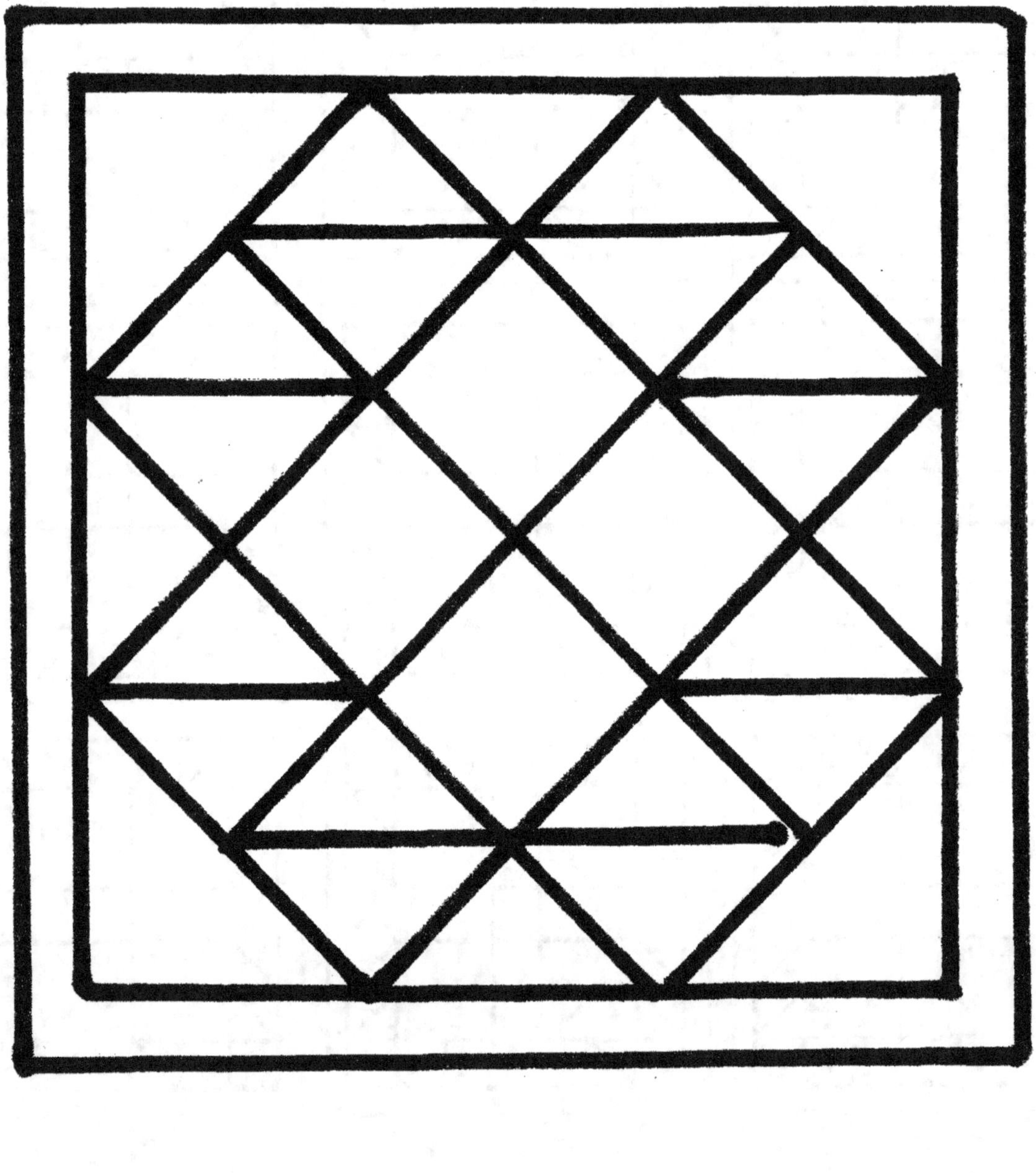

Frontier County Barn Quilt Buckwheat

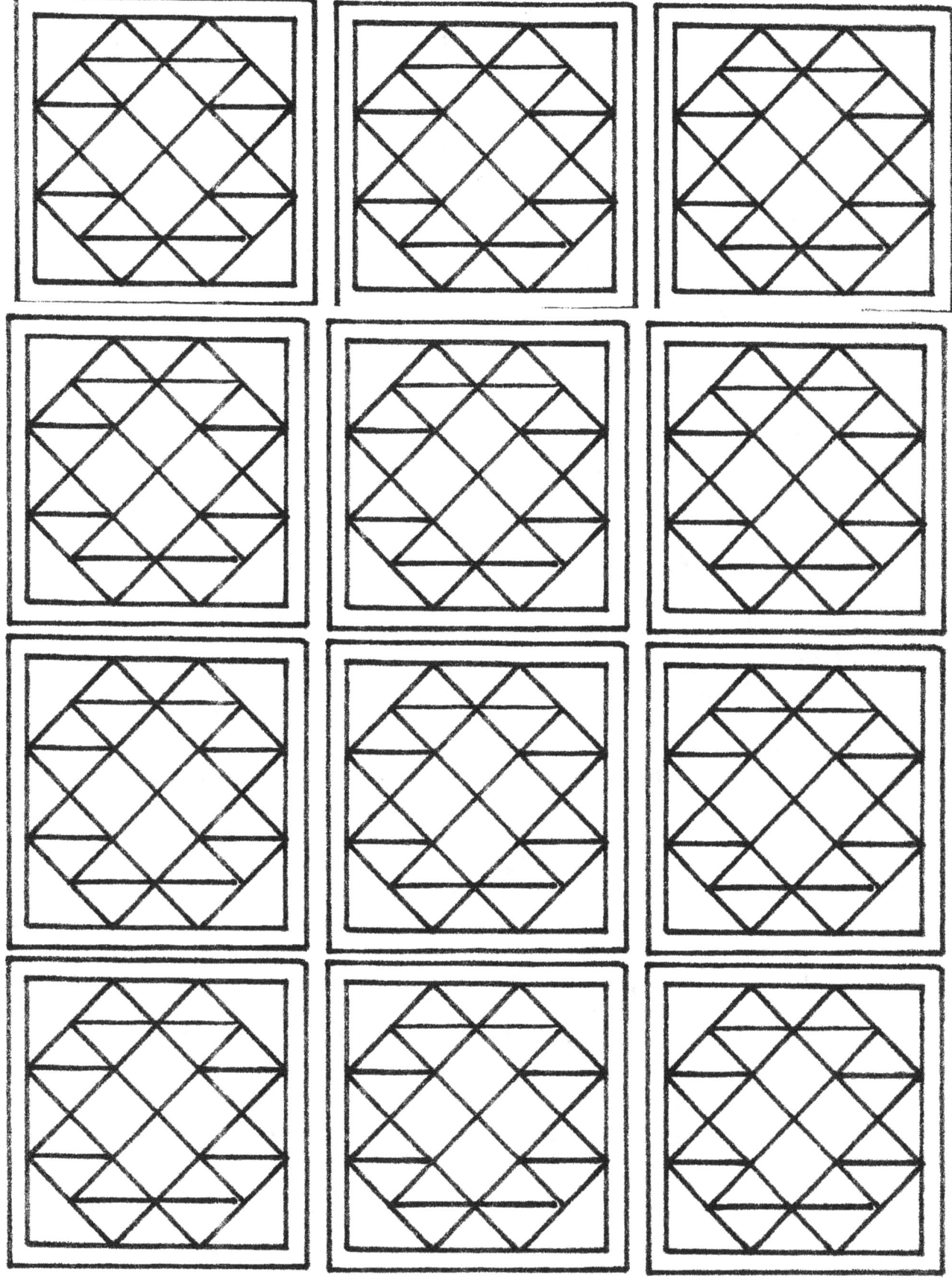

Barn Quilt America's Bird
Frontier County Barn Quilt Trail

Barn Quilt Location
Knobsville Road
Todd Township

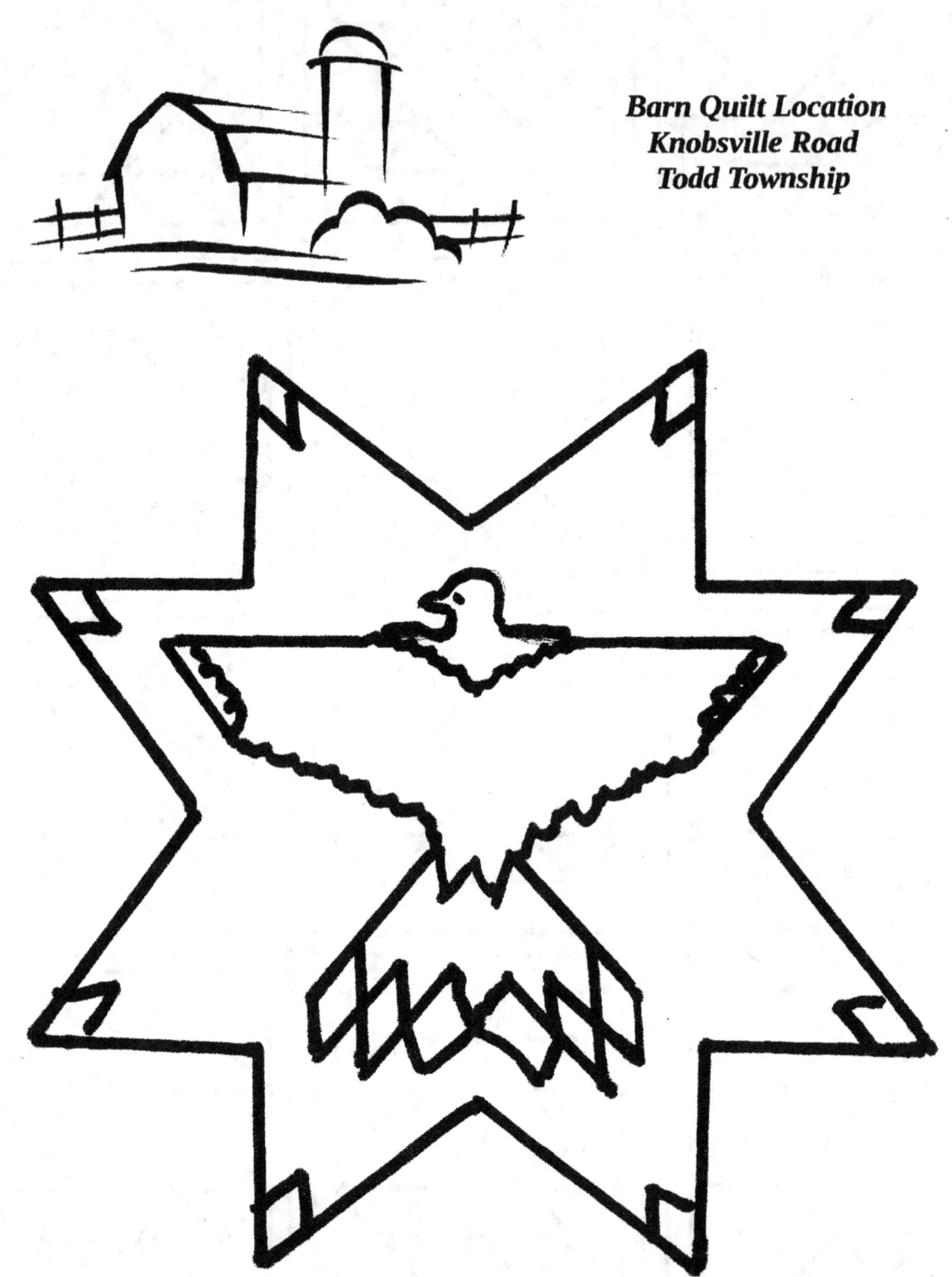

Frontier County Barn Quilt America's Bird

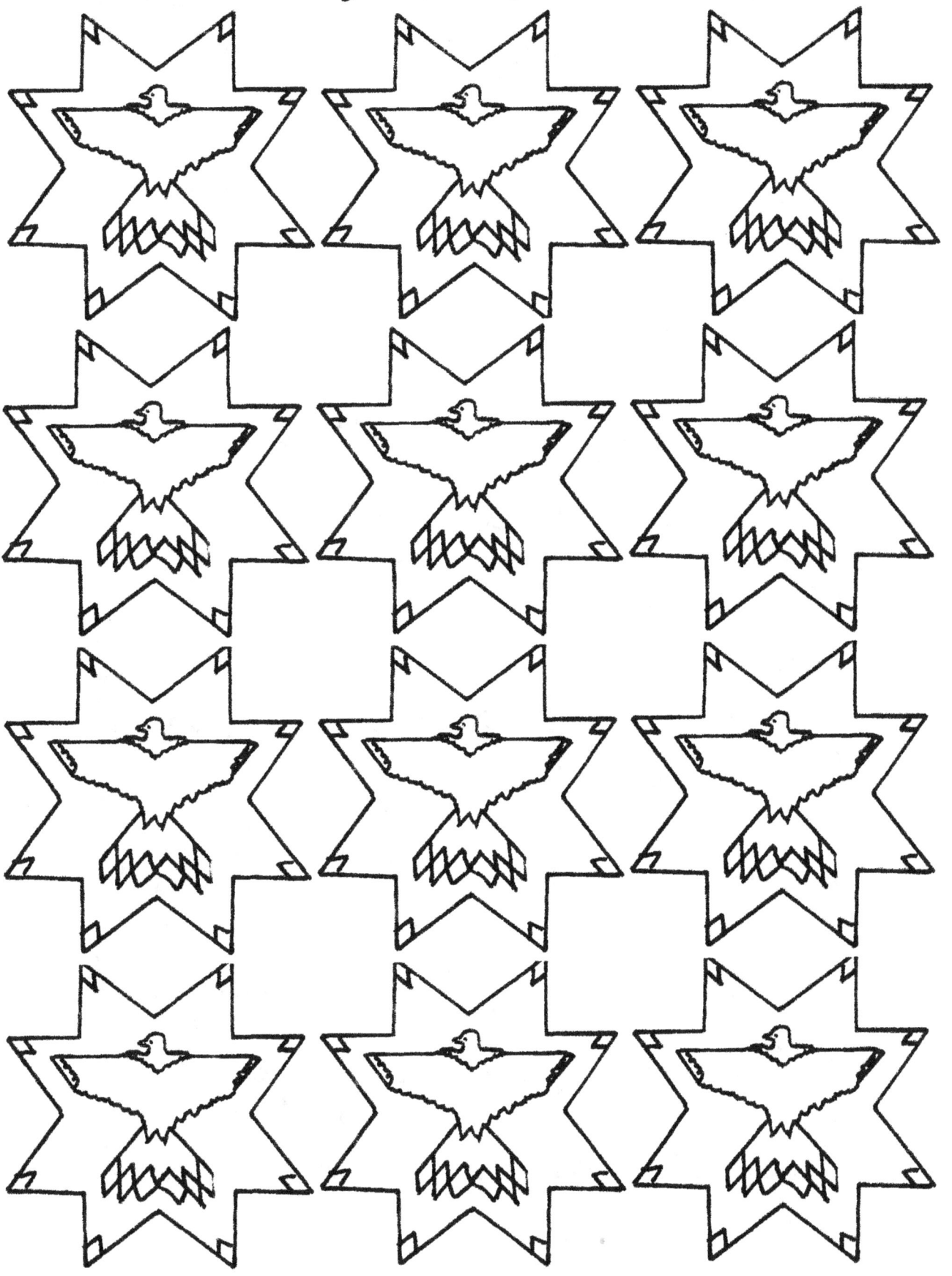

Barn Quilt Six Windows of Sunshine
Frontier County Barn Quilt Trail

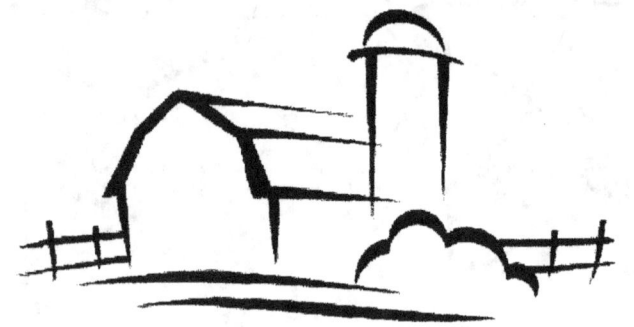

Barn Quilt Location
North 3rd Street
McConnellsburg Township

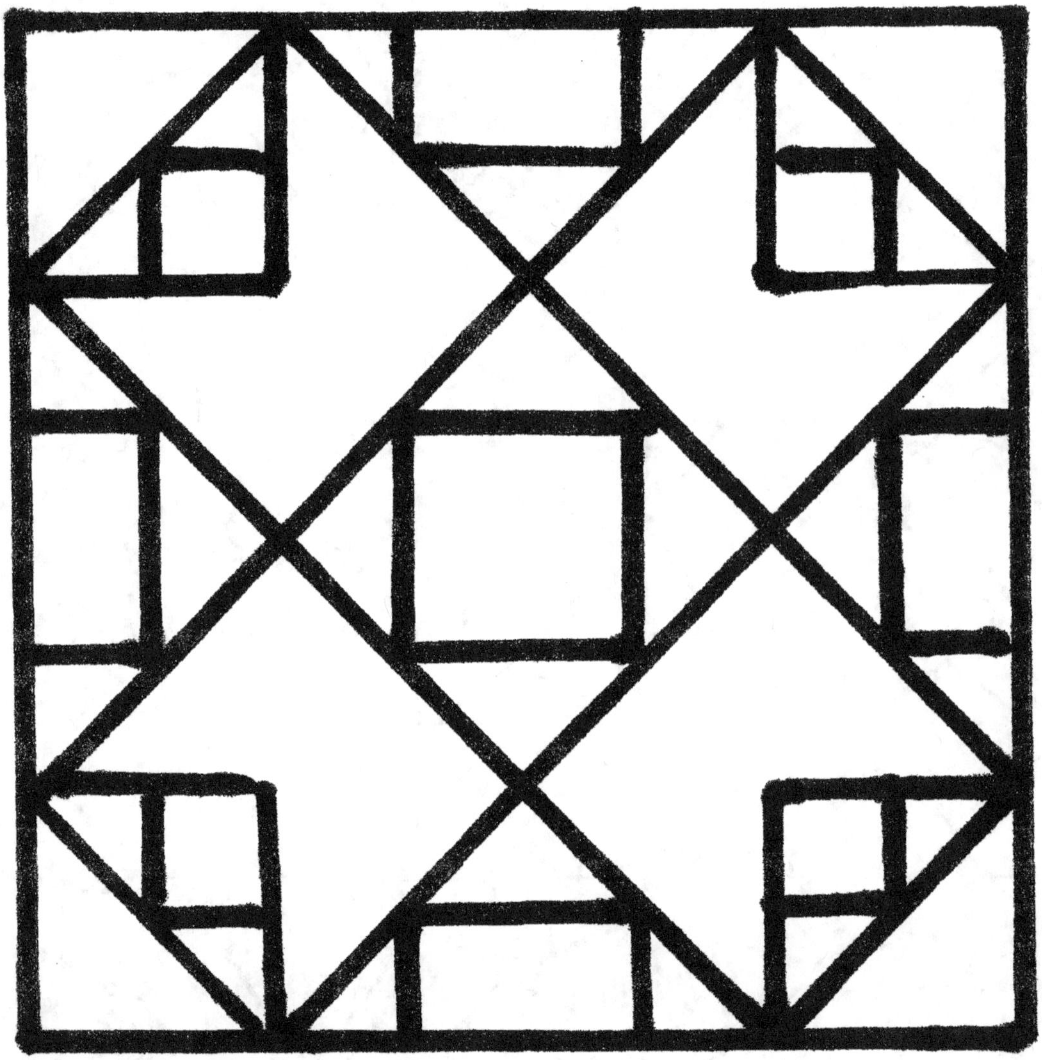

Frontier County Barn Quilt Six Windows of Sunshine

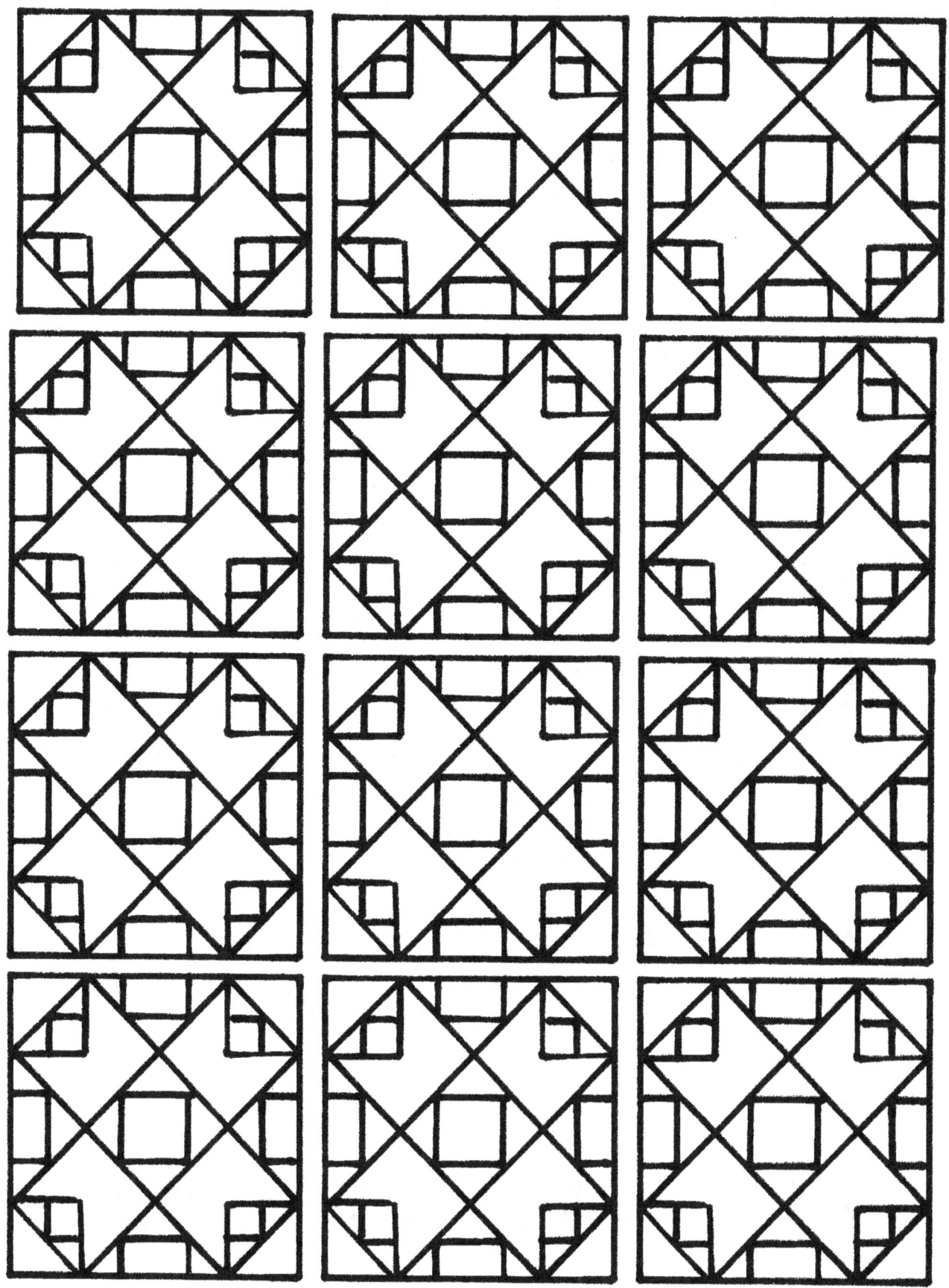

Barn Quilt Pig Tail
Frontier County Barn Quilt Trail

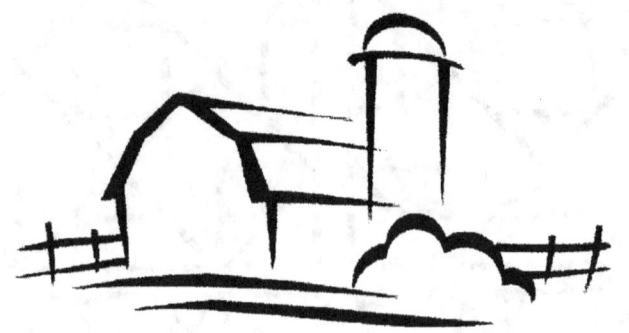

Barn Quilt Location
Great Cove Road
Todd Township

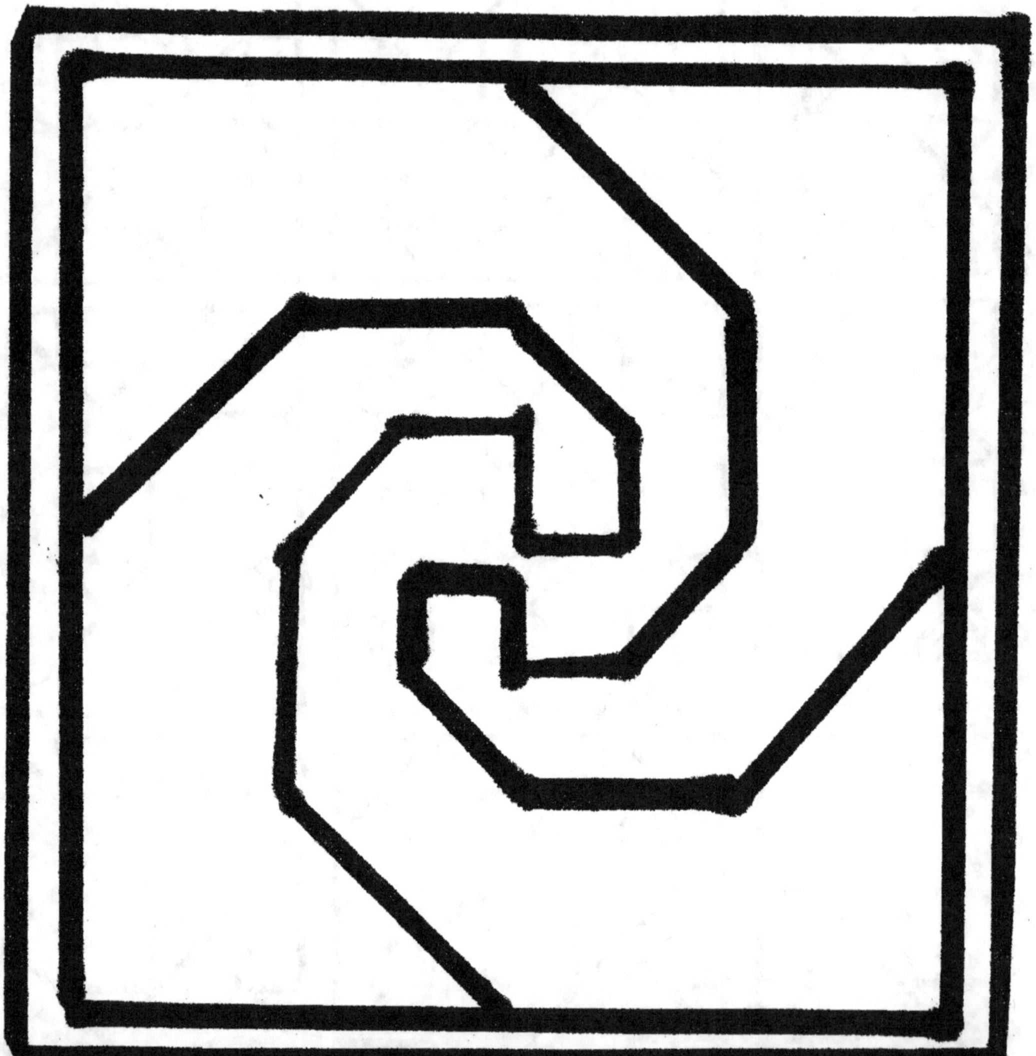

Frontier County Barn Quilt Pig Tail

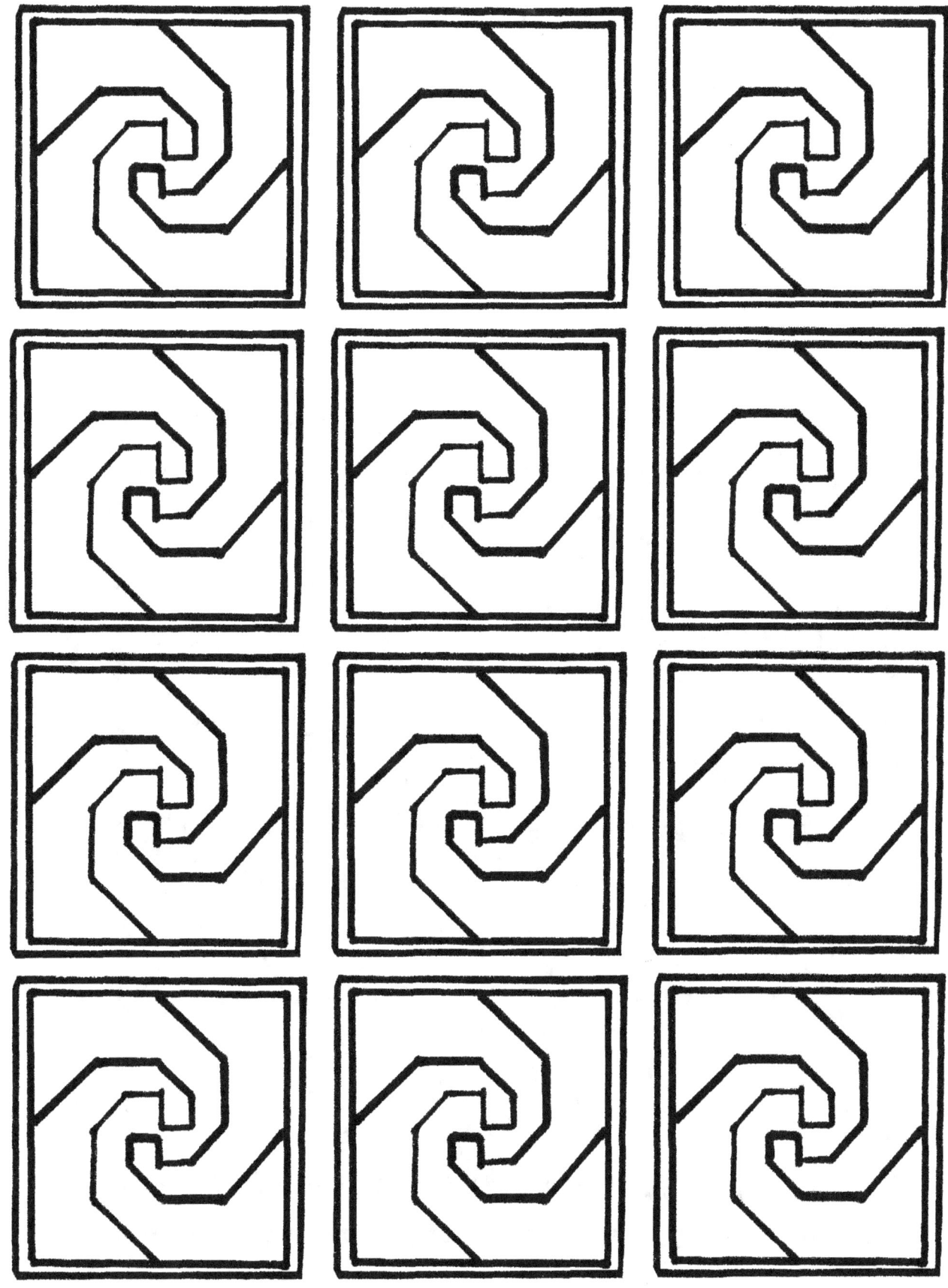

Barn Quilt North, South, East & West
Frontier County Barn Quilt Trail

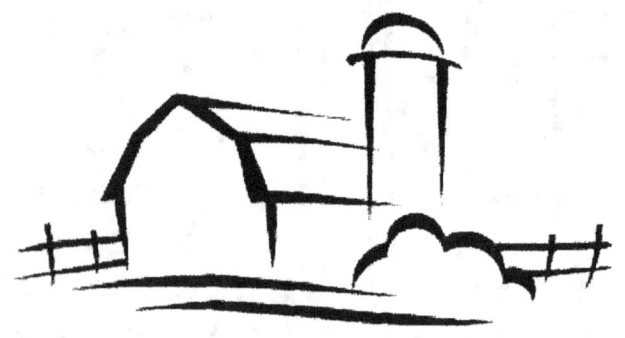

*Barn Quilt Location
North 3rd Street
McConnellsburg Township*

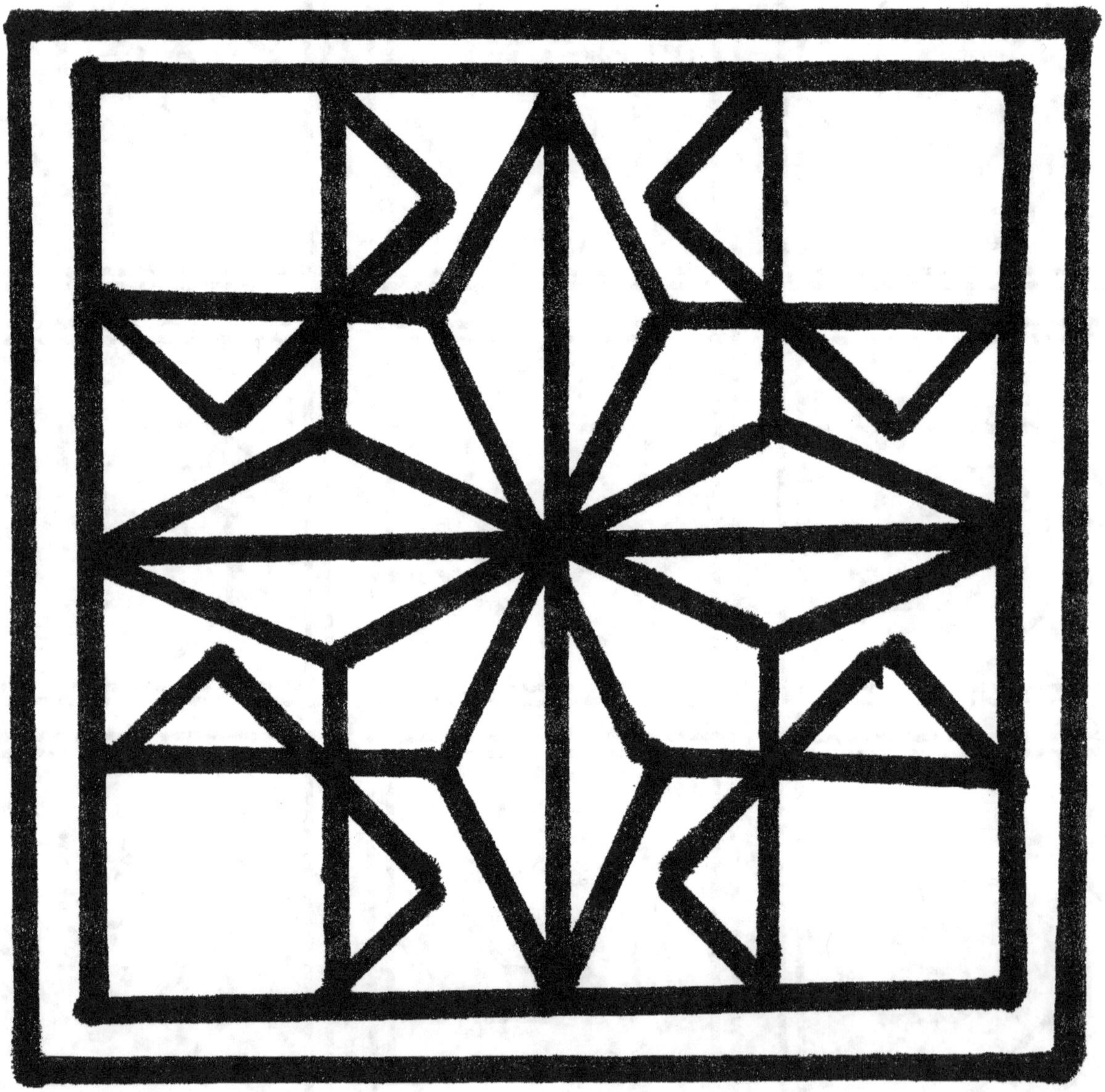

Frontier County Barn Quilt North, South, East & West

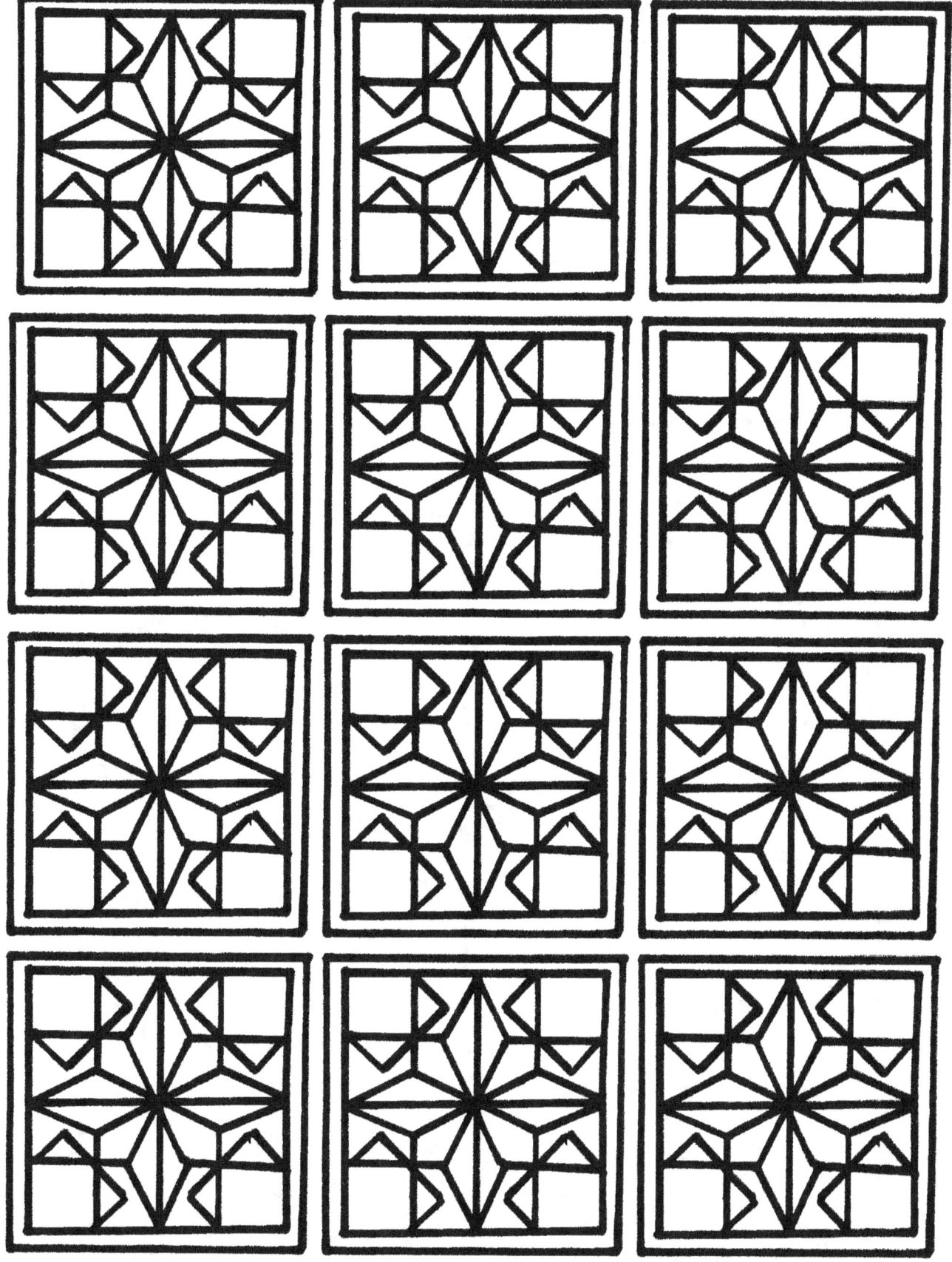

Barn Quilt Irish Green
Frontier County Barn Quilt Trail

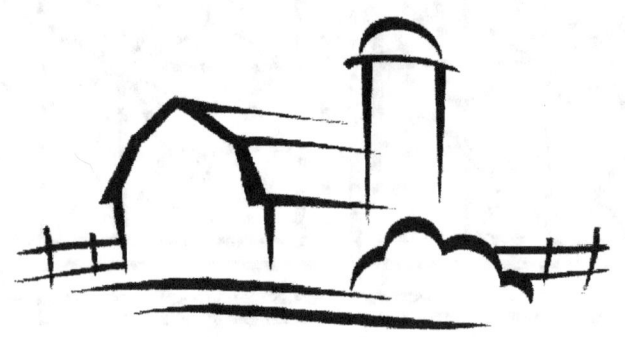

Barn Quilt Location
East Patterson Street
Todd Township

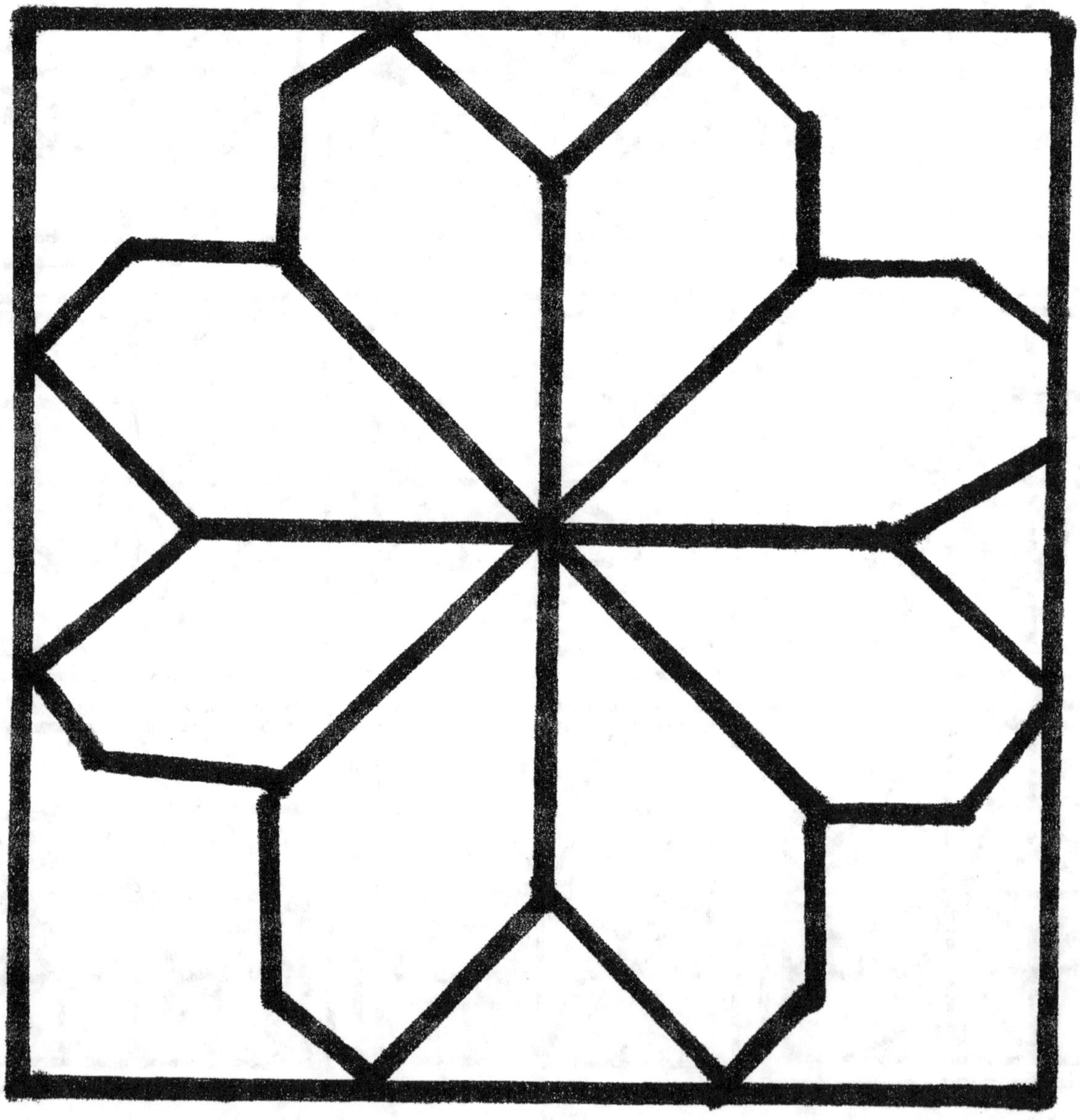

Frontier County Barn Quilt Irish Green

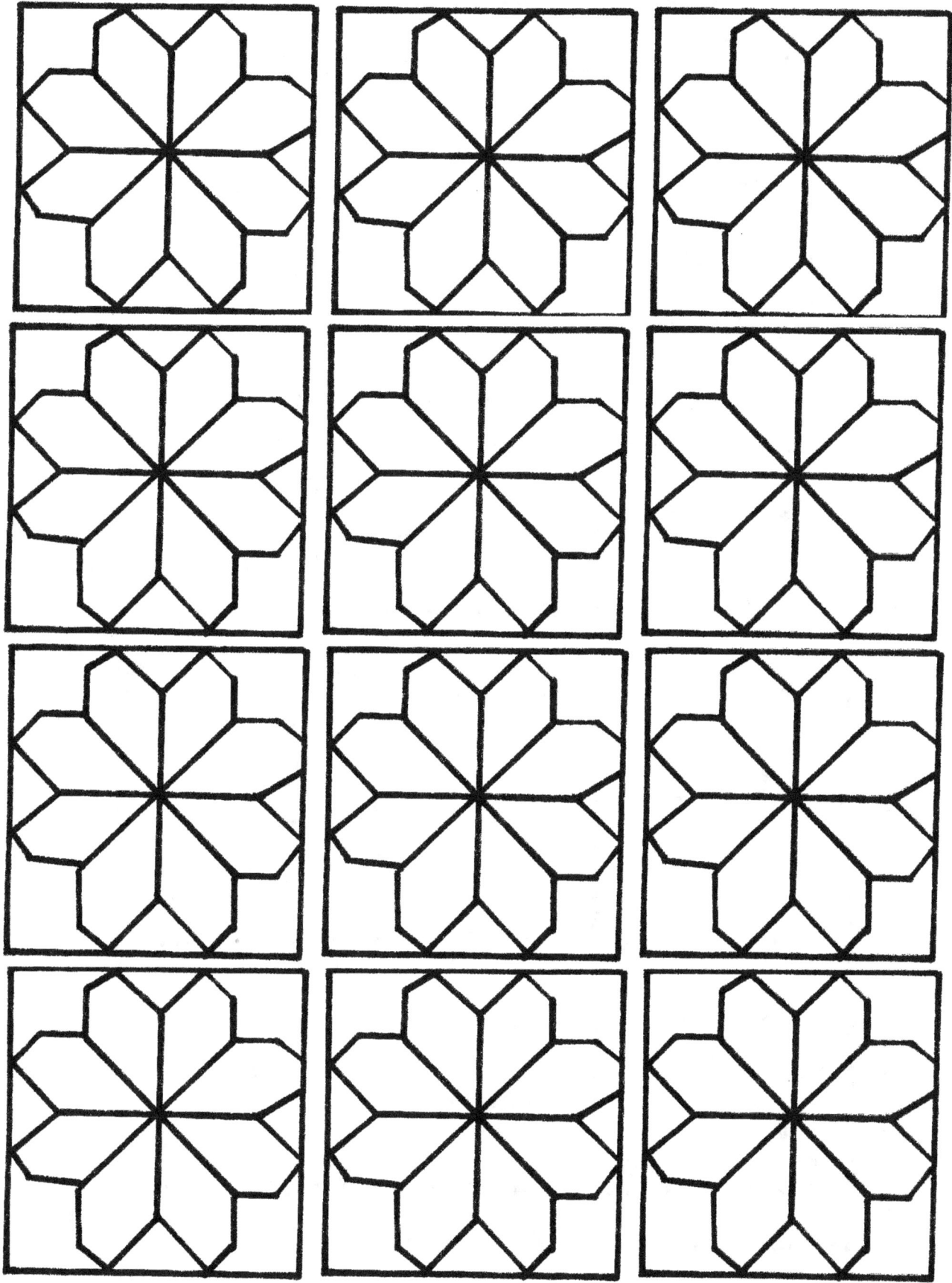

Barn Quilt Zelda's Ins & Outs
Frontier County Barn Quilt Trail

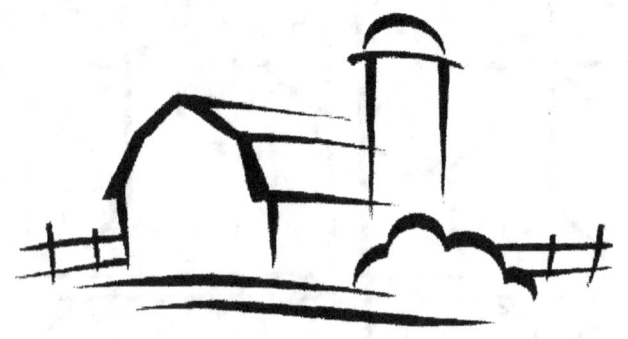

Barn Quilt Location
Black Bear Road
Belfast Township

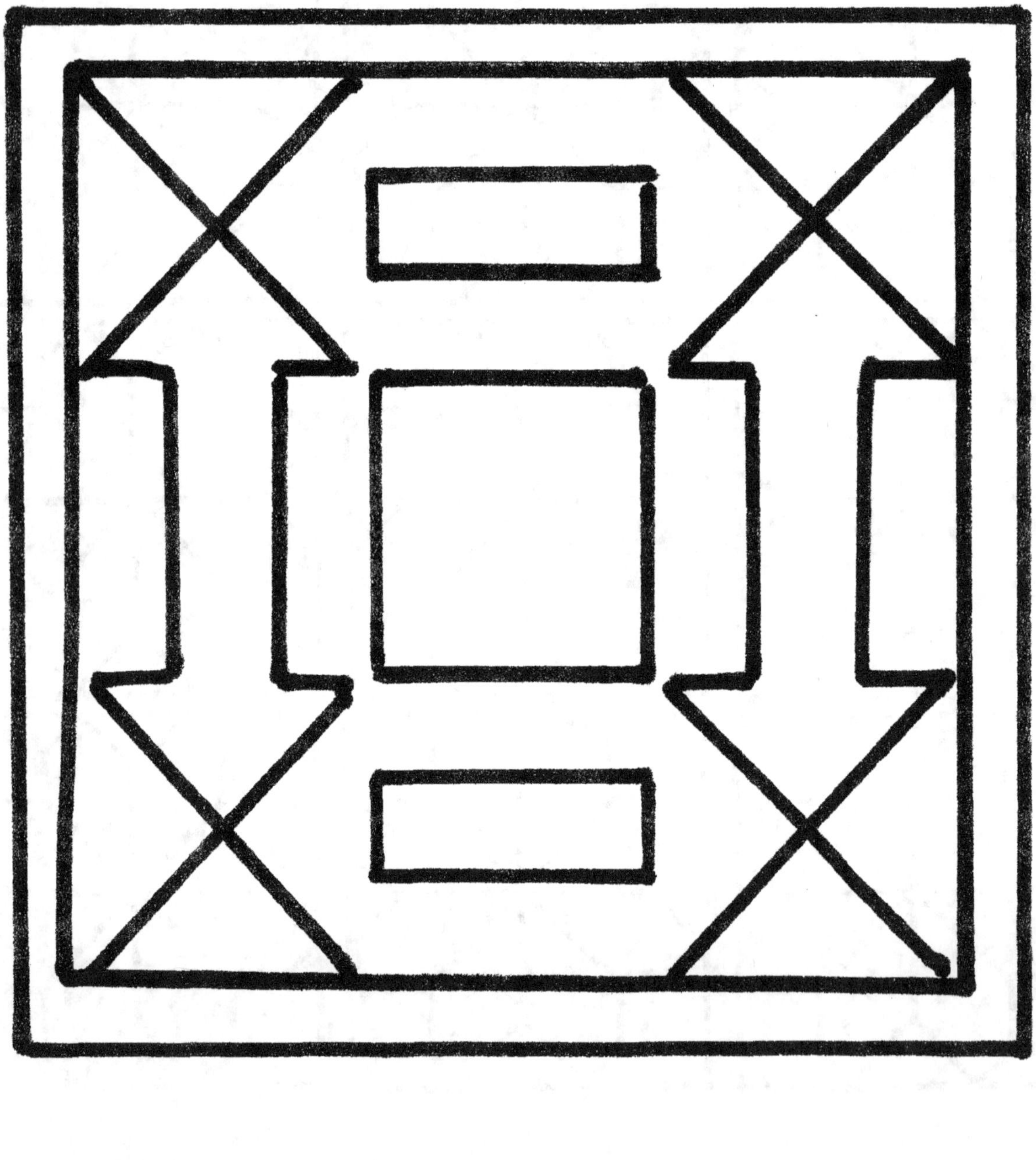

Frontier County Barn Quilt Zelda's Ins & Outs

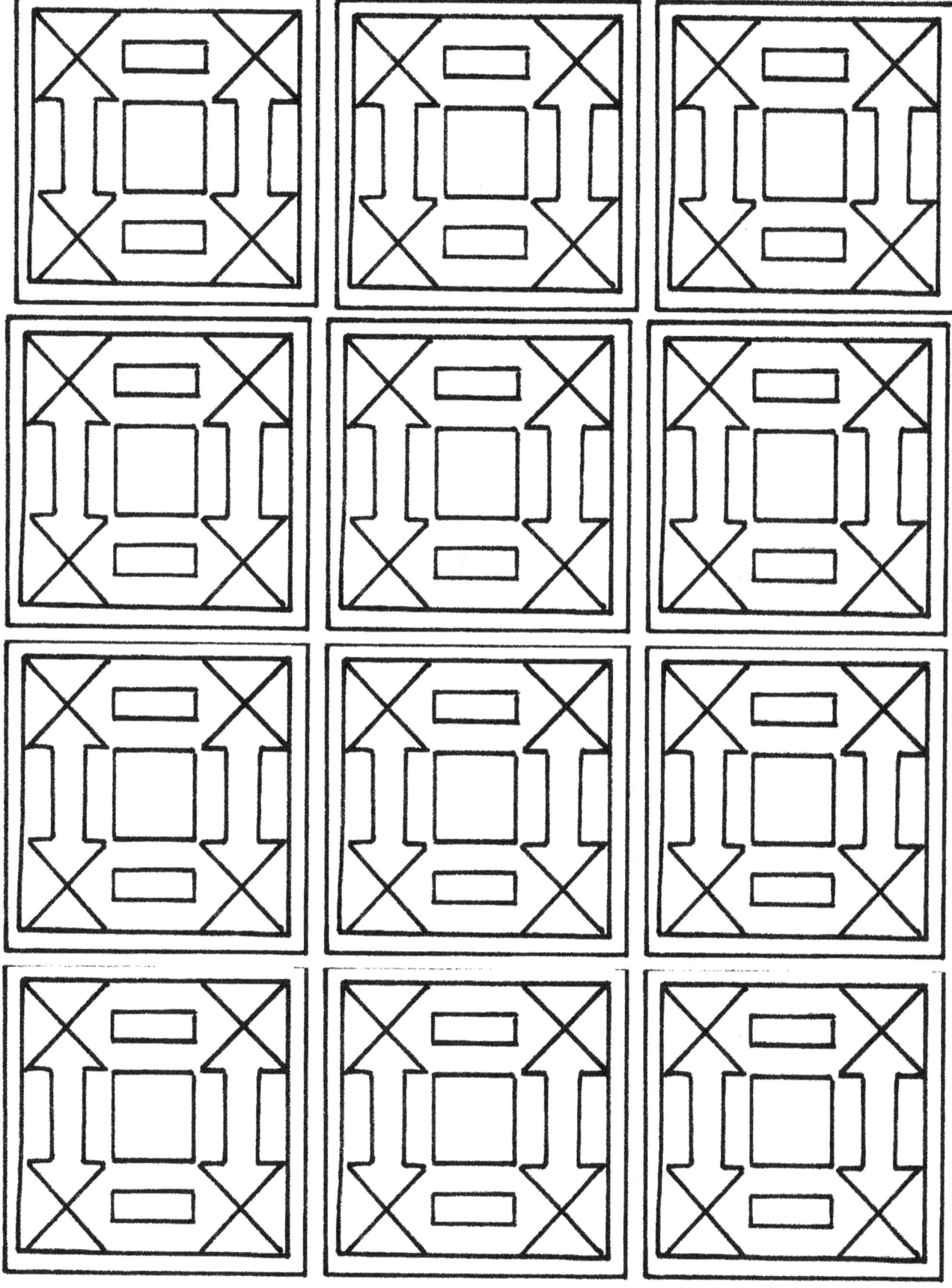

Barn Quilt J & B Star
Frontier County Barn Quilt Trail

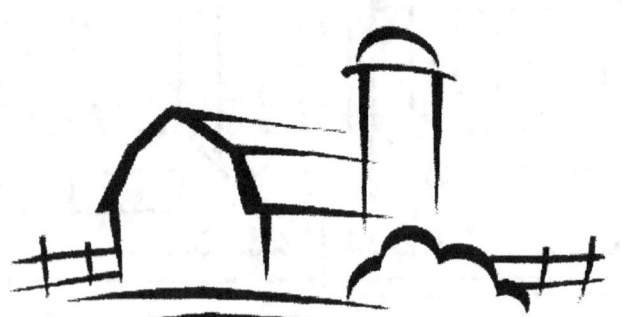

*Barn Quilt Location
Cito Road
Ayr Township*

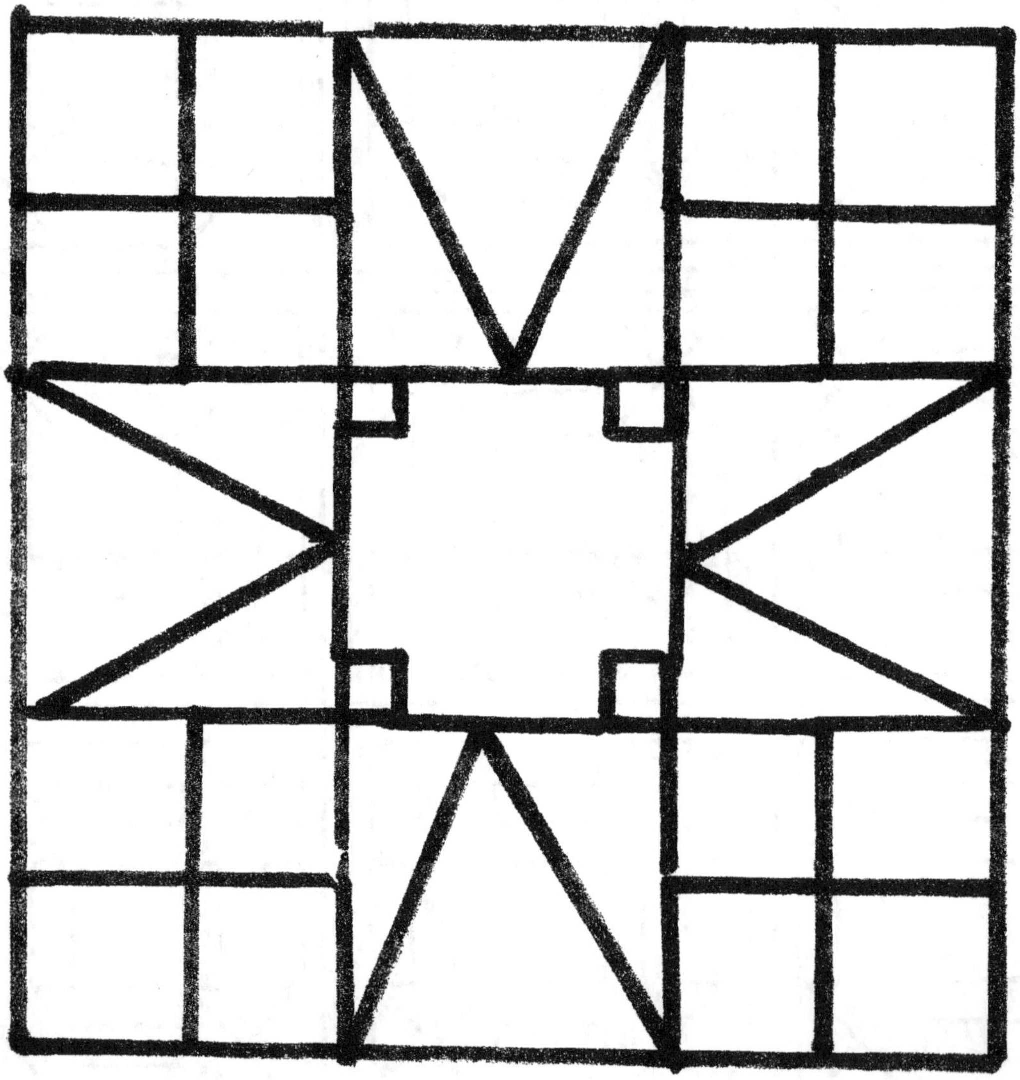

Frontier County Barn Quilt J & B Star

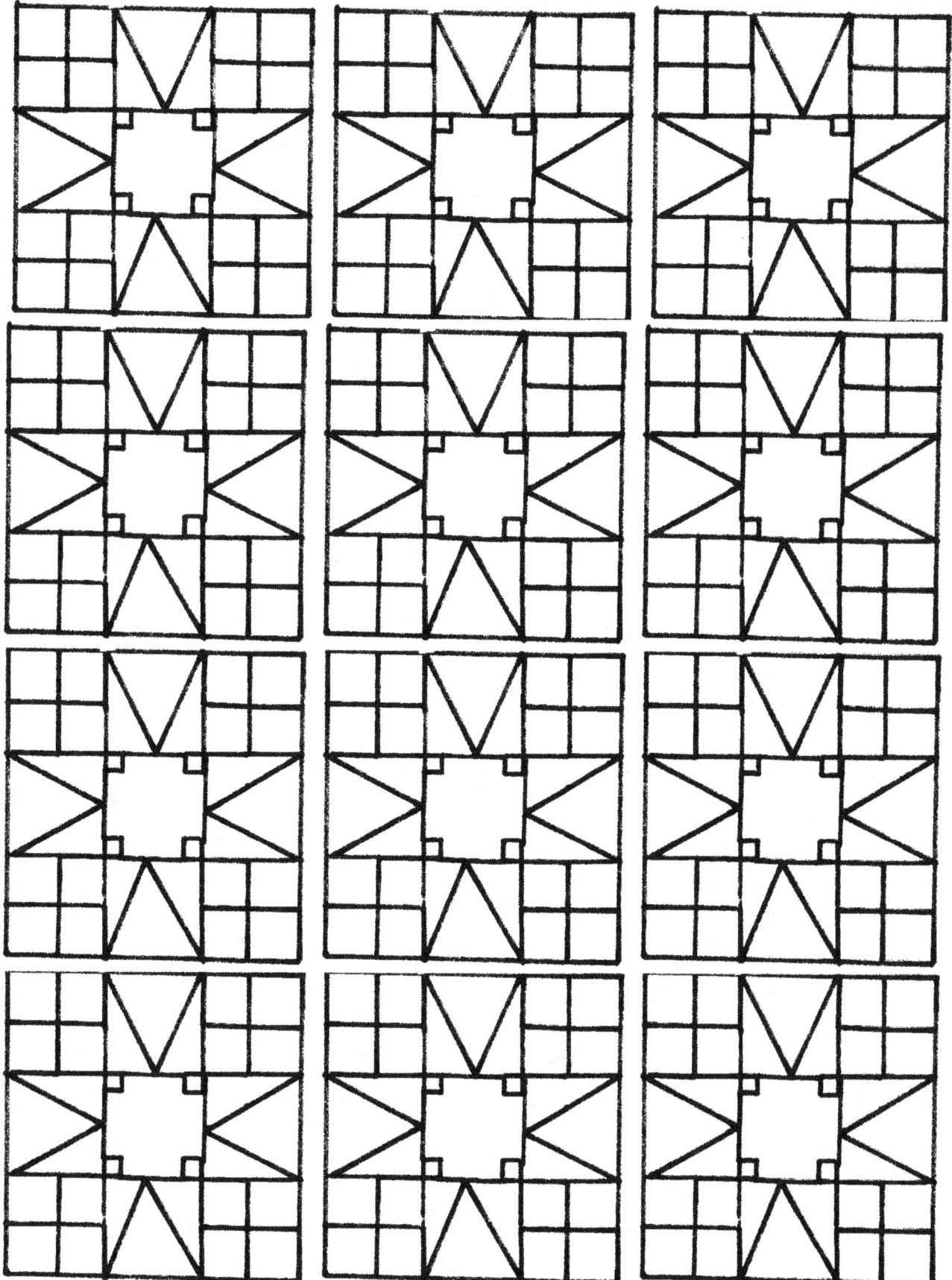

Barn Quilt Cathy's Star Patchwork
Frontier County Barn Quilt Trail

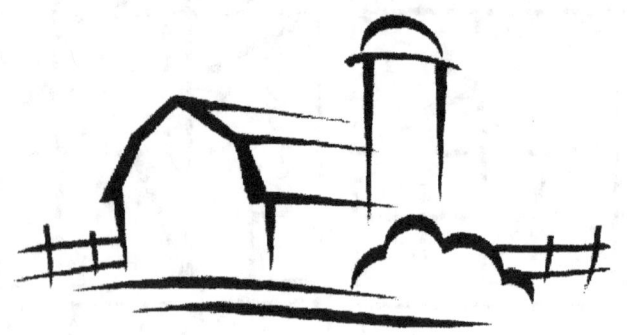

Barn Quilt Location
Timber Ridge Road
Thompson Township

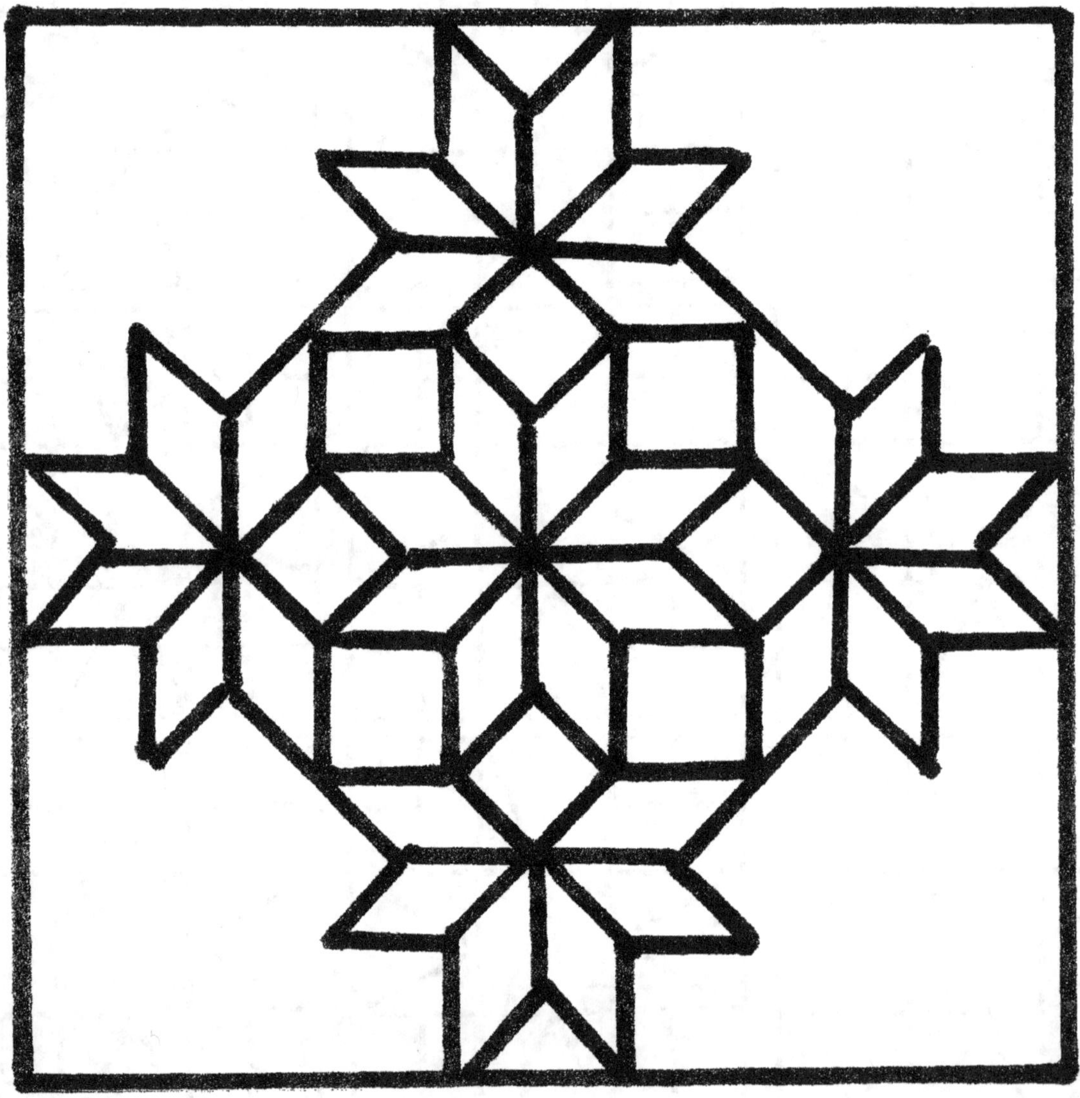

Frontier County Barn Quilt Cathy's Star Patchwork

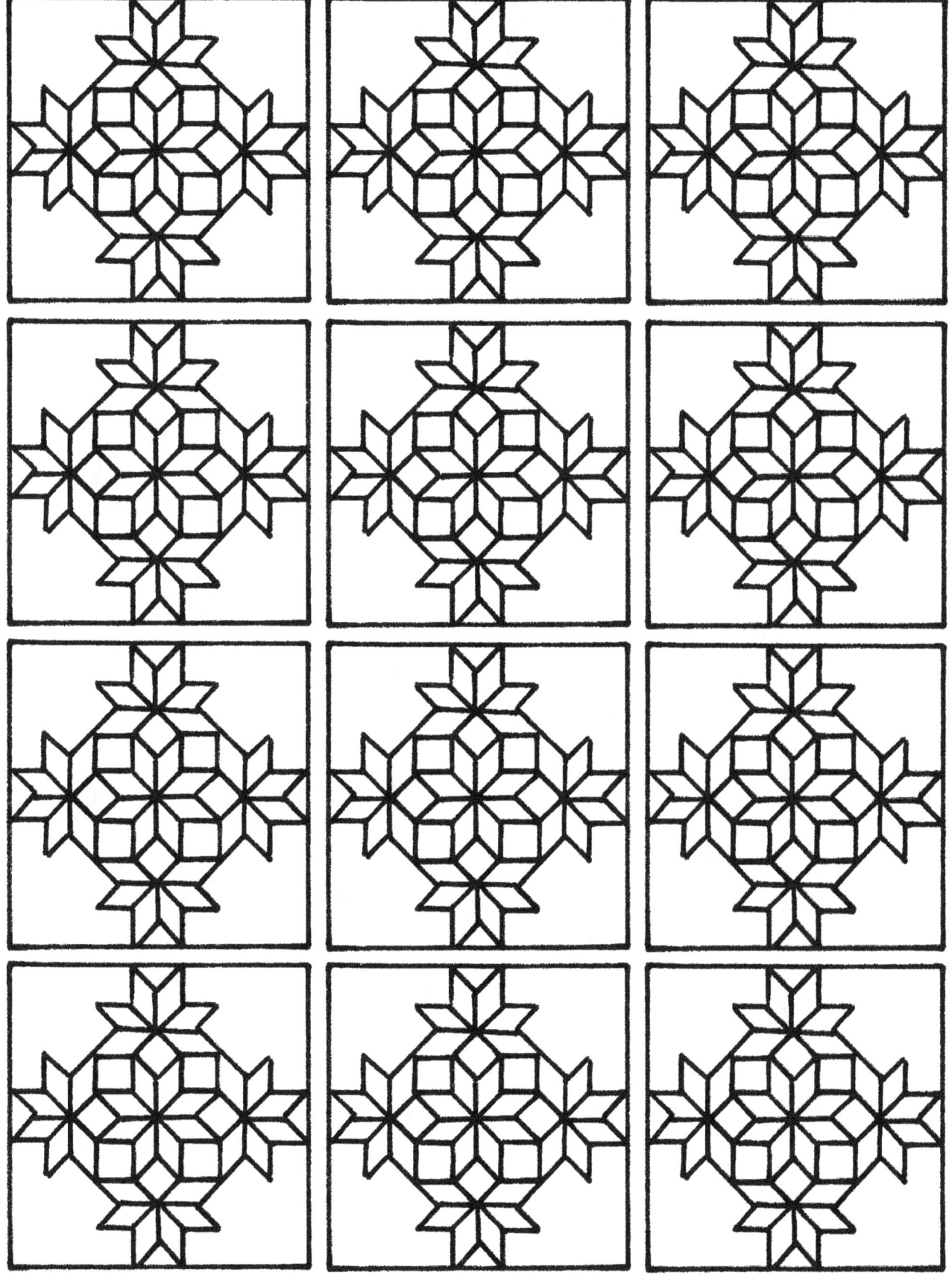

Barn Quilt Hands All Around
Frontier County Barn Quilt Trail

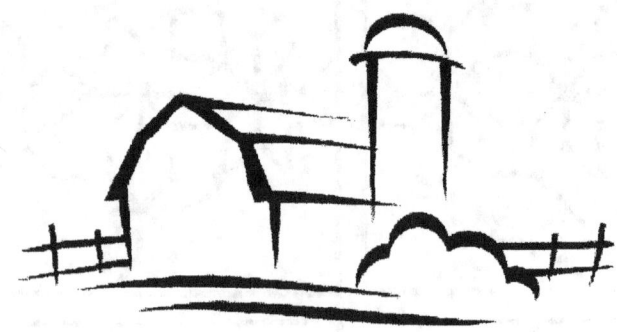

Barn Quilt Location
Great Cove Road
Belfast Township

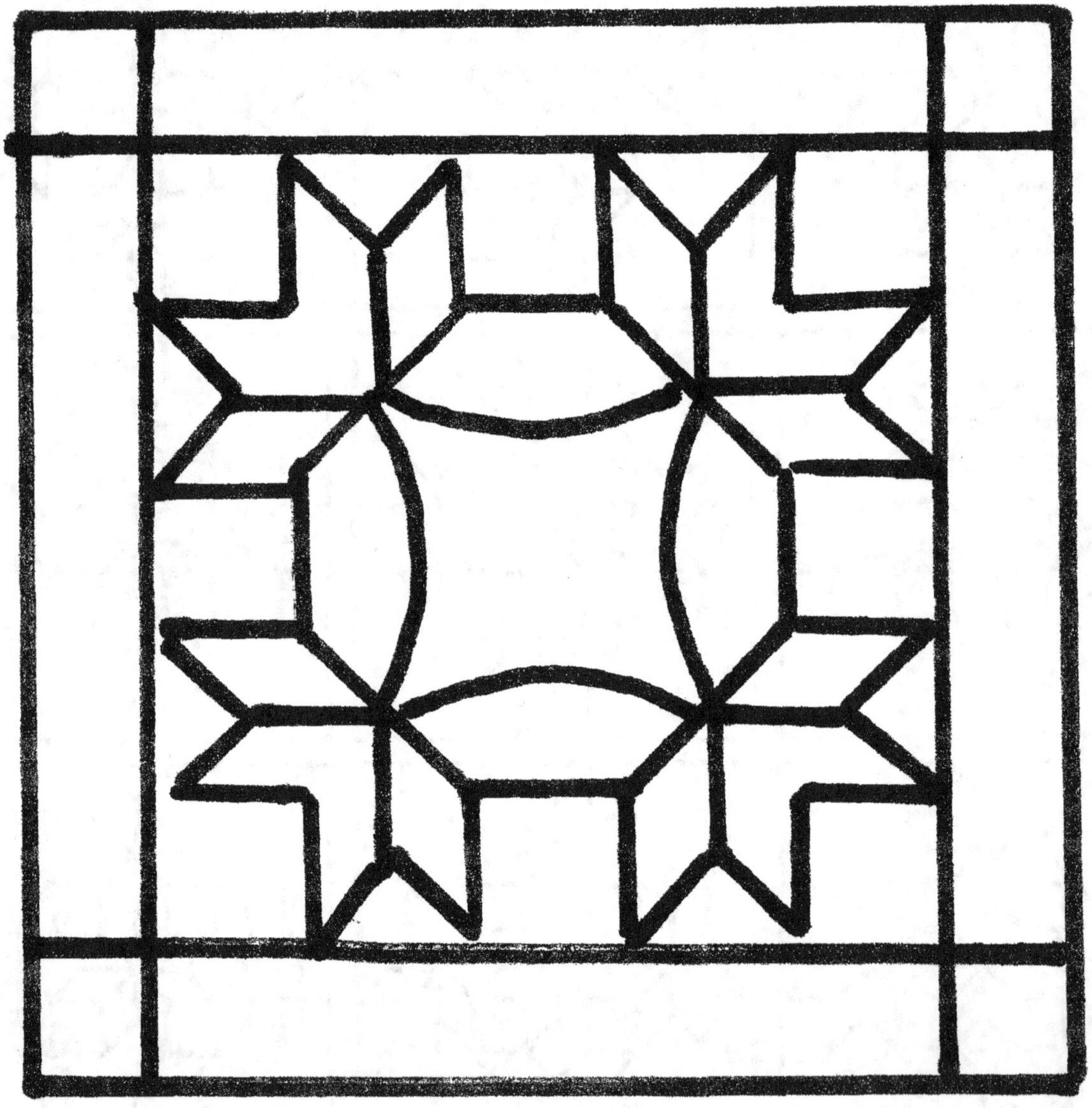

Frontier County Barn Quilt Hands All Around

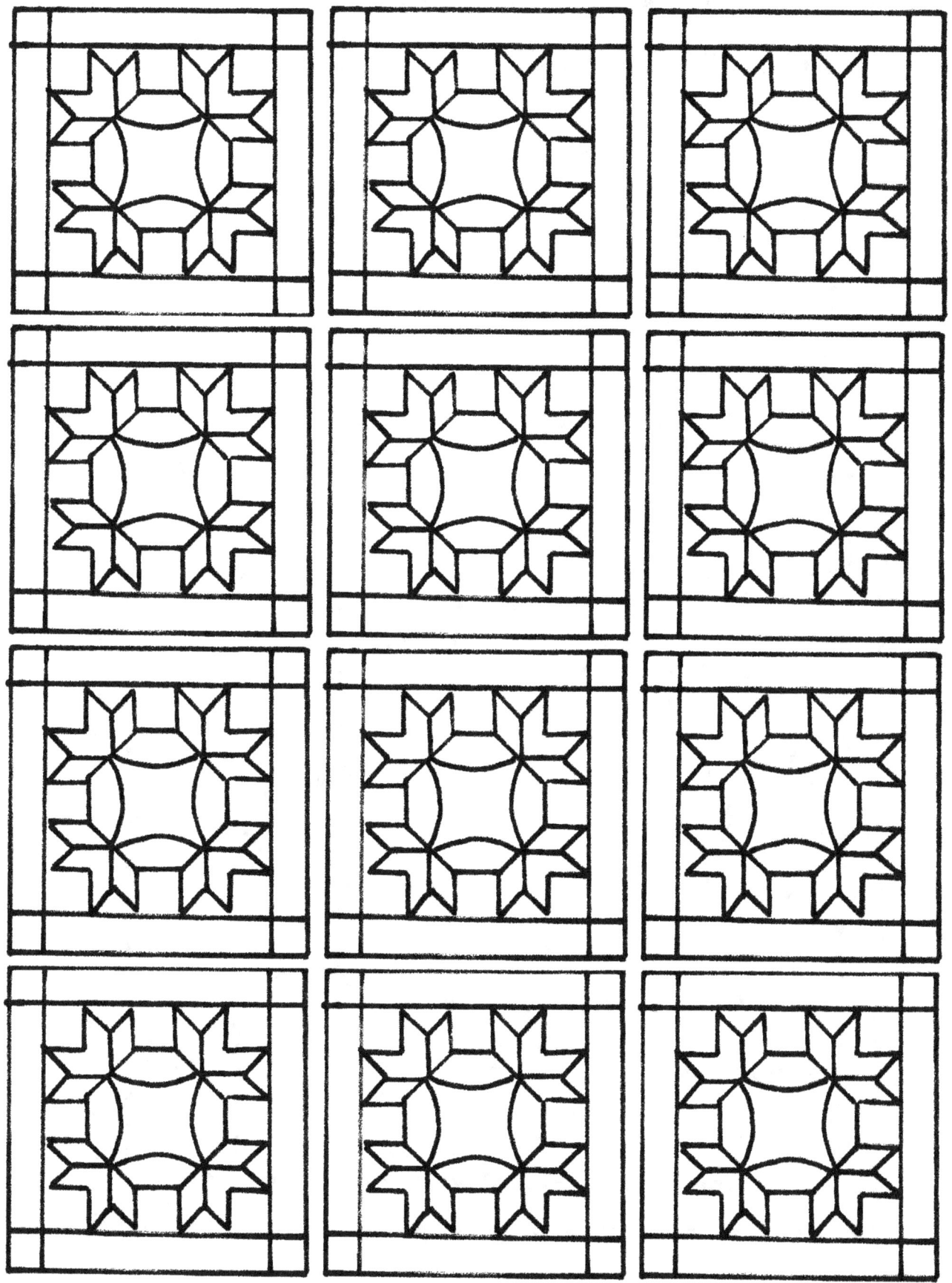

Barn Quilt Pigeon Cove Cross
Frontier County Barn Quilt Trail

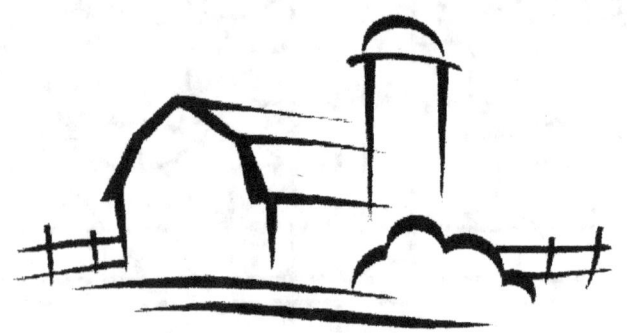

Barn Quilt Location
Alpine Road
Bethel Township

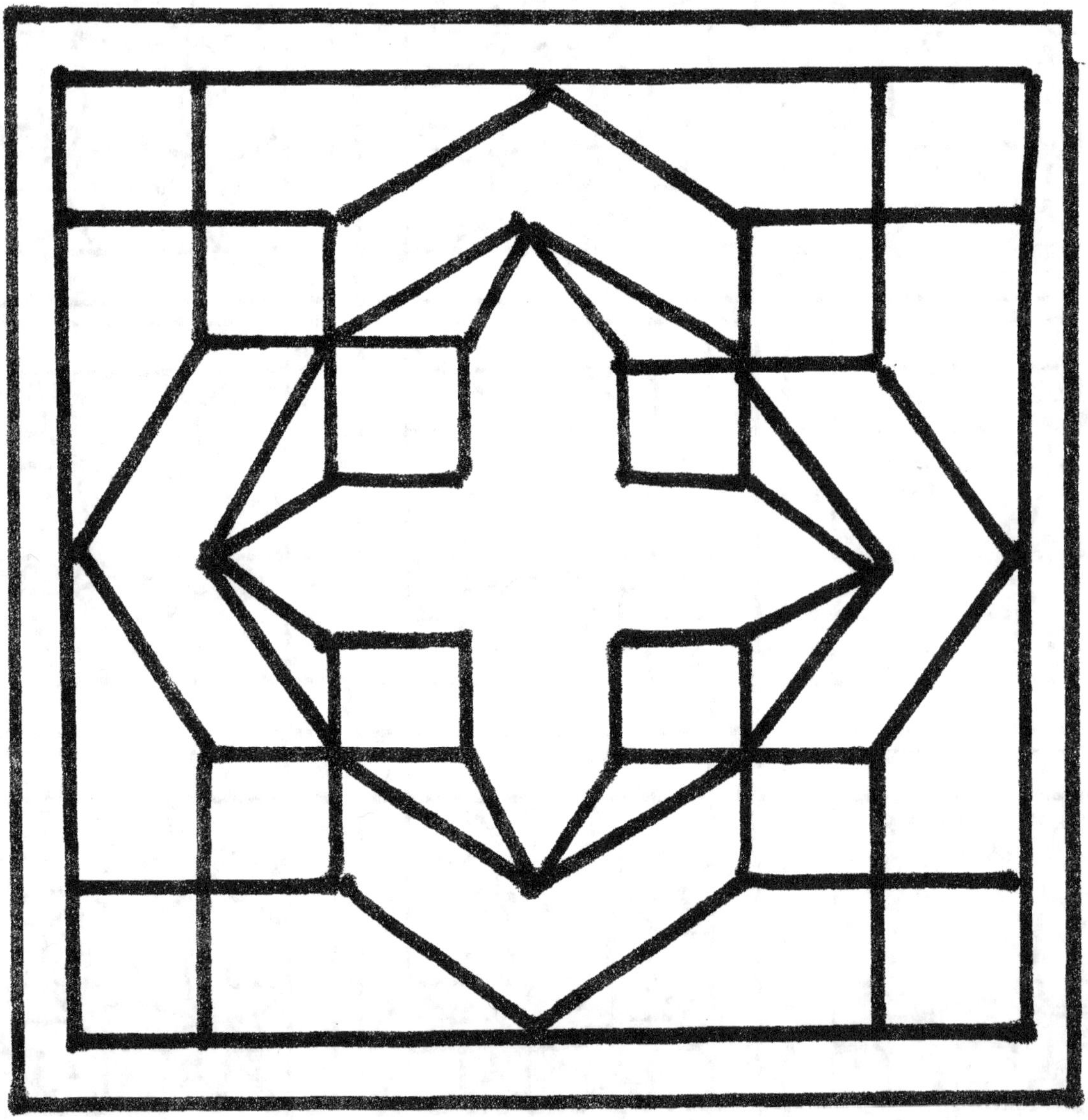

Frontier County Barn Quilt Pigeon Cove Cross

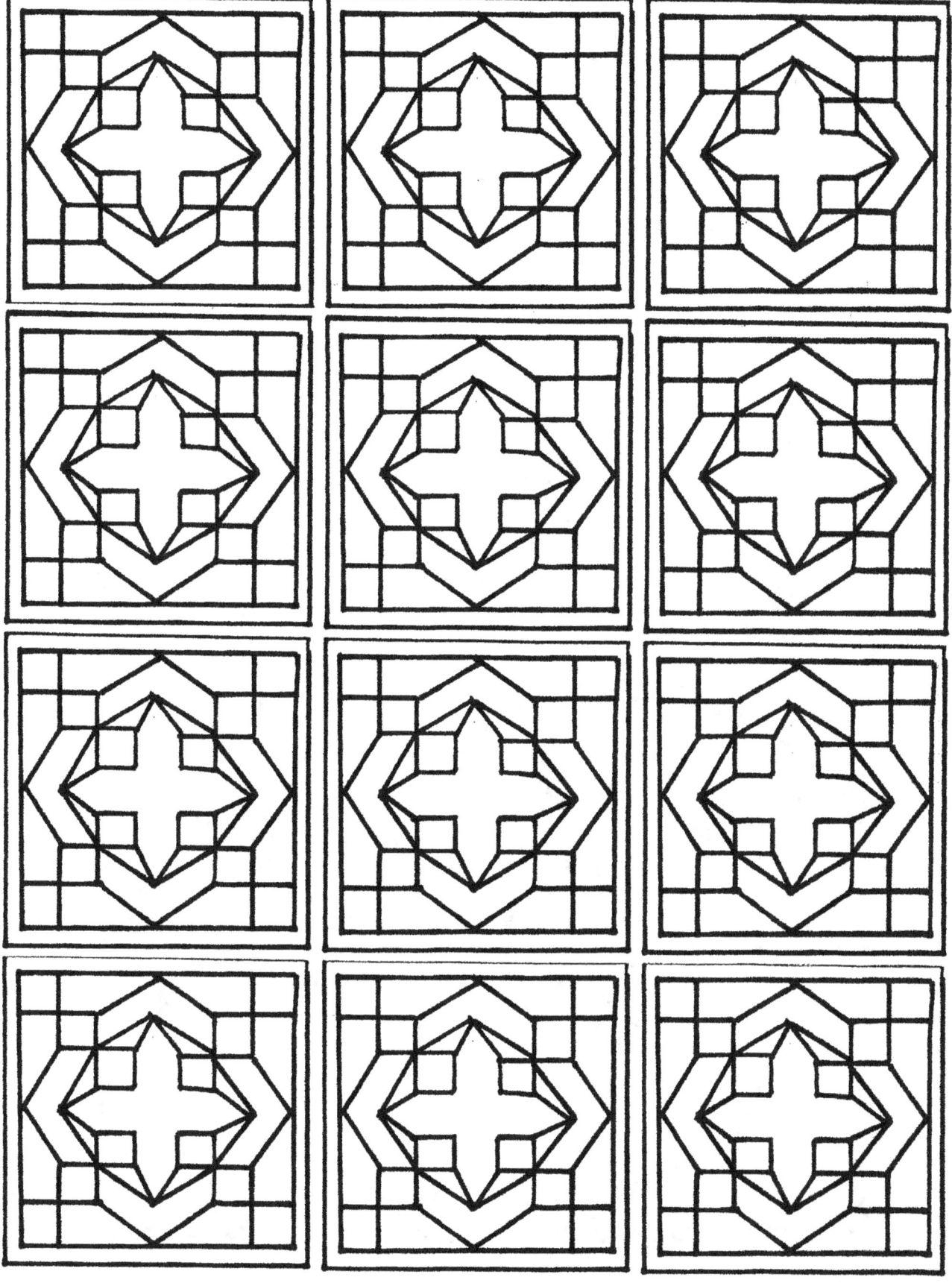

Barn Quilt Nova
Frontier County Barn Quilt Trail

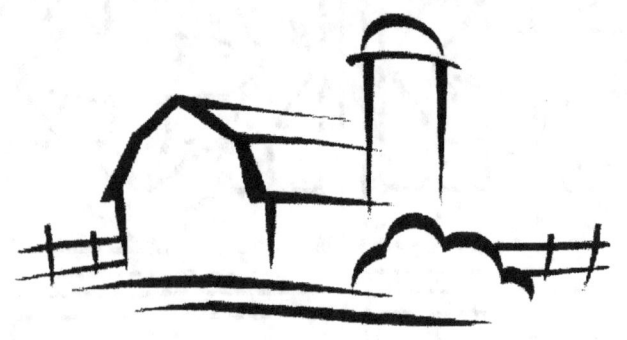

Barn Quilt Location
Great Cove Road
Belfast Township

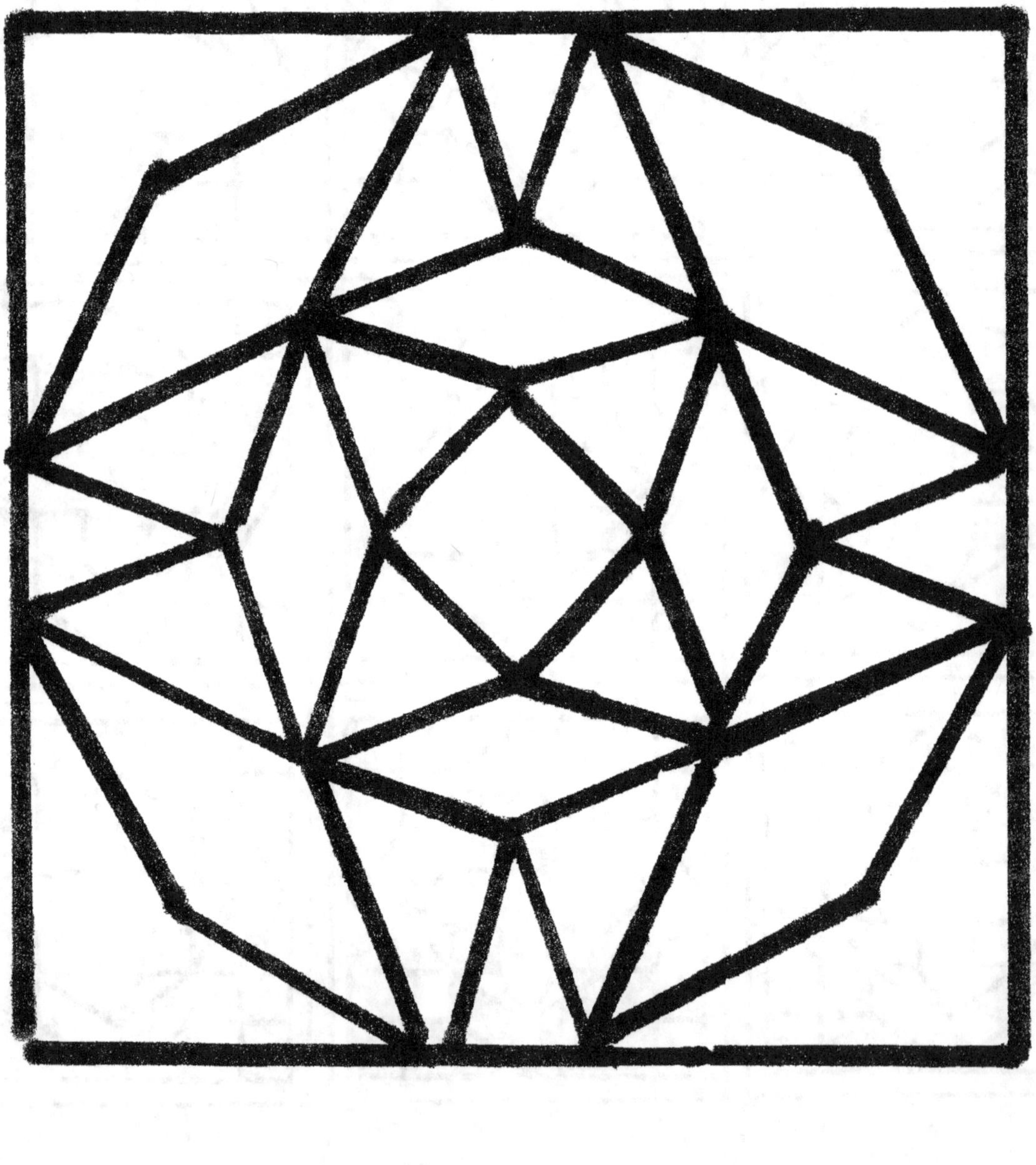

Frontier County Barn Quilt Nova

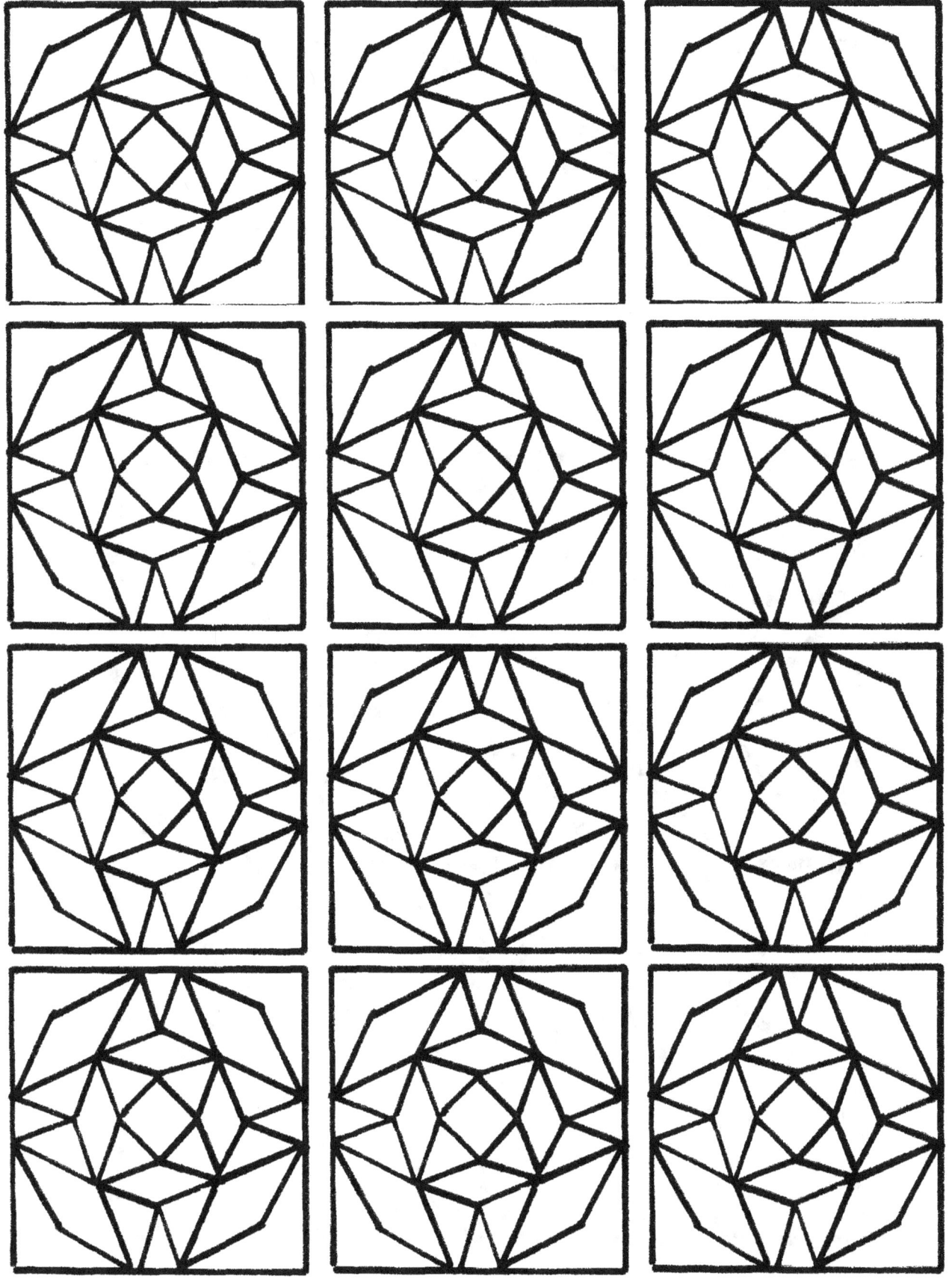

Barn Quilt Kansas
Frontier County Barn Quilt Trail

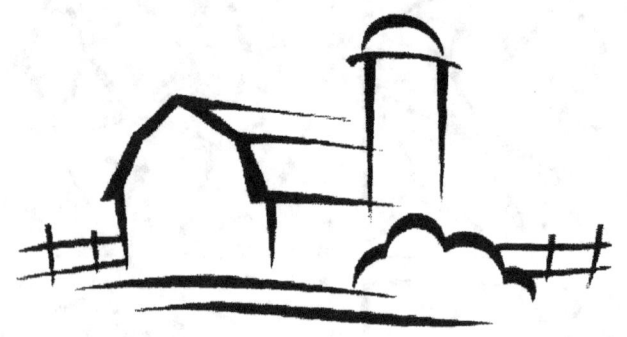

Barn Quilt Location
Black Mountain Road
Taylor Township

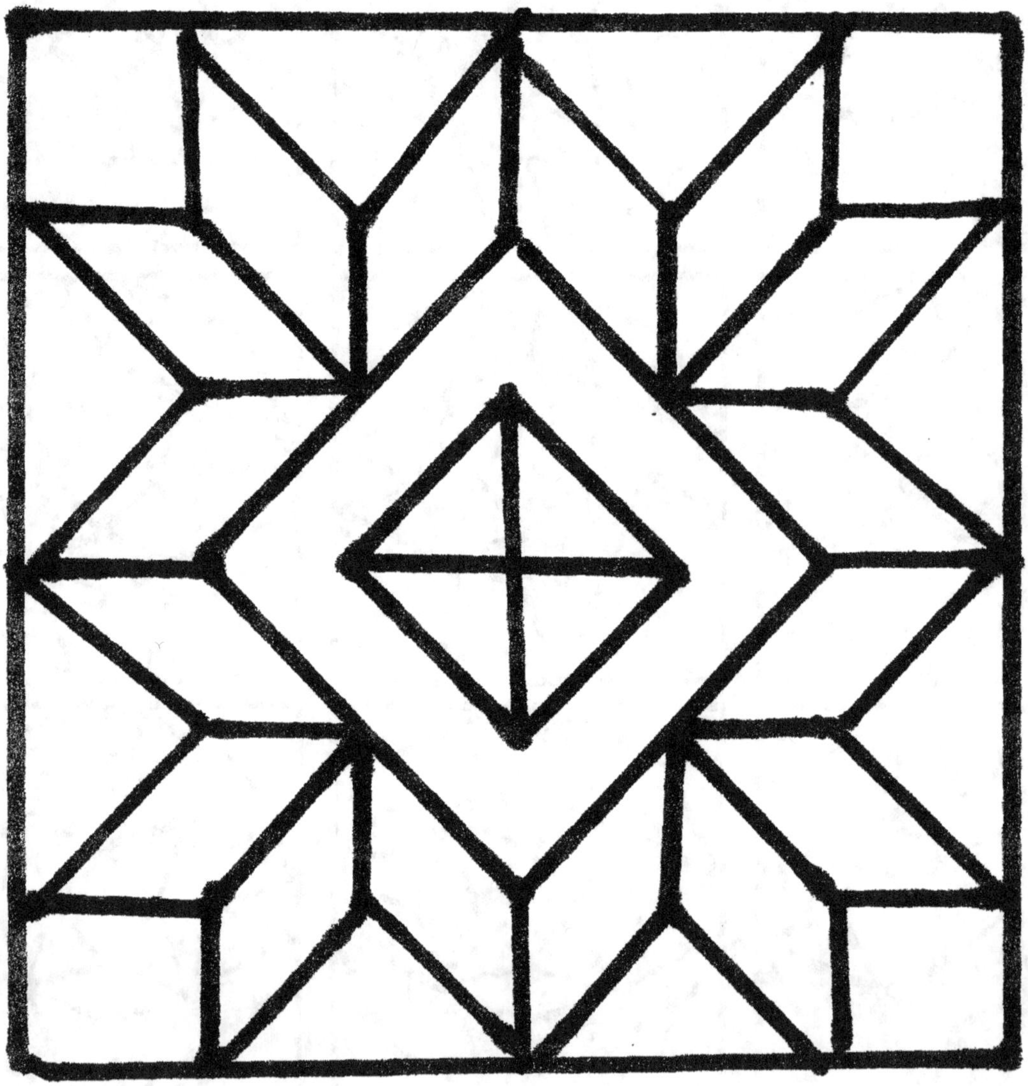

Frontier County Barn Quilt Kansas

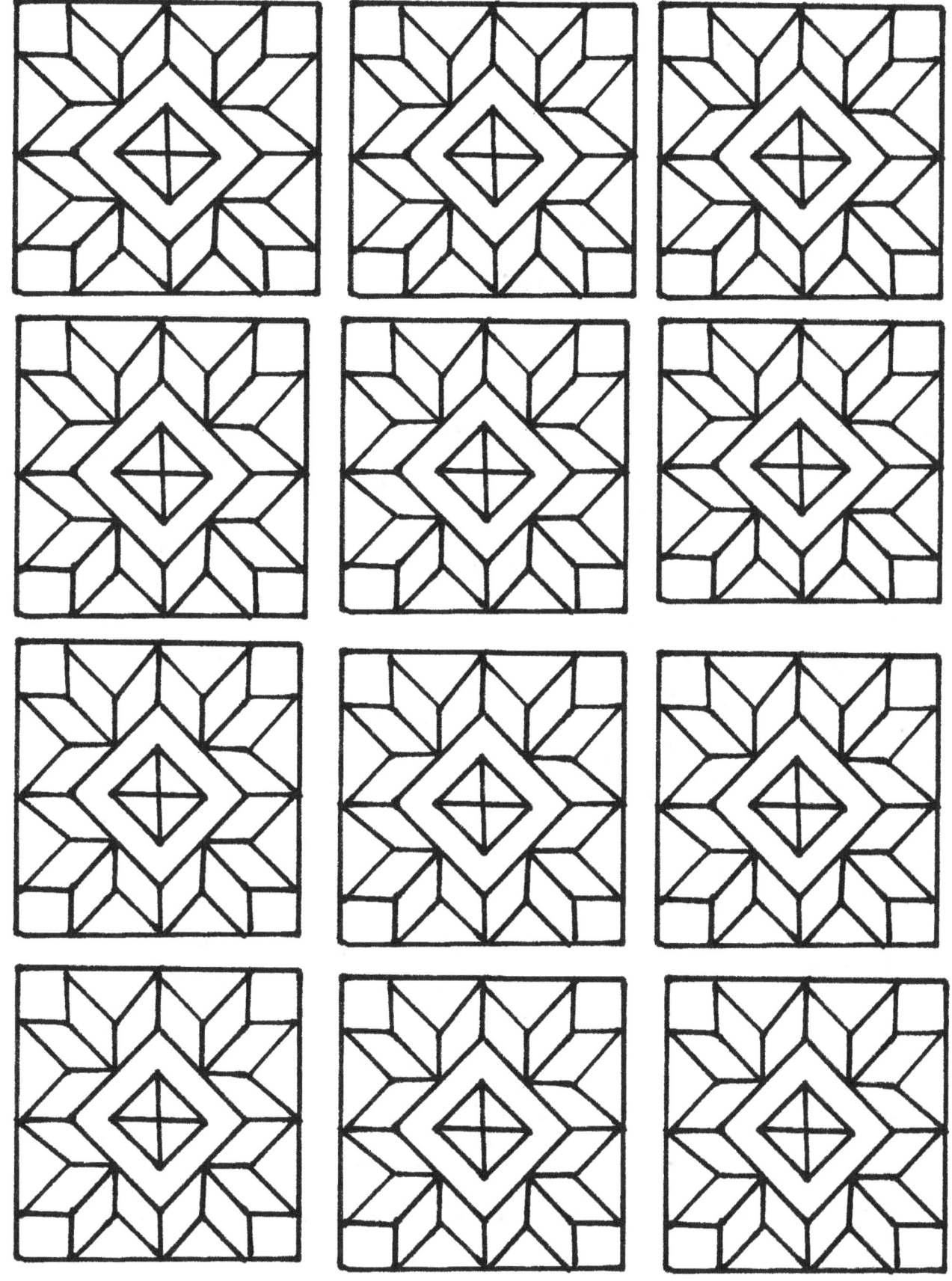

Barn Quilt Crown of Thorns
Frontier County Barn Quilt Trail

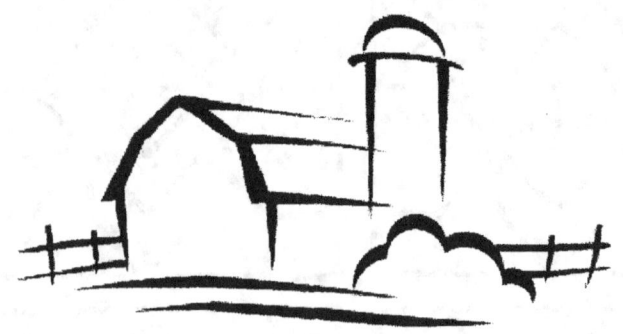

Barn Quilt Location
Cito Road
Ayr Township

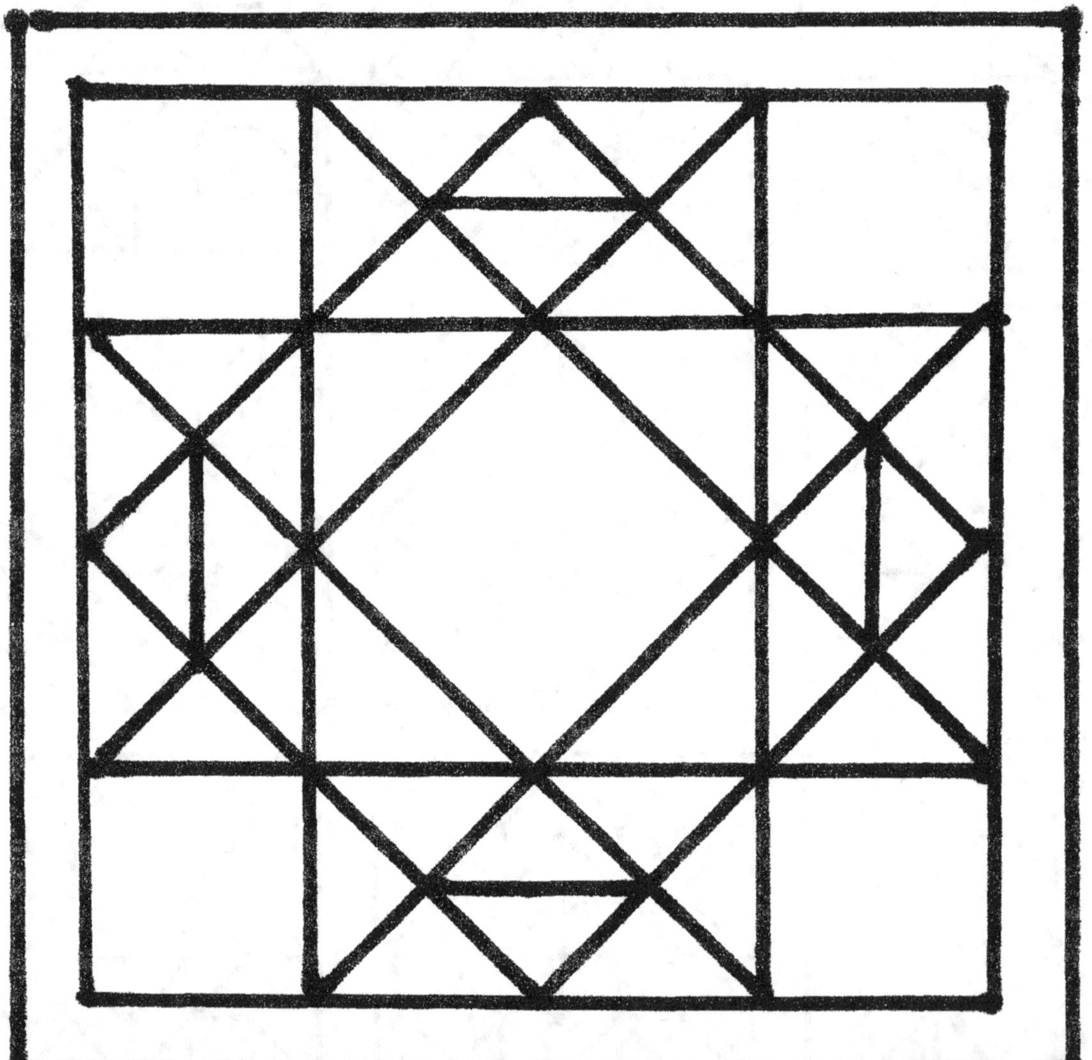

Frontier County Barn Quilt Crown of Thorns

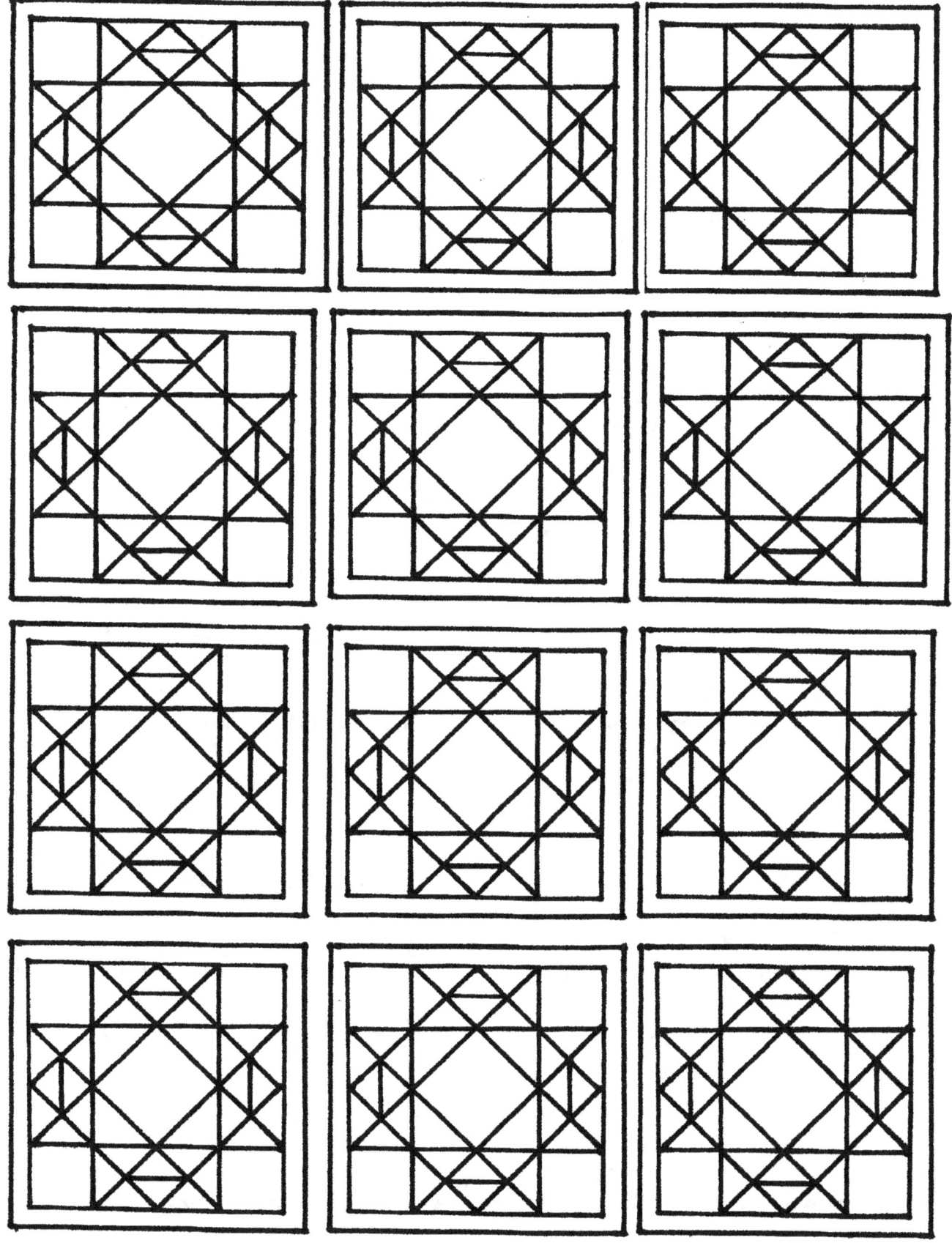

Barn Quilt Blazing Star
Frontier County Barn Quilt Trail

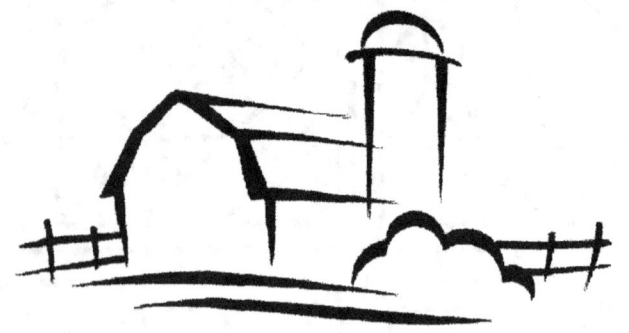

Barn Quilt Location
Circle Drive
Taylor Township

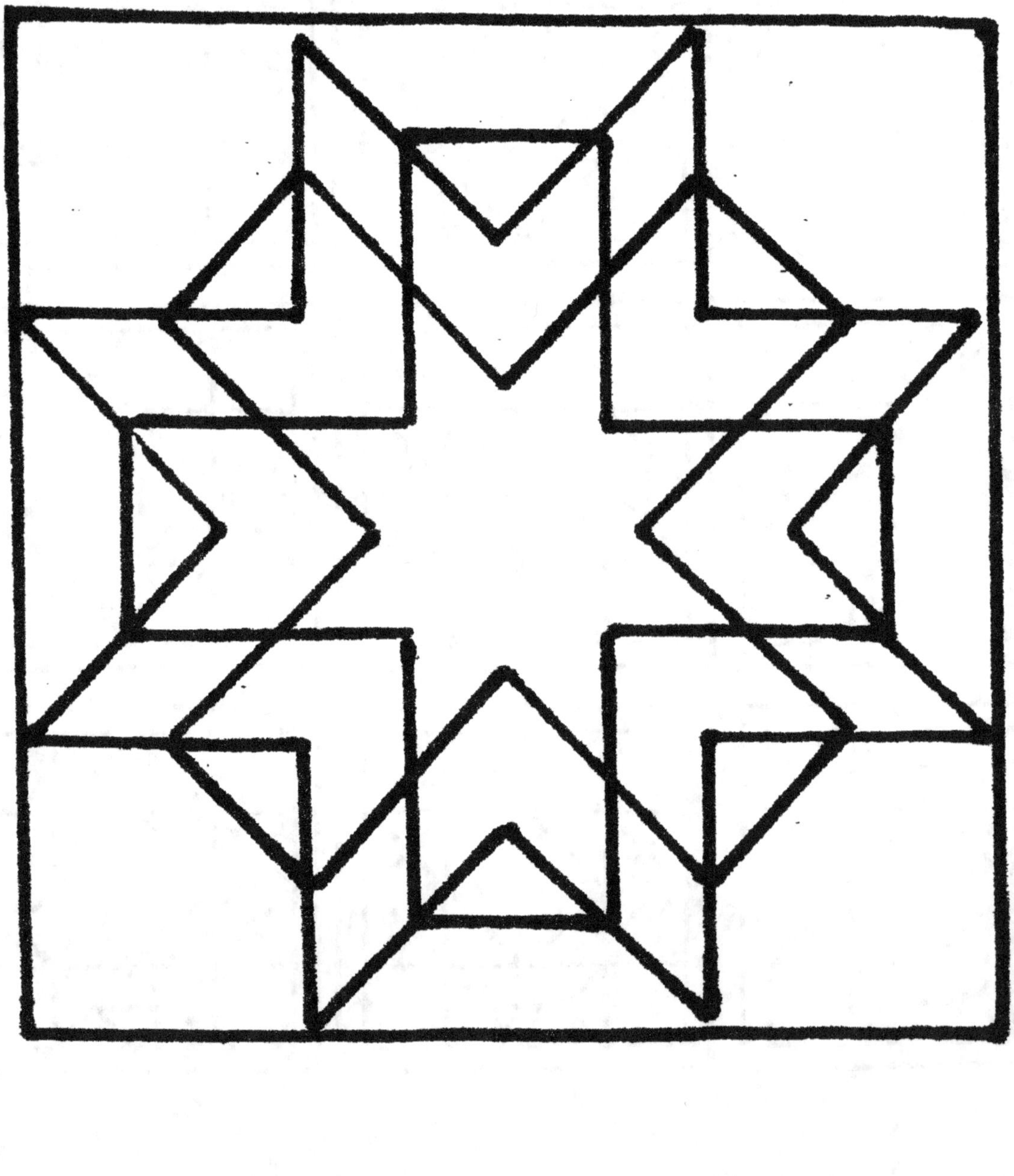

Frontier County Barn Quilt Blazing Star

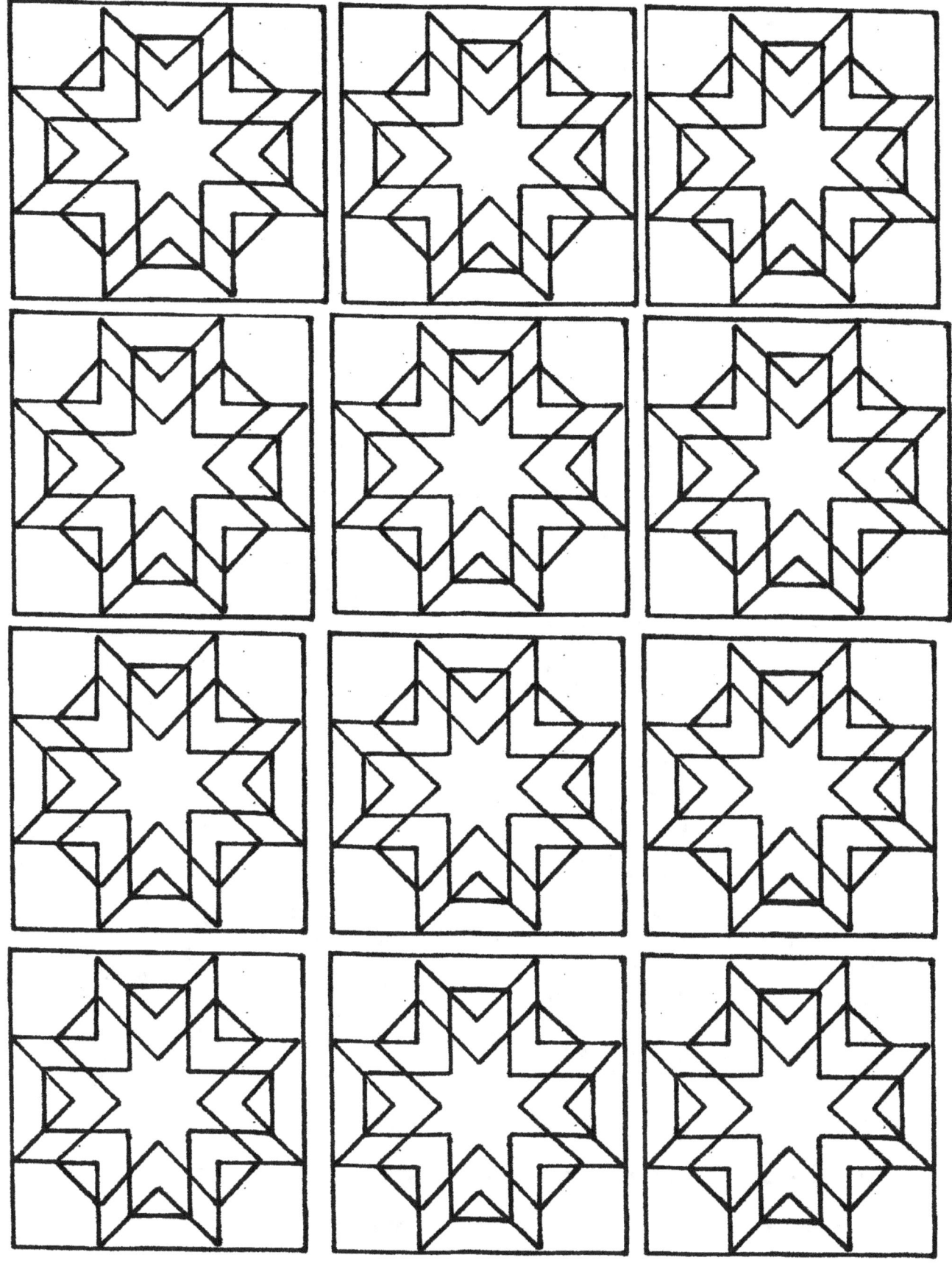

Barn Quilt County Fair
Frontier County Barn Quilt Trail

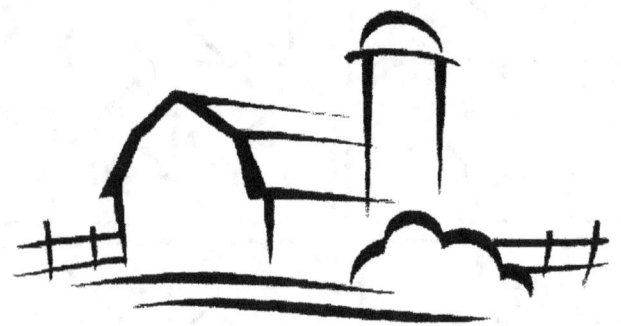

Barn Quilt Location
Lincoln Way East
Todd Township

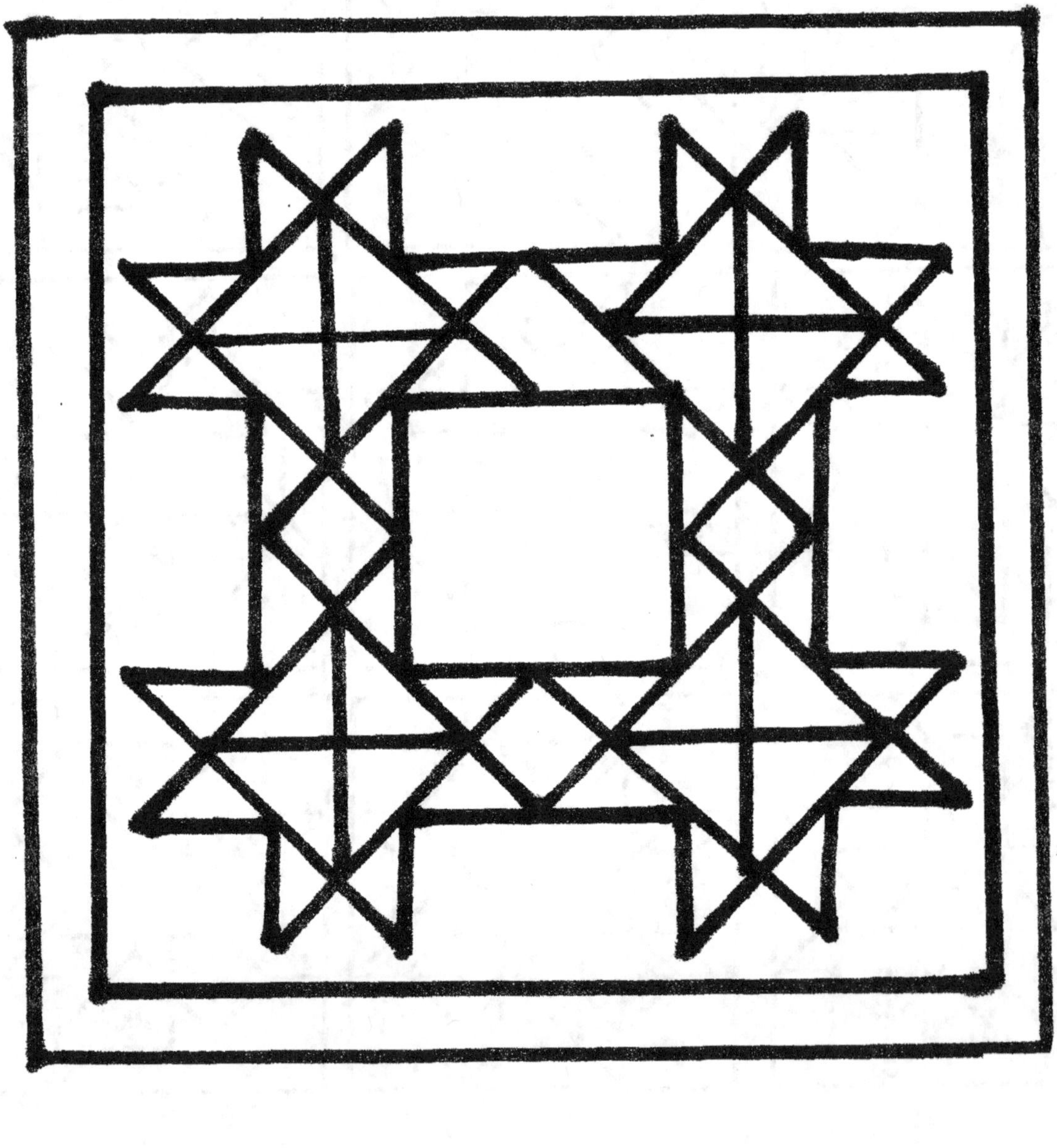

Frontier County Barn Quilt County Fair

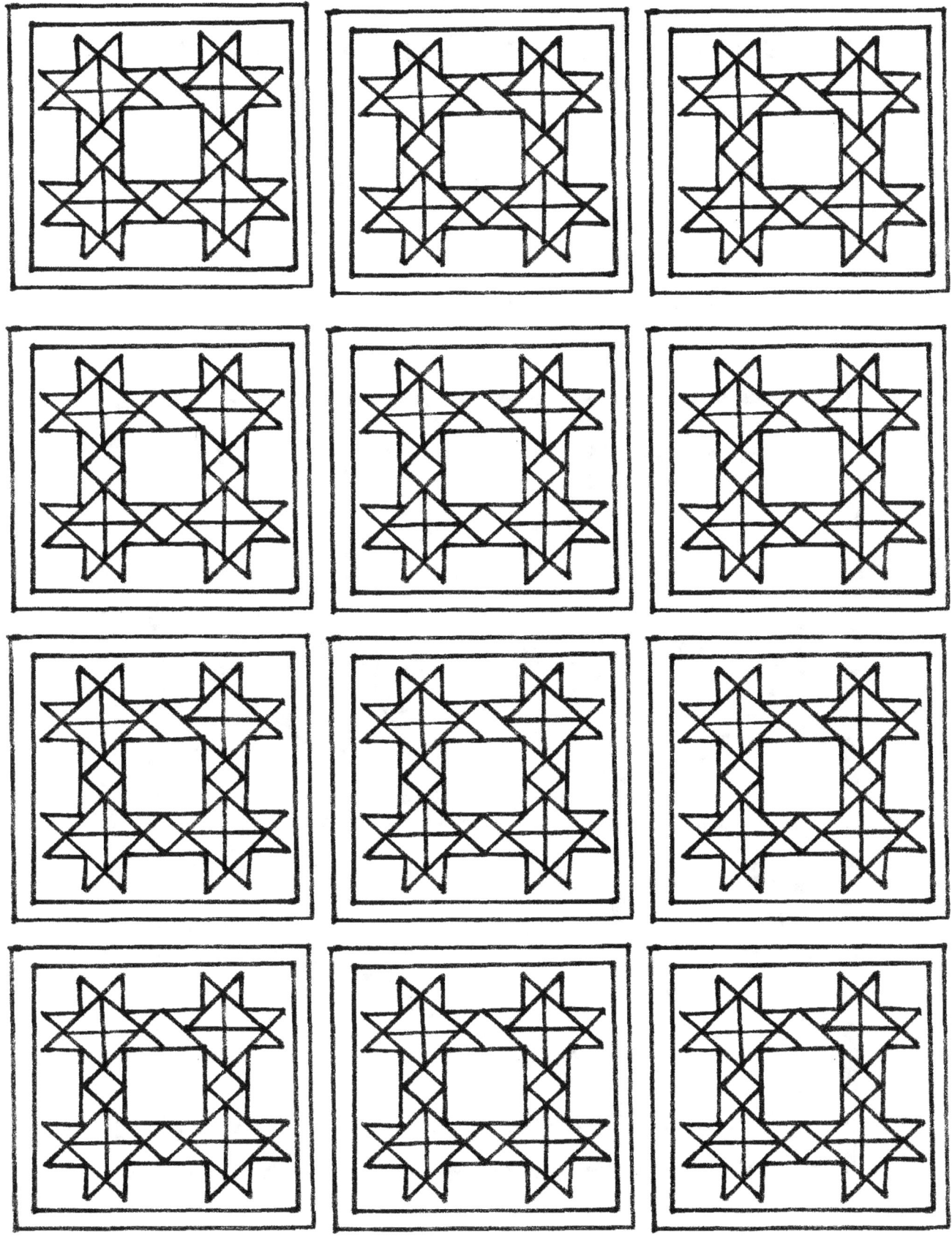

Barn Quilt Scout's Sunflower
Frontier County Barn Quilt Trail

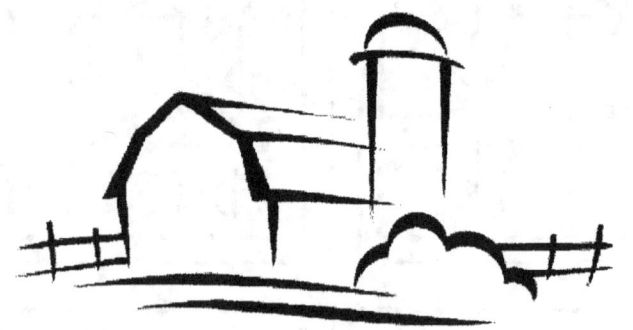

Barn Quilt Location
Big Cove Tannery Road
Ayr Township

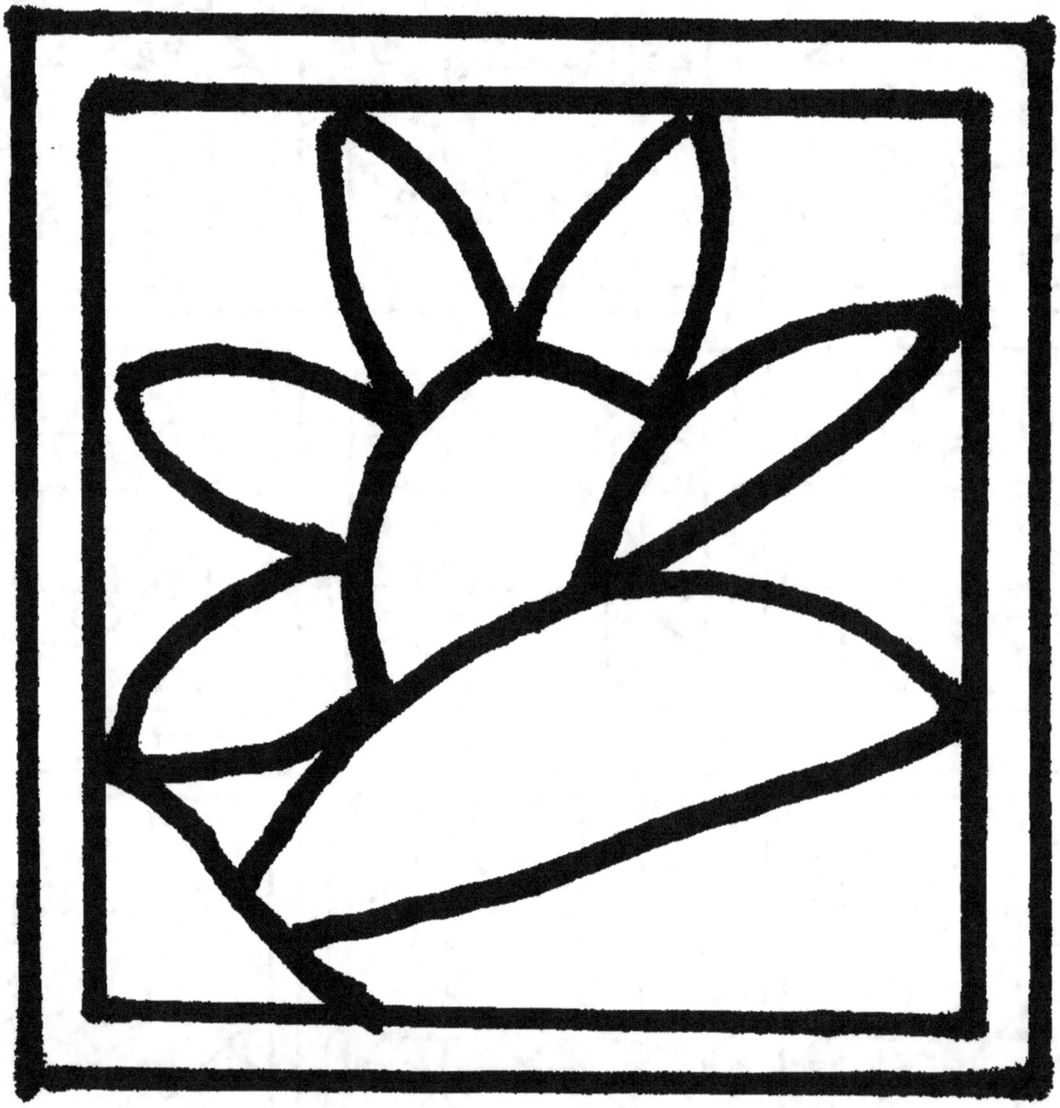

Frontier County Barn Quilt Scout's Sunflower

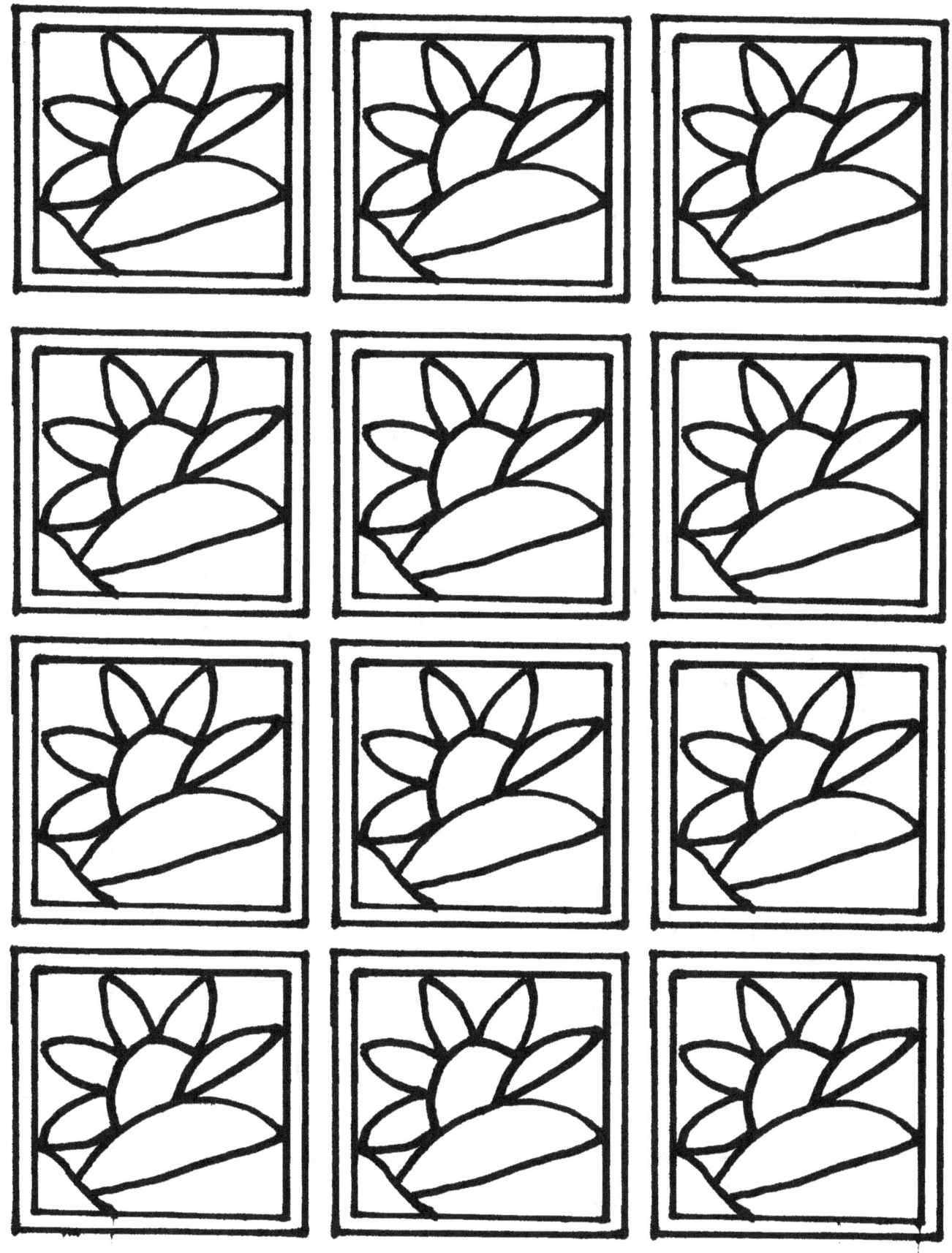

Barn Quilt Union Star
Frontier County Barn Quilt Trail

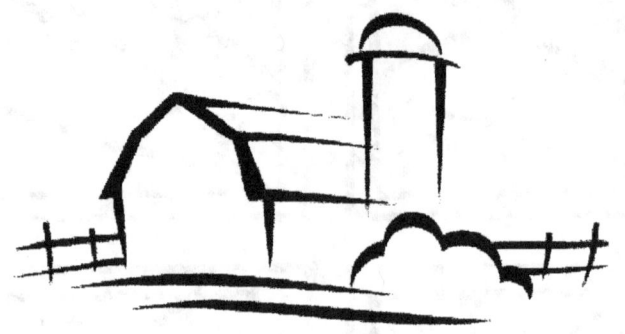

Barn Quilt Location
Spring Road
Bethel Township

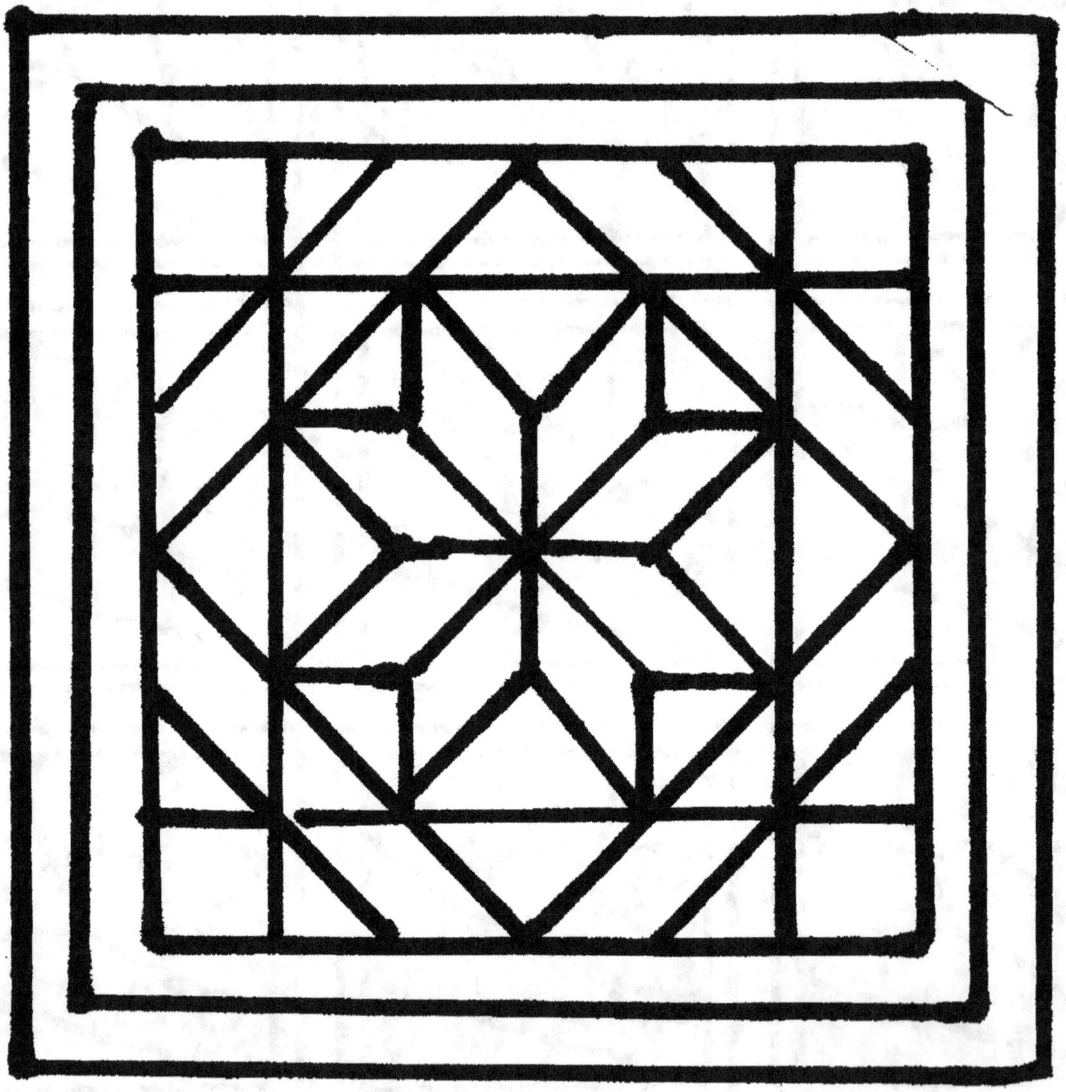

Frontier County Barn Quilt Union Star

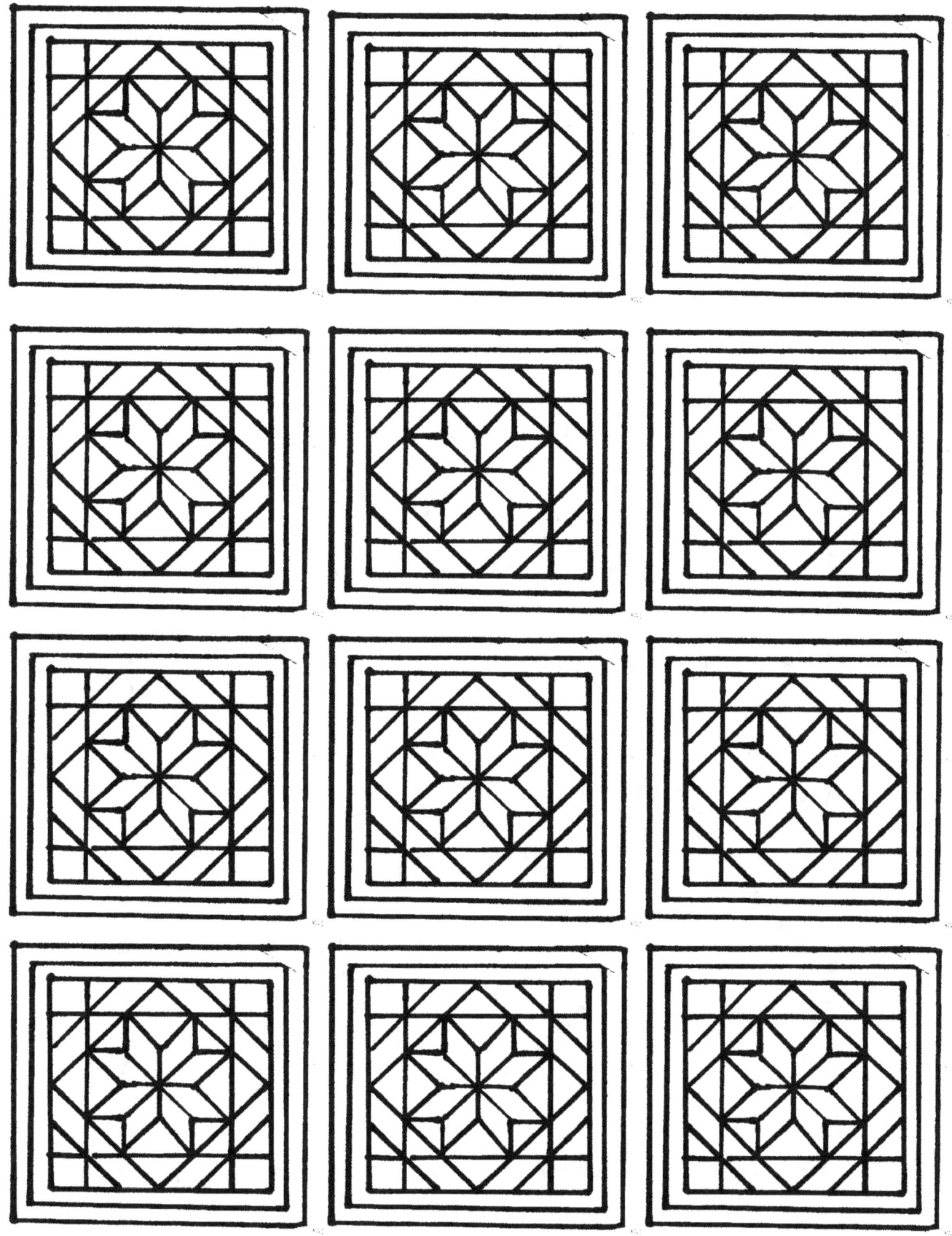

Barn Quilt Horn of Plenty
Frontier County Barn Quilt Trail

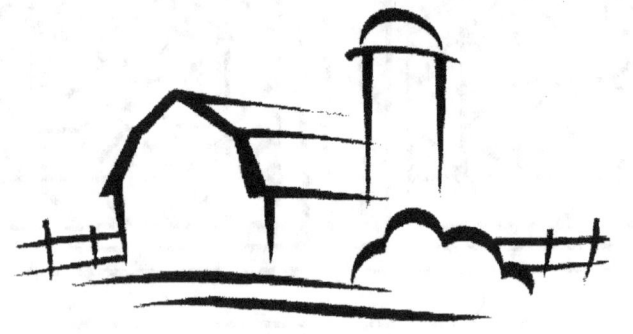

Barn Quilt Location
Horton Drive
Ayr Township

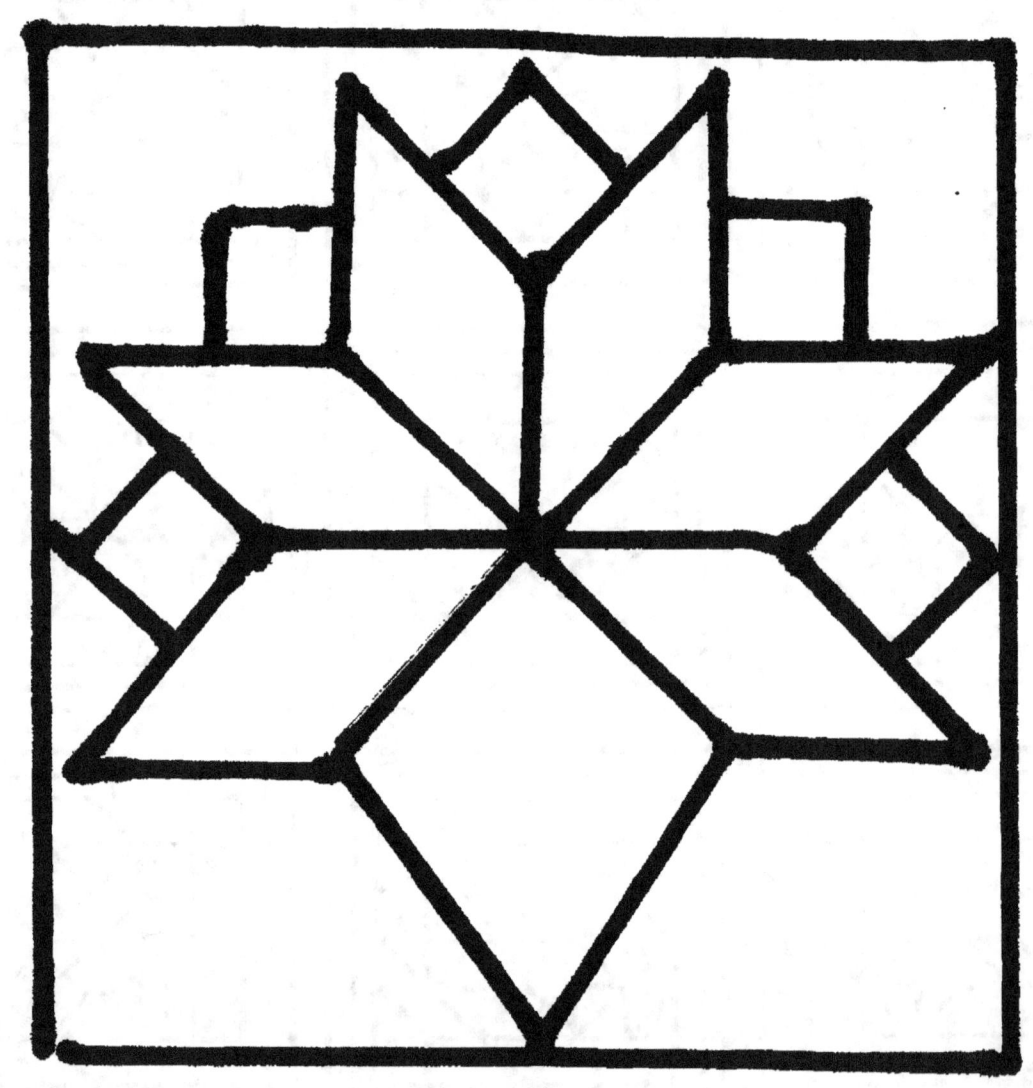

Frontier County Barn Quilt Horn of Plenty

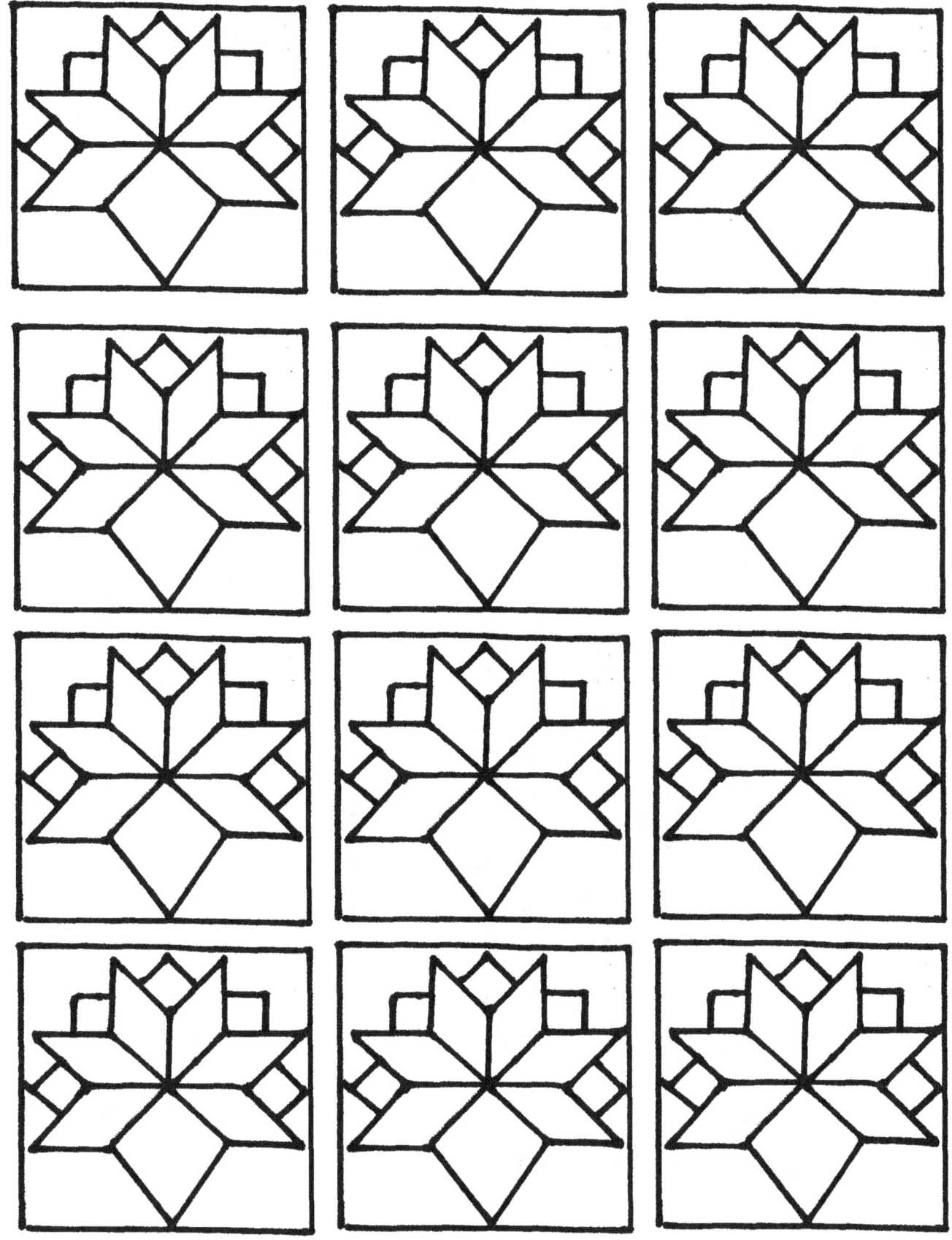

Barn Quilt Maryland, Old Line State
Frontier County Barn Quilt Trail

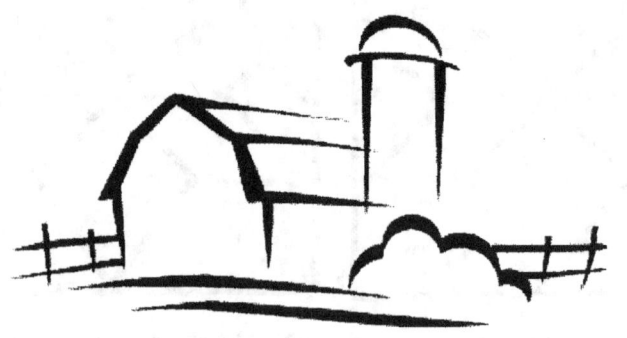

Barn Quilt Location
Battle Ridge Road
Dublin Township

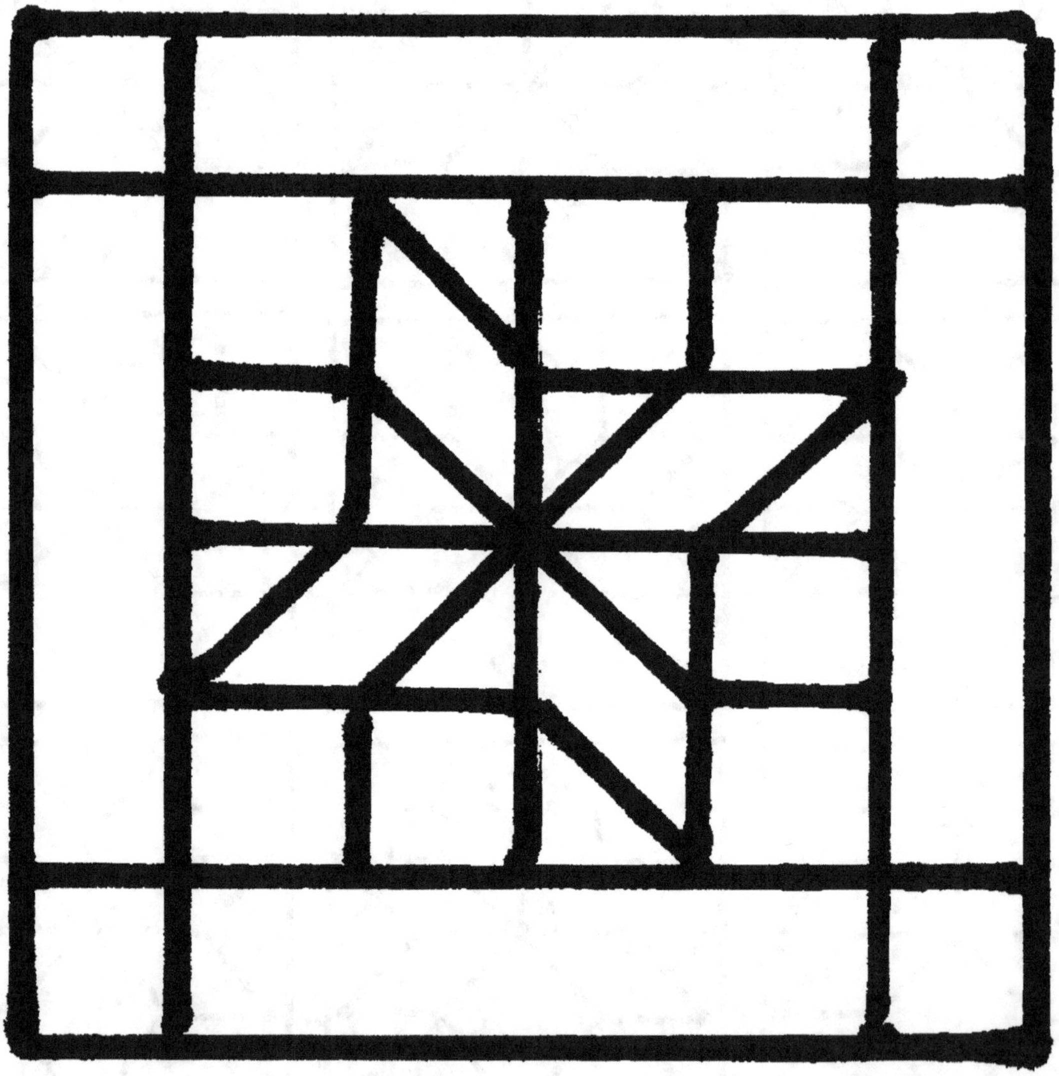

Frontier County Barn Quilt Maryland, Old Line State

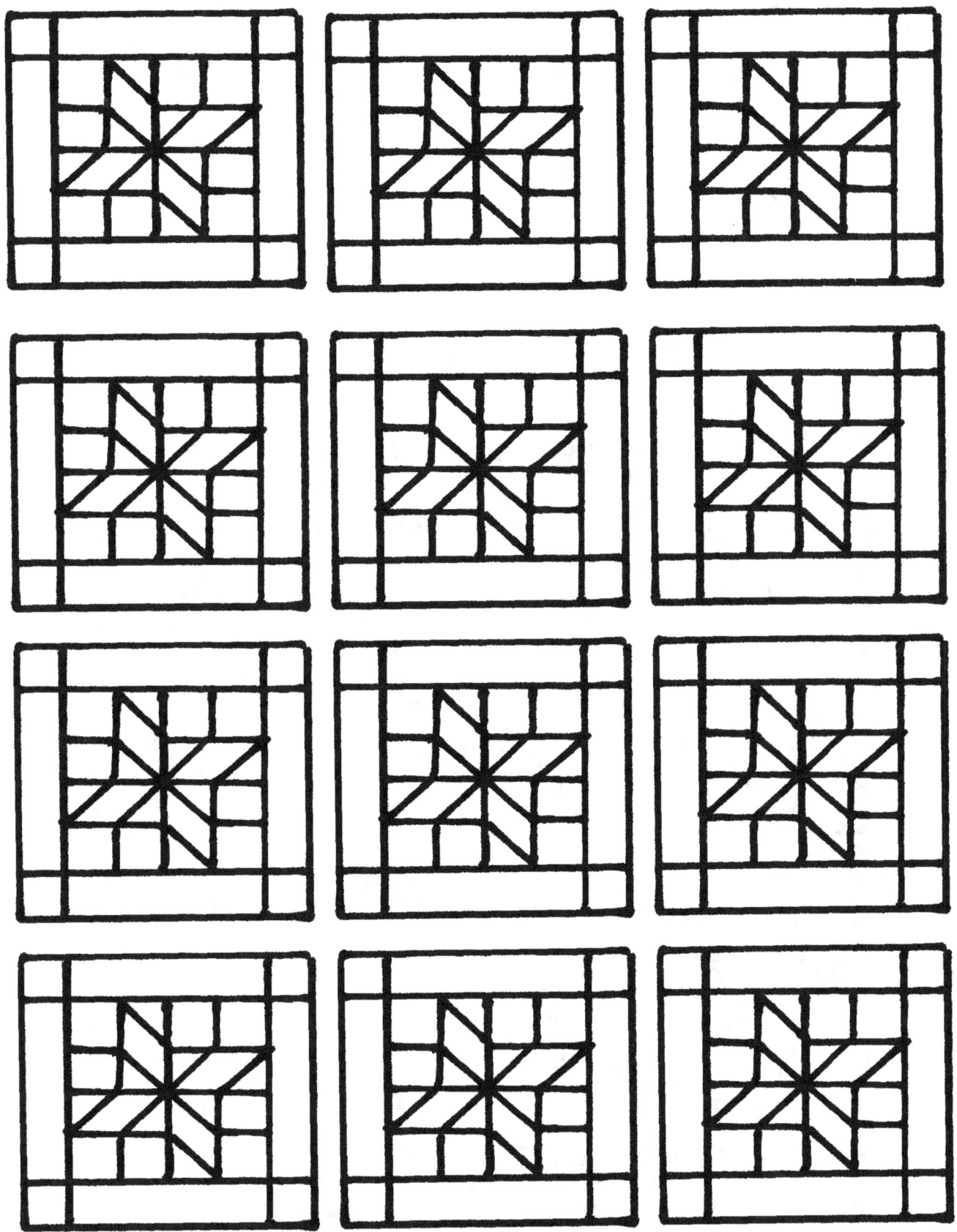

Barn Quilt Farmer Fields
Frontier County Barn Quilt Trail

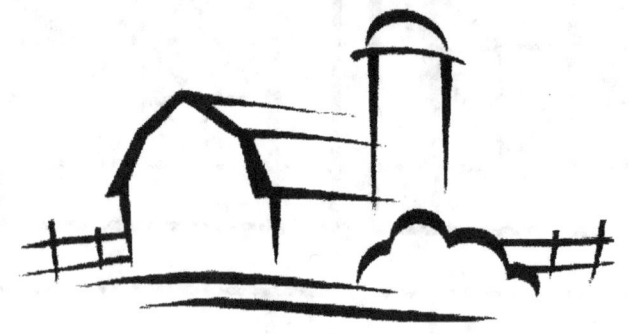

Barn Quilt Location
Great Cove Road
Ayr Township

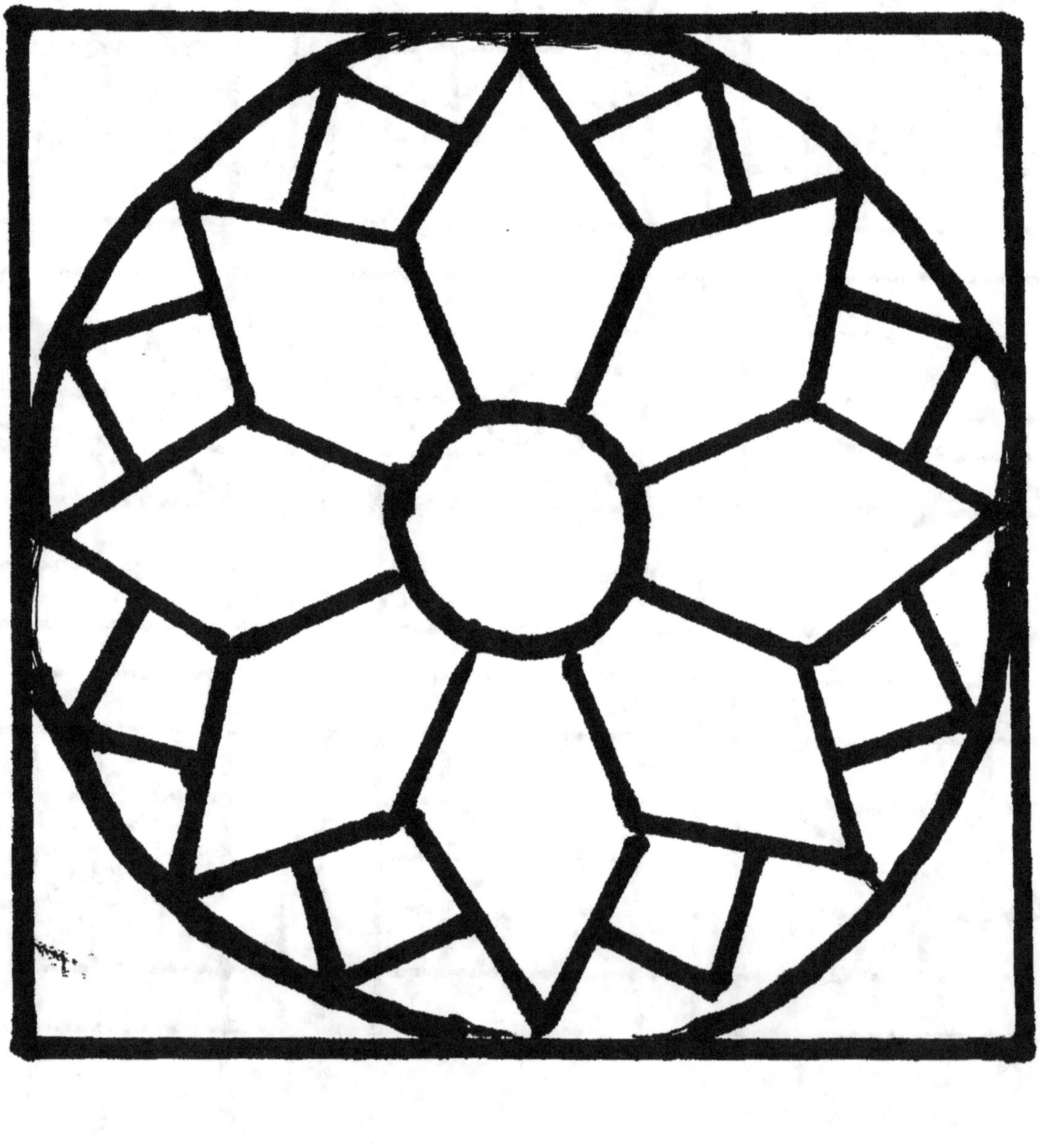

Frontier County Barn Quilt Farmer Fields

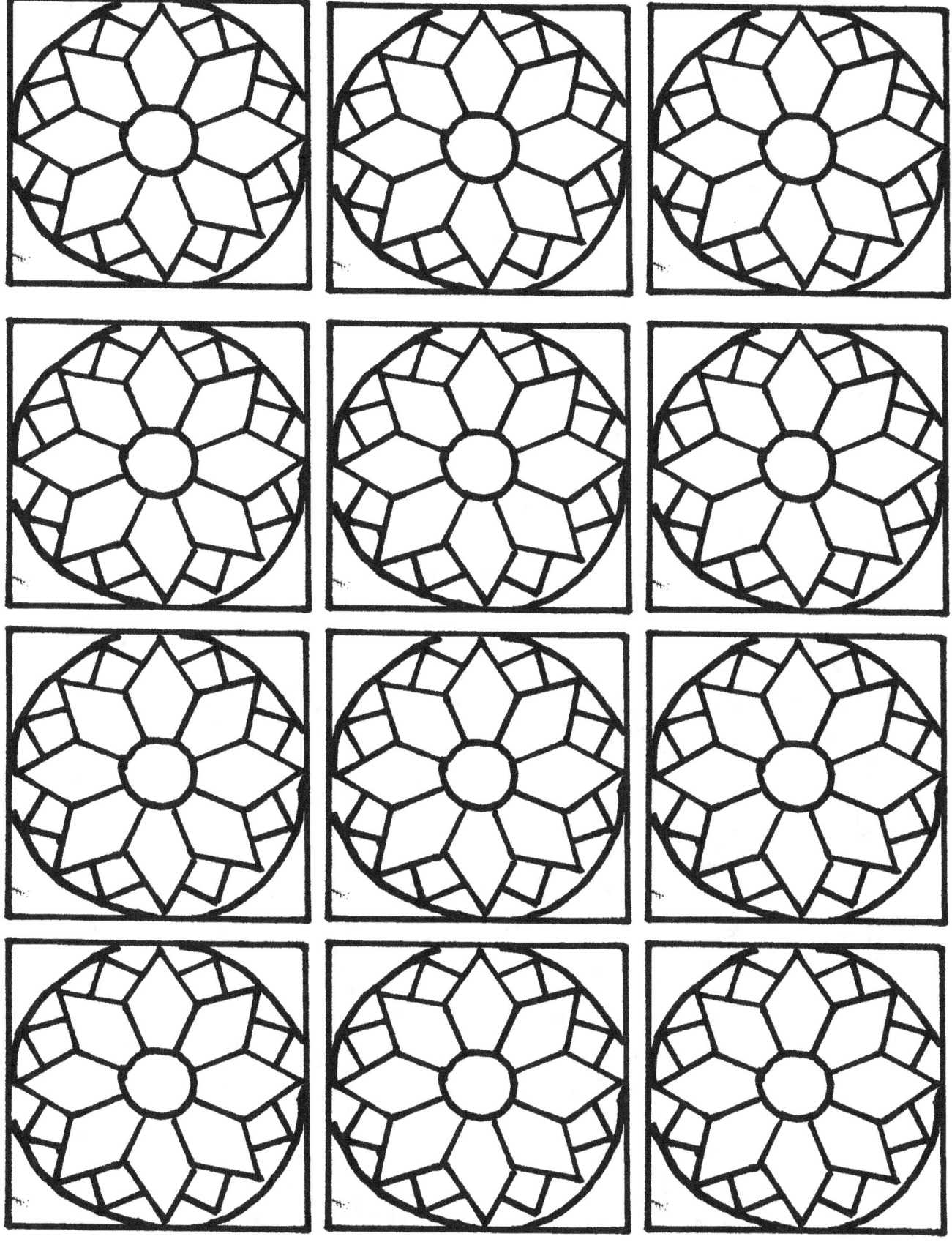

Barn Quilt Mill Wheel
Frontier County Barn Quilt Trail

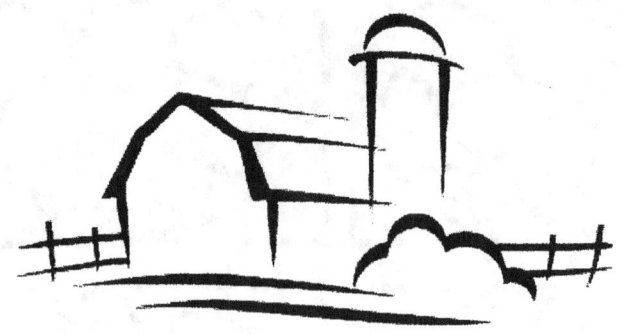

Barn Quilt Location
Grist Mill Road
Dublin Township

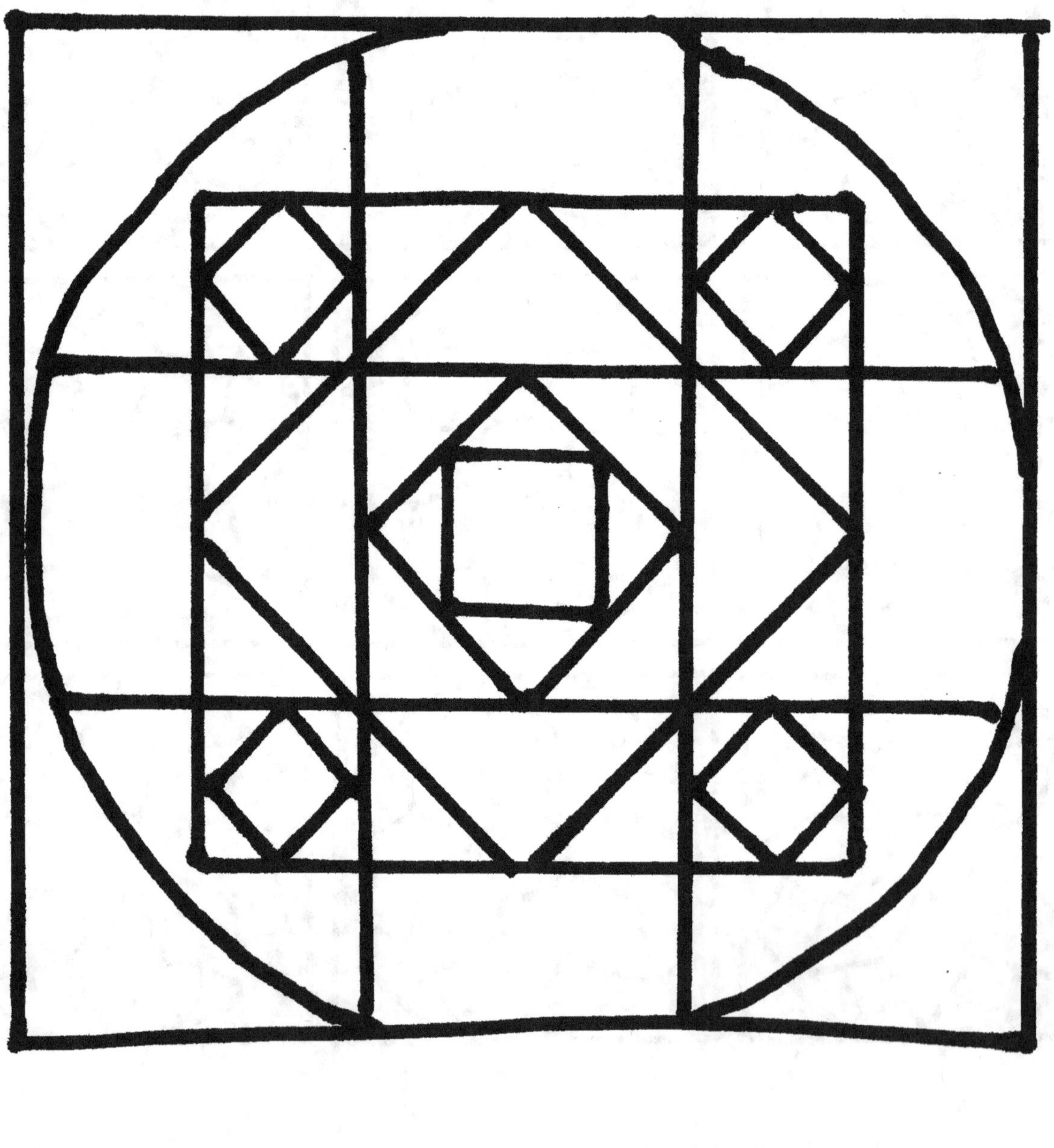

Frontier County Barn Quilt Mill Wheel

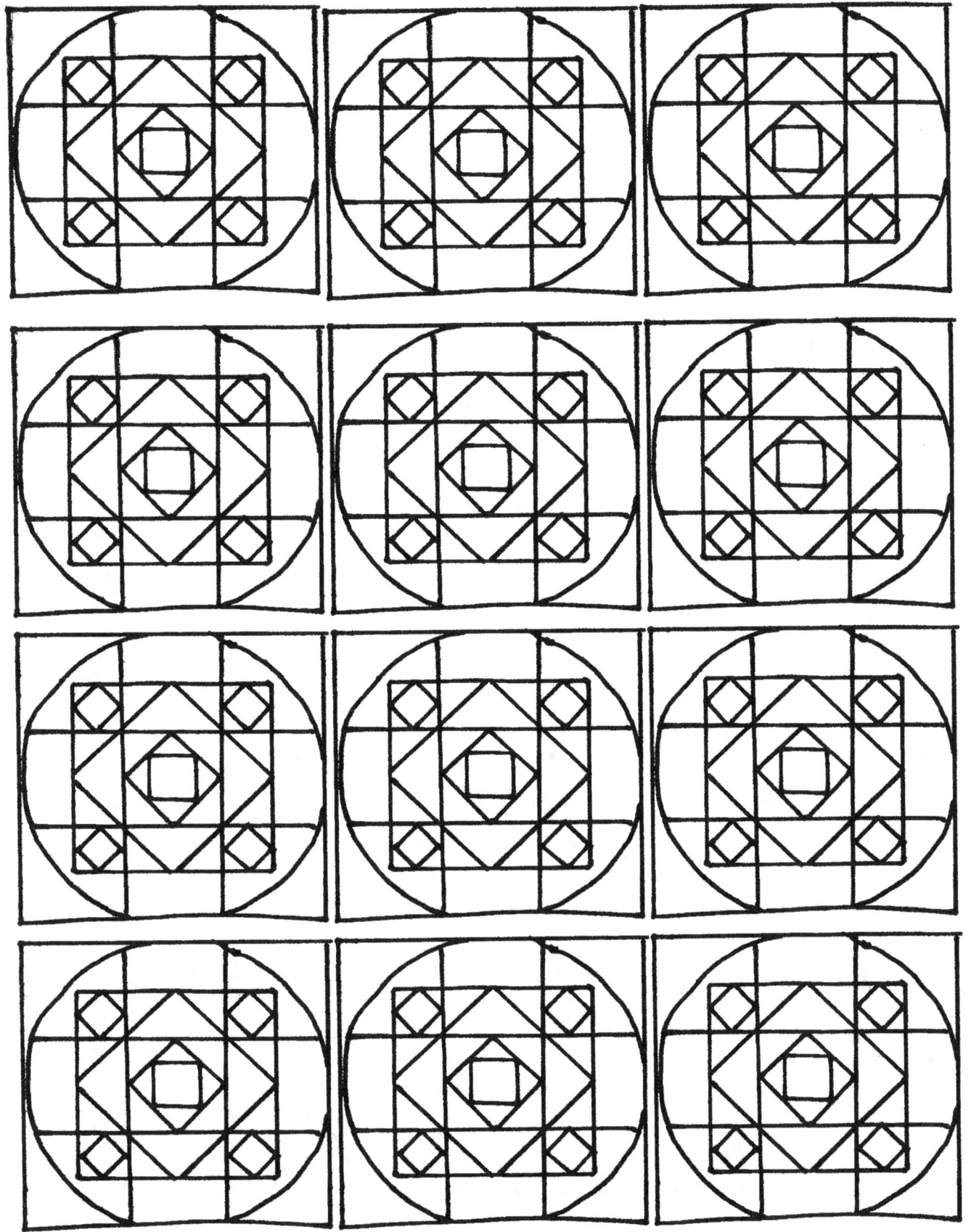

Barn Quilt Dickey's Mountain Star
Frontier County Barn Quilt Trail

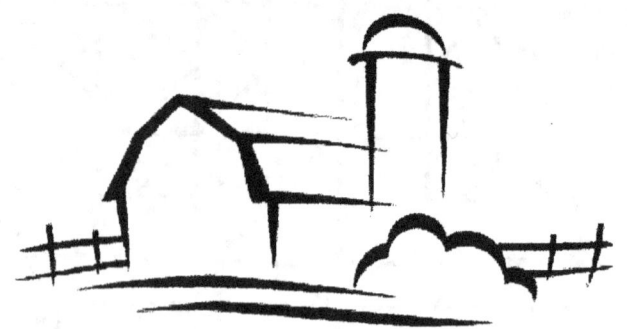

**Barn Quilt Location
Big Cove Tannery Road
Thompson Township**

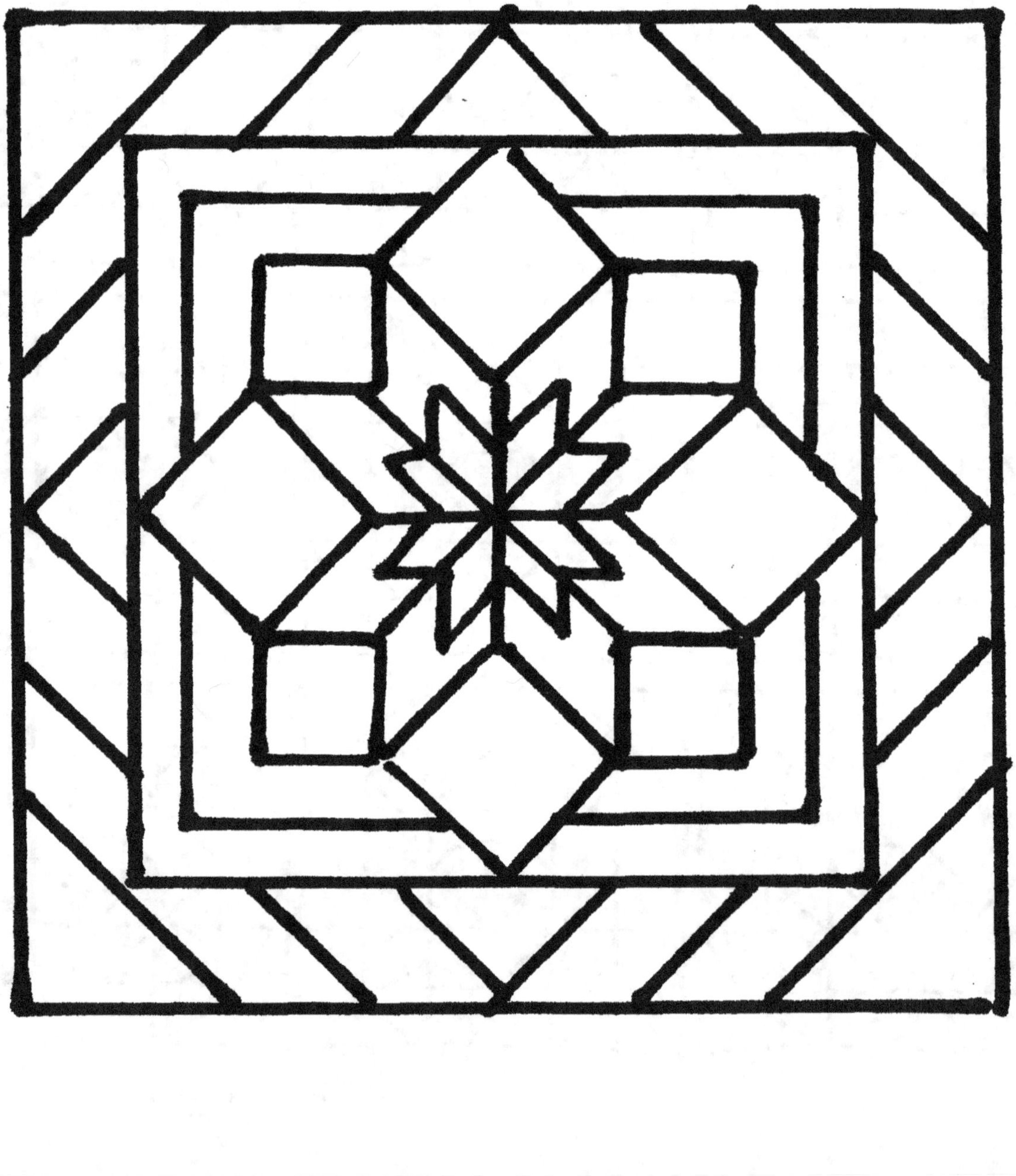

Frontier County Barn Quilt Dickey's Mountain

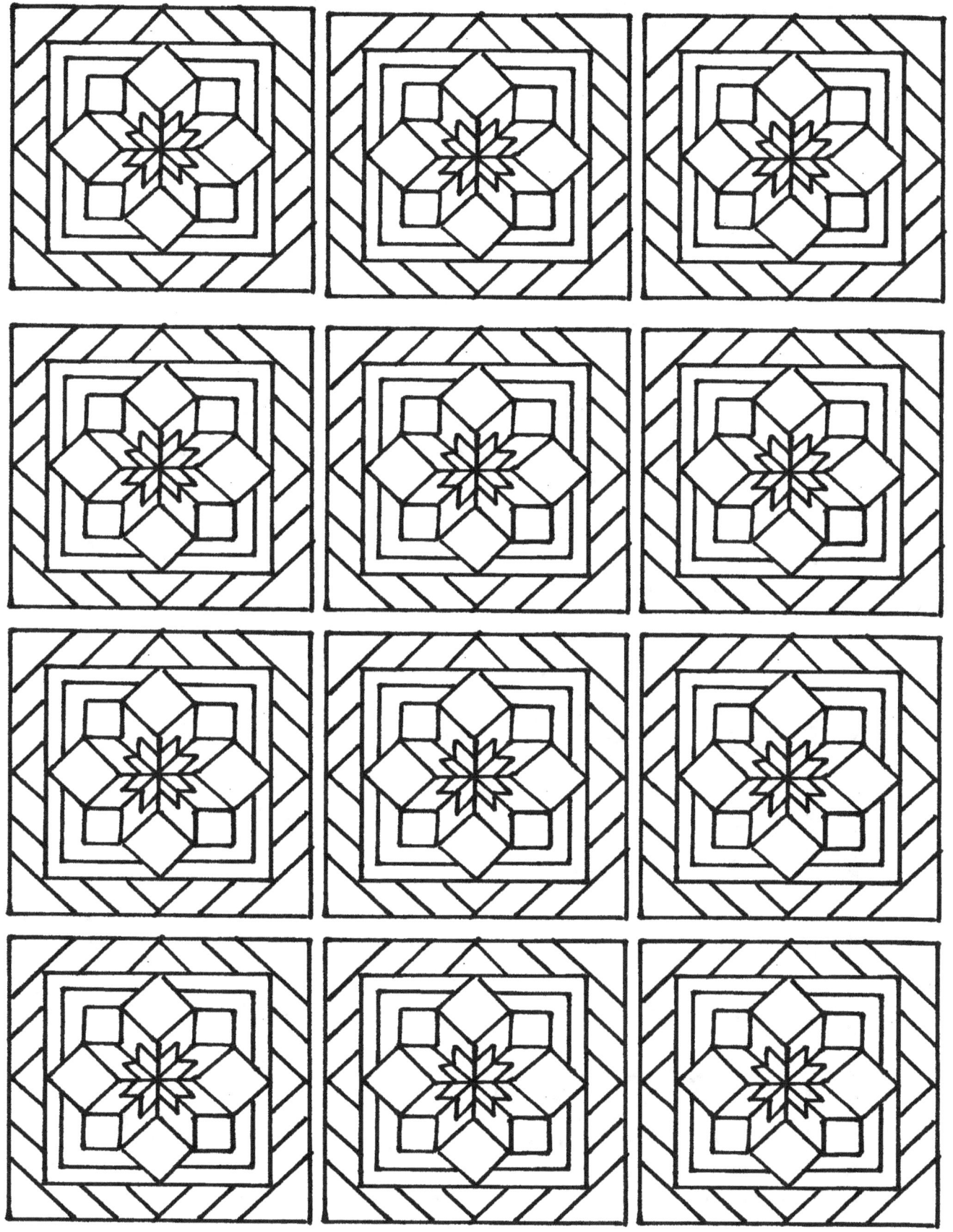

Barn Quilt Maltese Cross
Frontier County Barn Quilt Trail

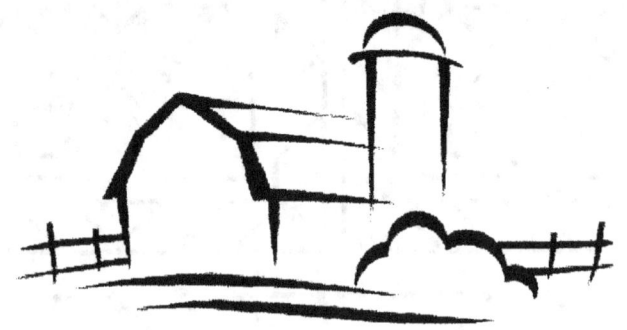

Barn Quilt Location
East Maple Street
McConnellsburg Township

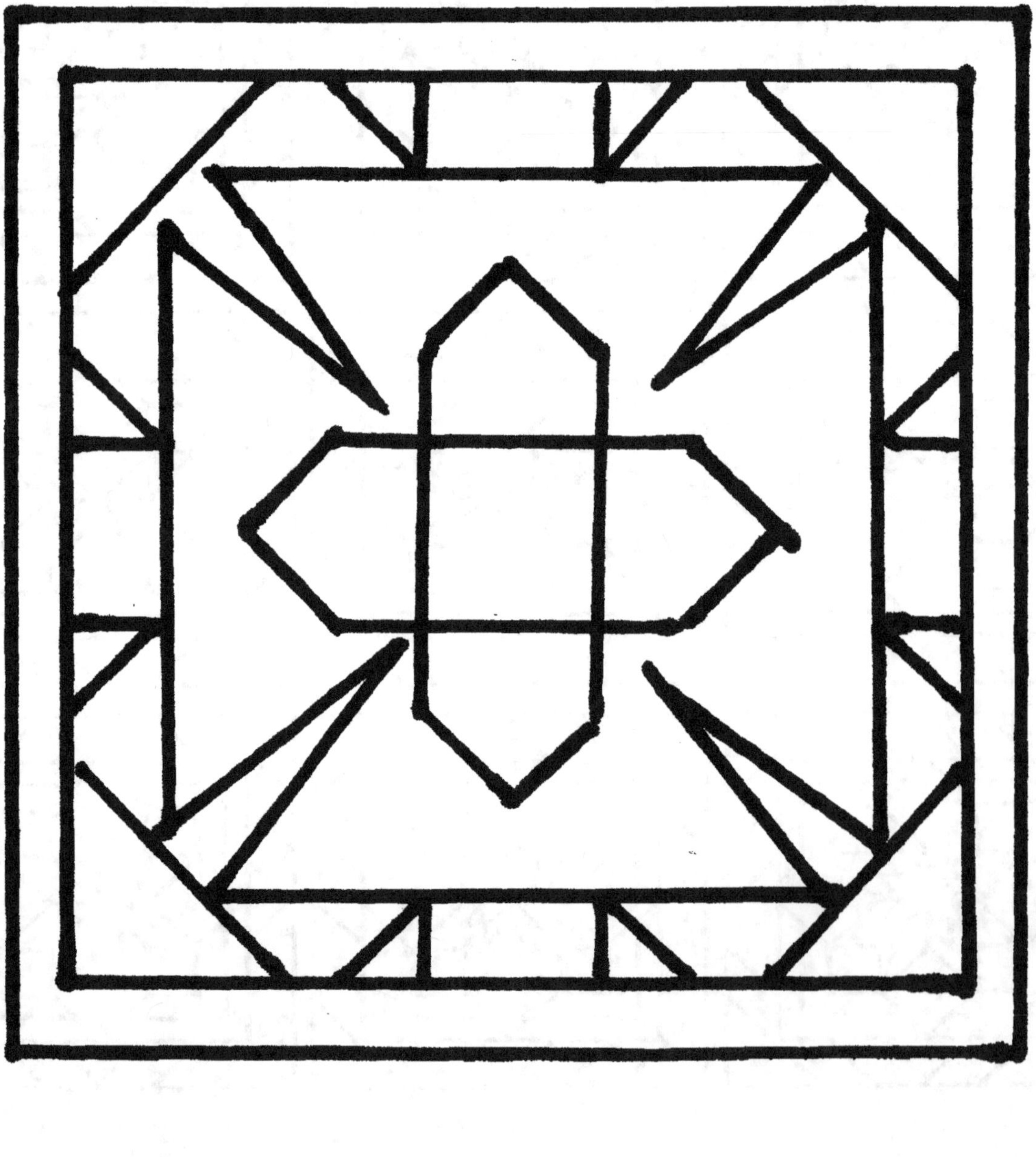

Frontier County Barn Quilt Maltese Cross

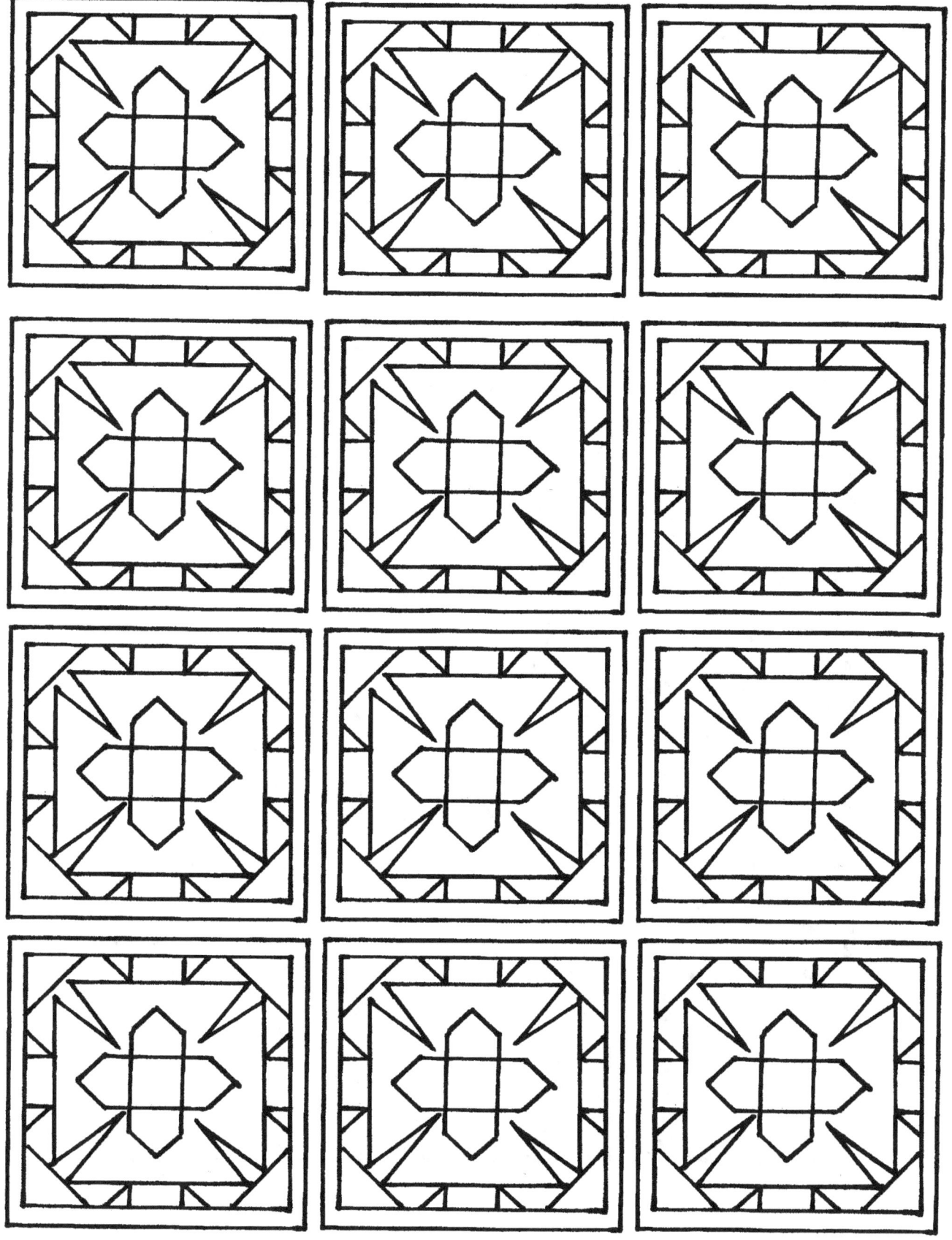

Barn Quilt Jaqcue Illinois Star
Frontier County Barn Quilt Trail

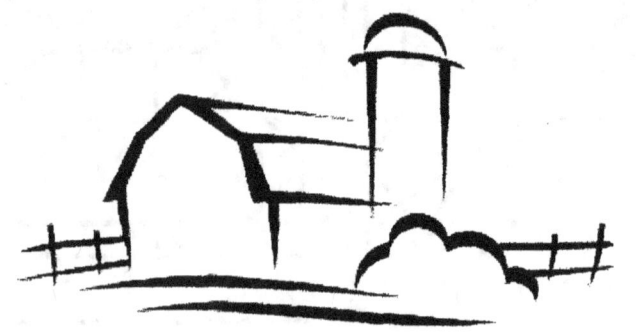

Barn Quilt Location
Circle Drive
Licking Creek Township

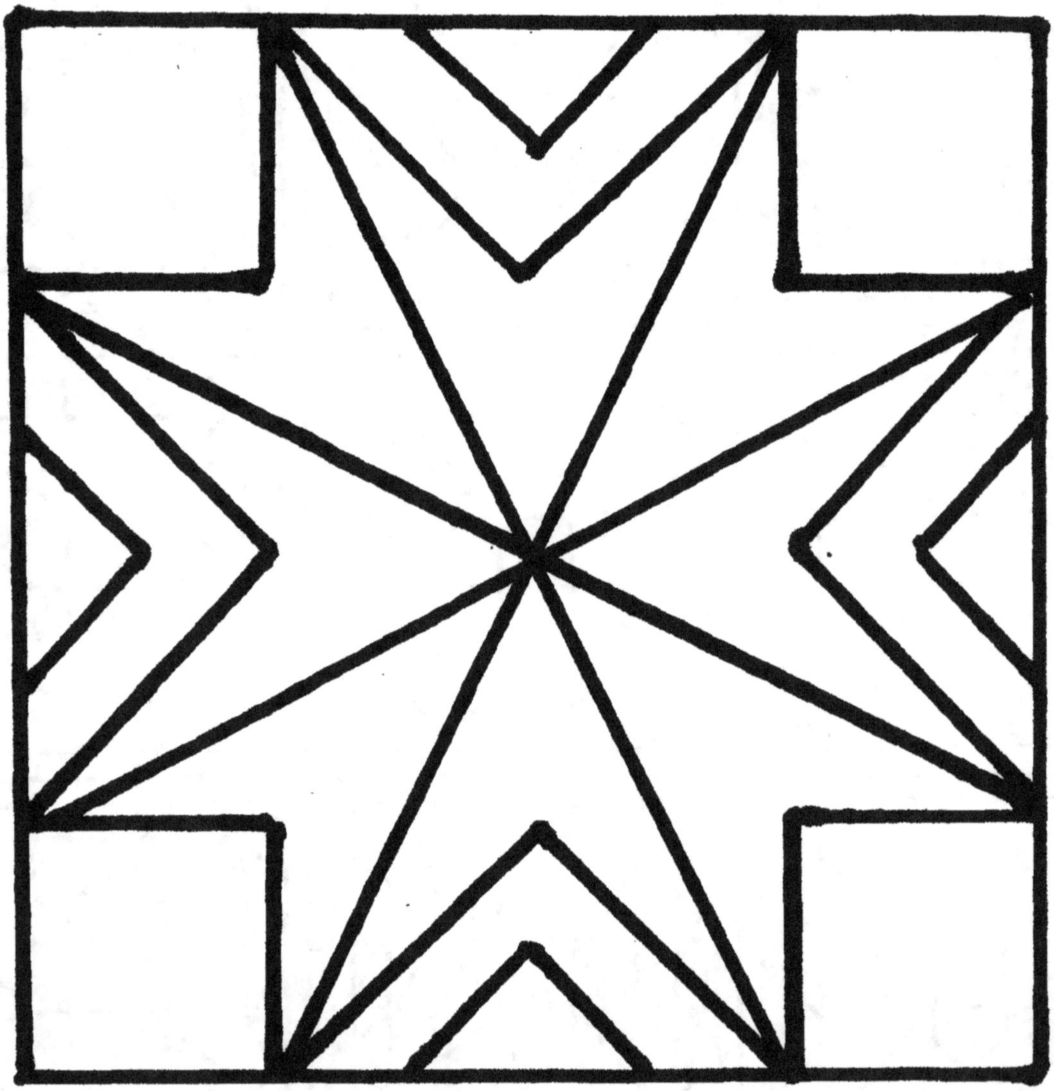

Frontier County Barn Quilt Jacque Illinois Star

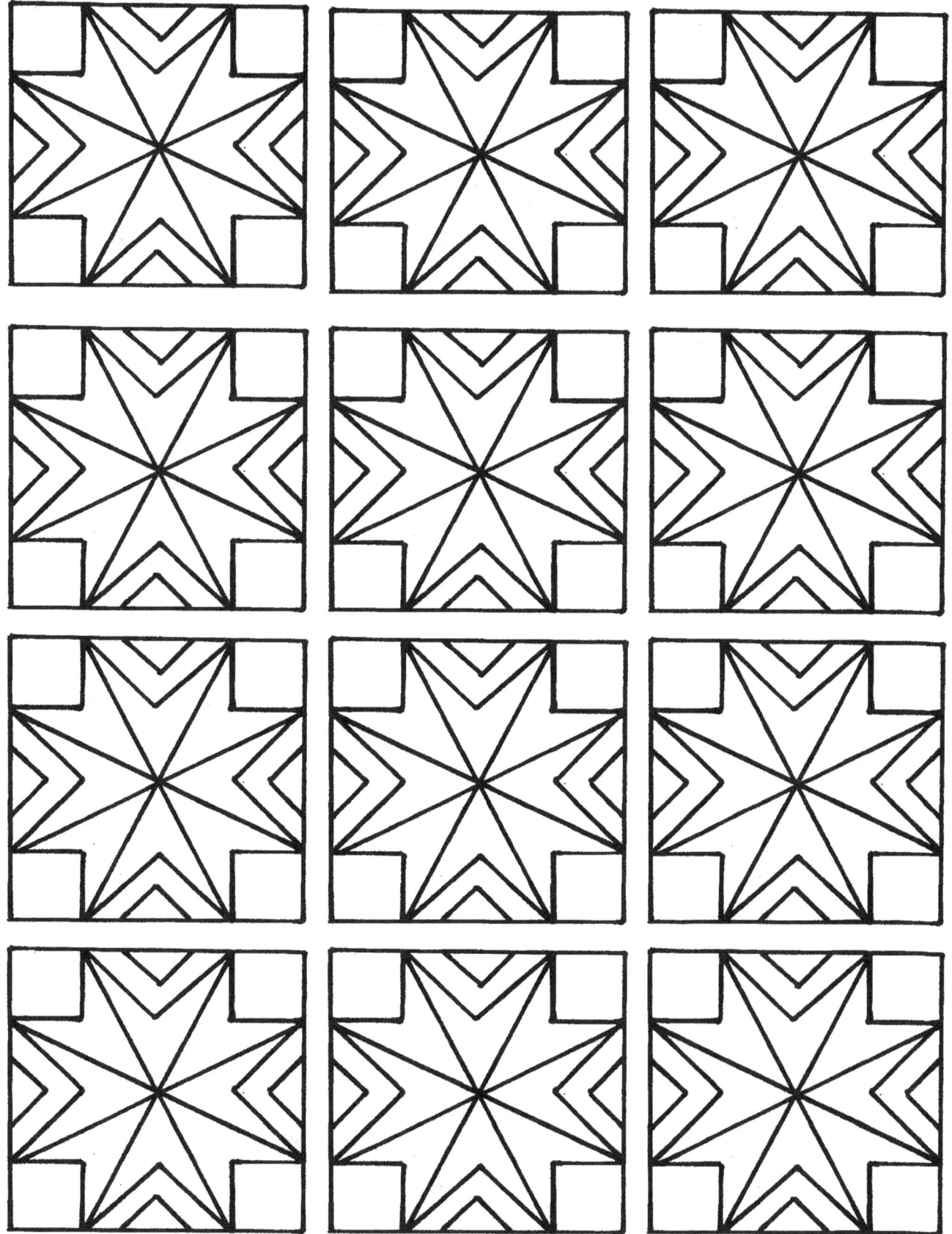

Barn Quilt Northcraft's
Frontier County Barn Quilt Trail

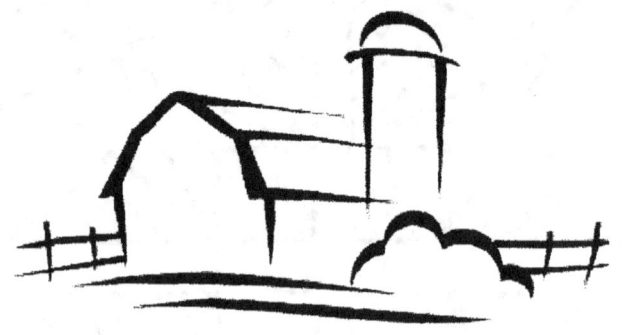

Barn Quilt Location
Buck Valley Road
Union Township

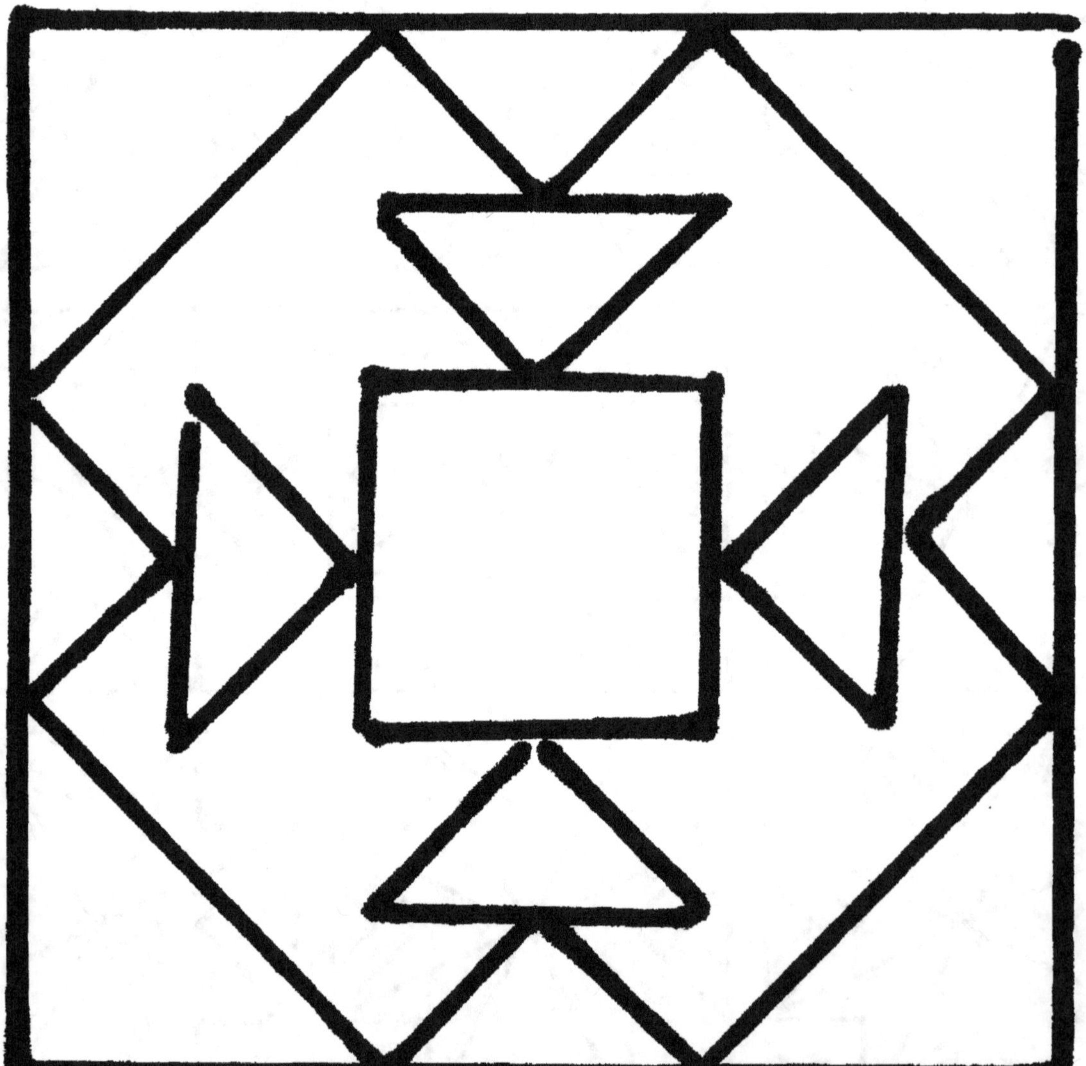

Frontier County Barn Quilt Northcraft's

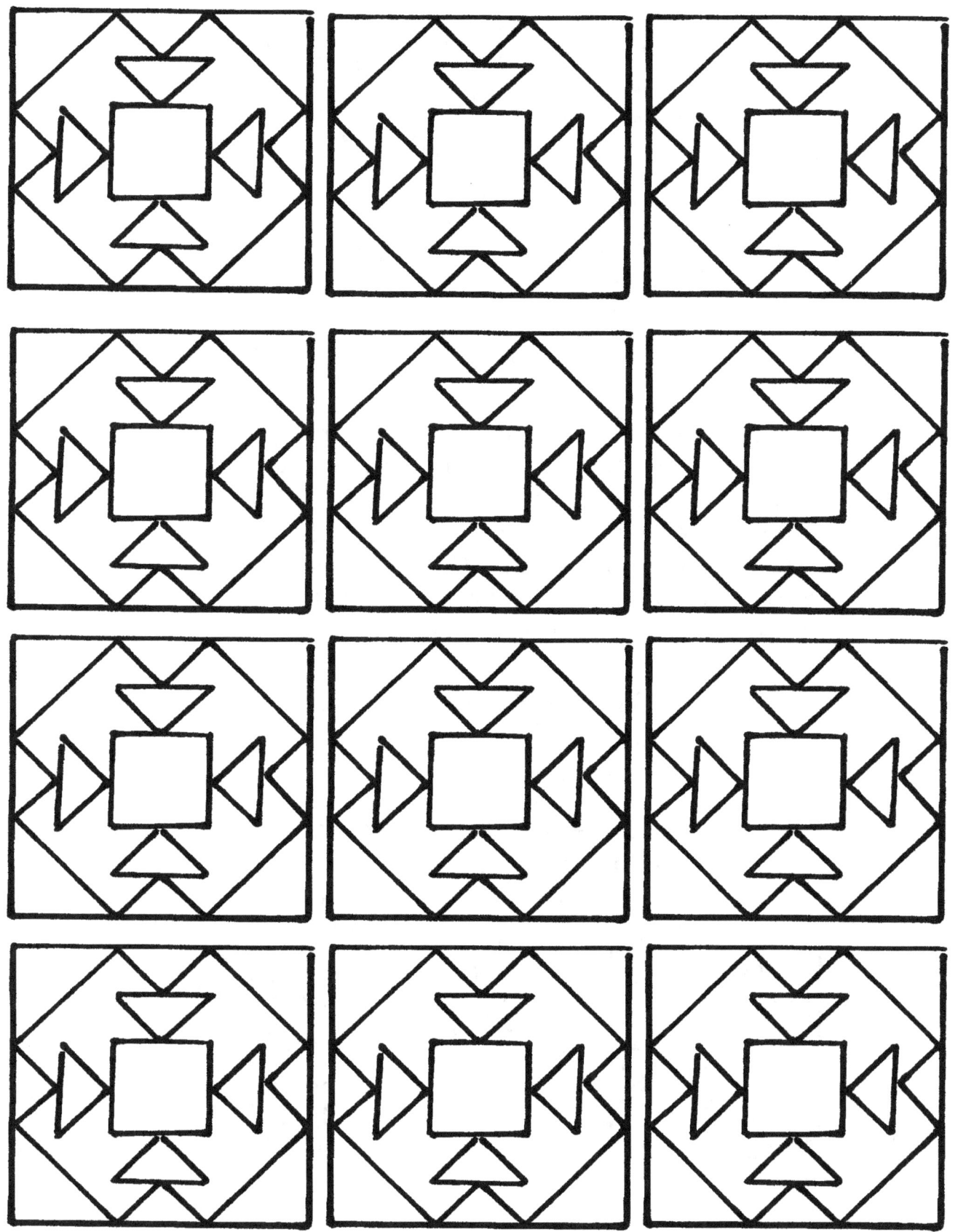

John Lettau Coloring Books

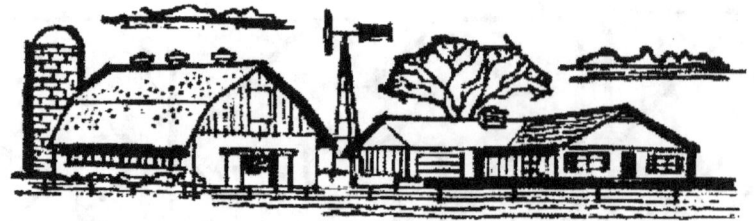

State Barn Quilt Coloring Books

Shawano Wisconsin Barn Quilt Coloring Books 1, 2, 3 & 4
Delaware County Iowa Barn Quilt Coloring Book
Lake County California Barn Quilt Coloring Book
Franklin County Vermont Barn Quilt Coloring Books 1, 2 & 3
Tennessee Barn Quilt Coloring Books 1 & 2
Indiana Barn Quilt Coloring Books 1 & 2
Delaware County Iowa Barn Quilt Coloring Book
Greene County Wisconsin Barn Quilt Coloring Books 1 & 2
Franklin County Vermont Barn Quilt Coloring Books 1, 2 & 3
Cozad County Nebraska Barn Quilt Coloring Book
Frontier County Colorado Barn Quilt Coloring Book
Kansas Barn Quilt Coloring Books 1, 2, 3 & 4
Kentucky Barn Quilt Coloring Book

Related Coloring Books

Geometric Design Coloring Books 1, 2, 3, 4 & 5
Barn Quilt Around America Coloring Book

Graph Paper Designs

Learn how to create your own geometric
designs and/or quilt patterns.

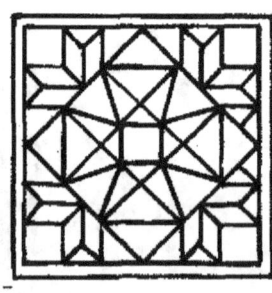

READING & MATH BOOKS by JOHN H. LETTAU

1st Dimension	Grades 3-6
2nd Dimension	Grades 3-6
Primary Dimension	Grades 1-4
Aztec Math Primary Book One	Grades 1-3
Aztec Math Primary Book Two	Grades 1-3
Aztec Math Intermediate Book One	Grades 3-6
Aztec Math Intermediate Book Two	Grades 3-6
Aztec Math Jr. High Book One	Grades 5-8
Aztec Math Jr. High Book Two	Grades 5-8
Aztec Math Decimal Book	Grades 4-8
Aztec Math Fraction Book	Grades 4-8
Sum-Action Number Puzzle Book One	Grades 3-6
Sum-Action Number Puzzle Book Two	Grades 3-6
Sum-Action Number Puzzle Primary Book One	Grades 1-3
Sum-Action Number Puzzle Primary Book Two	Grades 1-3
Multiplication Number Puzzles	Grades 3-6
Geometric Design Puzzle Book One	Grades 3-6
Geometric Design Puzzle Book Two	Grades 3-6
Aztec Reading Primary Book One	Grades 1-3
Aztec Reading Primary Book Two	Grades 1-3
Math in Action	Grades 3-6
A-Maze-ing Number Puzzles	Grades 3-6
Graph Paper Designs	Grades 2-6
Pick-A-Dilly Papers	Grades 3-6
Awards for All Reasons	Grades 1-6
Time Marches On	Grades 1-3
Pennies, Nickels & Dimes	Grades 1-3
Super-Sum Activity Cards	Grades 3-6
Learning Center Game Boards	Grades 1-3
Aztec Design Coloring Book	Grades 1-6

www.ingramcontent.com/pod-product-compliance
Lightning Source LLC
Chambersburg PA
CBHW081438220526
45466CB00008B/2429